T0164071

Servitors
of
Empire

Studies in the Dark Side of Asian America

Darrell Y. Hamamoto

Published by:
Trine Day LLC
PO Box 577
Walterville, OR 97489
1-800-556-2012
www.TrineDay.com
publisher@TrineDay.net

Library of Congress Control Number: 2014934104

Hamamoto, Darrell Y.
Servitors of Empire–1st ed.
p. cm.
Includes index and references.
Epud (ISBN-13) 978-1-937584-87-0
Mobi (ISBN-13) 978-1-937584-88-7
Print (ISBN-13) 978-1-937584-86-3
1. Asian Americans -- Politics and government. 2. Asian Americans --
Social conditions. 3. Asian Americans -- Cultural assimilation. 4. Asian
Americans -- History. 5. Immigrants -- United States. I. Hamamoto,
Darrell Y. II. Title

First Edition
10 9 8 7 6 5 4 3 2 1
Printed in the USA
Distribution to the Trade by:
Independent Publishers Group (IPG)
814 North Franklin Street
Chicago, Illinois 60610
312.337.0747
www.ipgbook.com

For Joan K. Hamamoto, my dear mother

Acknowledgments

Because work such as this is a solitary undertaking, the support of special individuals make the task both easier to endure and a pleasure to engage in conversation. This book represents a departure from orthodoxy on many different levels, on many different fronts. As such, I am grateful to Mike Davis, Joan Mellen, Kurt Nimmo, and Rudy Torres for suggesting different publishers that might be interested in taking this book on. It was the intrepidly independent publisher Kris Millegan, however, who gave me this opportunity to present a wildly different view on contemporary Asian America and the integral role of a certain subset within it that has contributed to the development of the US national security state.

Valerie Katagiri argued strenuously on my behalf against detractors that would have preferred a more modulated approach in pointing to the mental health establishment and the university-pharmaceutical complex as the source—not the cure—of the unnecessary torment and angst experienced by far too many of its victims. Connie Zeiller prior to her premature retirement from UC Davis was patient enough to hear hour upon hour of rants that coalesced into major sections of the present book. Dave Williams, a friend and musical band-mate since seventh grade at Brookhurst Junior High School, similarly was subjected to many of the themes that permeate this current work of mine. Another music buddy Mike Kobayashi got bits and pieces of the puzzle as well.

It has been a wild past few years at UC Davis. I am appreciative of the friendship and professional relationship I have forged with Caroline Kieu-Linh Valverde during this time. She endured unimaginably harsh treatment inflicted by individuals at the university but prevailed through the love of her husband Brian Turner. I was joyfully in attendance when they were wed one perfect summer day in Oakland, California.

I had the good fortune of meeting in person a good number of experts in their respective fields. Matthias Chang was most welcoming and generous with his time when we met in Kuala Lumpur. He continues to produce provocative and well-considered work. I had been an ardent reader of the eminent British writer Gordon Thomas before being invited into his home for lunch and a long chat. His life and amazing career warrants a book-length study in itself.

Michael Omi at UC Berkeley is one of the major theorists of race and ethnicity in the US. He is one of the more giving and likeable gentlemen one might encounter in the academic world. His comments and criticism of an earlier draft of the present book were invaluable in bringing it up to snuff. We both share a deep appreciation for the artistry of Hank Williams. I have been pestering Doug Kellner at UCLA for a number of years regarding this current project. He remained patient with my monomaniacal enthusiasms and suggested several publishers for this book. Importantly, spanning many years I have been influenced by the sheer scope and intellectual depth of his scholarship that ranges far more widely than usually is accepted in the academy. Much of his early independent TV and critical media work now can be found online. Appreciation to Madeline Y. Hsu at the University of Texas at Austin for inviting me to present new concepts in Asian American Studies.

During the writing of this book my daughter Gena S. Hamamoto married Chuong T. Bui on a perfect summer day in Pasadena, California. They too were subjected to the obsessive thoughts of the author but listened anyway. Thank you both for indulging me. In attendance at the wedding was Itsuki Charles Igawa-*sensei* and wife Yuko. I have known them both since graduate school and am thankful for their friendship.

My father died peacefully at age ninety-four before publication of this book. He was a man of grand ambitions and dreams but highly resistant to regimentation. In family lore, it is told that he entered in the US Army as a buck private and then sent overseas to Japan during the US Occupation. But he kept getting busted in rank so that he achieved the dubious distinction of being mustered out of the military at the very same rank he held upon induction: buck private. In this, I might unwittingly have followed his personal example. But Joel Koichi Hamamoto approached life with zeal and excitement and I thank him posthumously for passing on these traits to me. My mother Joan Kimiko Hamamoto (née Kakazu) sometimes would buy me DC Comics or *Mad Magazine* (less often due to the cost and irreverent content) when as a child I tagged along with her to the supermarket. This prepared me well for a university career. Thank you, Mother.

Darrell Y. Hamamoto
Sacramento, California

TABLE OF CONTENTS

Preface

This book began quite conventionally. The topic was to be "Asian American criminality." A number of titles on Asian-specific crime such as those by Martin Booth, Sterling Seagrave, David E. Kaplan, and Gerald L. Posner provided a solid foundation along with related literature that dealt more specifically with criminality in the US setting. The body of work by Ko-Lin Chin was useful in this latter regard although it suffered from the normative biases characteristic of the sub-field within sociology called criminology. His work on criminality in Taiwan, for example, notes the interpenetration of underworld organizations with the mainstream political system.[1] Chin, however, stops short of understanding criminal networks as complementary or even integral to the larger social system rather than existing in an antagonistic relationship to it.

Irish American best-selling writer T. J. English has probed the ethnic dimension of modern criminality in his compelling studies of mobster-led entities whether they be the Westies of Hell's Kitchen, Vietnamese American "BTK" (Born To Kill) in Chinatown of New York, or the legendary Jewish and Italian American syndicates that once ran Havana as part of a larger hemispheric enterprise along with an appreciable segment of the corporate, government, and political establishment.[2]

The fall of the Soviet Union saw criminal finance oligarchs setting up operations throughout Europe and the US. Fine work in investigative journalism has begun to emerge on the "red mafiya" including that by the late Robert I. Friedman, who died at age fifty-one of cardiac arrest.[3] US-born Russian writer Anna Politkovskaya investigated the highest reaches of post-Soviet government and was a prominent critic of Vladimir Putin.[4] She survived more than one attempt at murder, including a near-fatal poisoning, before being shot dead in her apartment building on October 07, 2006. Mischa Glenny, former BBC World Service correspondent for Central Europe and author of award winning books on the Yugoslav Wars and specialist on the Balkans, writes of the "new Silk Road" being traversed by transnational criminals exploiting the fluidity and chaos following the Anglo-American economic liberalization policies of the 1980s. The British-educated reporter refers to these globally linked networks as "McMafia" in homage to multinational corporate chains that exert a presence almost everywhere on earth.[5]

The "Mustache Petes" of yesteryear and the classic *goombata* that predominated for much of the postwar period by now are woven into the fabric of American popular culture. Beginning with the mass commercial breakthrough of writer Mario Puzo (*The Godfather*) at the end of the 1960s, Italian American writers such as Nicholas Pileggi and more recently David Chase (DeCesare) – creator of the critically acclaimed *The Sopranos* – have built careers portraying co-ethnic kinsmen within the criminal underworld.[6]

Though the subjects of his books is varied, ranging from reportage on contemporary American sexuality to a study of his former employer the *New York Times*, the estimable Gay Talese has drawn deeply from his Italian American heritage. He drew upon such existential knowledge in crafting his profile of Salvatore "Bill" Bonanno, which in turn inspired an autobiography by his father, the famed "godfather" Joseph "Joe Bananas" Bonanno.[7]

Films of operatic proportions by Francis Ford Coppola and Martin Scorcese stand collectively as the romantic epitaph for a heroic era now gone. Today, individuals such as Rudy Giuliani (his family past connections notwithstanding), Nancy Pelosi, or Janet Napolitano exemplify the era of the assimilated Italian American that serve the interests of the State as political insiders.[8]

Lest organized crime be understood as being in permanent decline, however, former *New York Times* reporter Selwyn Raab concludes his nearly 800-page best-selling account of the Five Families by raising the possibility for revitalization and renewal with the arrival of ambitious Asian and Latino immigrants.[9]

Currently, the dean of Italian American true crime writers is Gus Russo. His research skills concerning political assassination and state-level criminality helped shape "Who Was Lee Harvey Oswald" (1993) as part of the peerless PBS *Frontline* investigative documentary series founded by David A. Fanning.[10]

Independent writer Charles Bowden has written lyrically of the brutality and carnage inspired by drug war rivalries and gun-running operations that have become pervasive in many communities of the American Southwest.[11] The undeclared war and underreported systemic violence along the porous US-Mexico border where approximately 40,000 people have been murdered "in drug-related violence" since 2006 (according to the Council on Foreign Relations) is the manifestation of the robust state-level drug trade that bears more than superficial similarity to that once administered by the East India Company.[12]

Government agencies under US Atty. General Eric Holder have been accused of supplying weapons to Mexican drug cartels through the gun-walking operation code-named "Fast and Furious." As Bowden argues, the US-Mexico borderlands violence has less to do with ethnicity than destructive globalist economic policy initiatives such as the North American Free Trade Agreement (NAFTA). Moreover, the US-Mexico "war on drugs" fills the coffers of the banking establishment that is the ultimate beneficiary of a profit-system which, as historian Carl A. Trocki has documented, was pioneered by Anglo-American trading companies throughout much of Asia beginning in the mid-eighteenth century.[13]

The "first family" of Asian America – which independent historian Sterling Seagrave titled the "Soong Dynasty" – accumulated a healthy portion of its wealth through the robust international trade in opium.[14] They are given extended treatment in Chapter Three. One member of the clan in particular, Mei-ling Soong (Madame Jiang Jieshi), perhaps out of misplaced ethnic pride has been credited with advancing the lives of Chinese Americans by her having challenged "orientalist assumptions" concerning race and the status of the "new women" and race-based while successfully negotiating "whiteness."[15] By drawing upon research resources and material that largely has gone ignored within this academic specialty, however, startling and revelatory historical connections are revealed that hopefully will inspire a new level of intellectual honesty in future scholarship. The immature phase of heroic ethno-nationalist narrative in Asian American Studies is over.

The prime example of the liberal multiculturalism steeped in race-guilt used as a grand distraction from real and pressing crises within both the US and the larger globalist complex is seen in the cynical positioning of Barack Hussein Obama as "America's first Pacific president."[16] In truth, evidence is emerging from credible media sources that Obama aka Barry Soetoro is a third-generation intelligence asset brought forward to occupy the office of the presidency as were his predecessors George H. W. Bush and William Jefferson Clinton.[17] The apotheosis of Soetoro/Obama and the majority of Asian Americans, Latinos, and African Americans that supported him politically exemplifies the successful cooptation and redirecting of contentious postwar racial politics into a new multiethnic power bloc dependent upon an ever-expanding welfare state holding out the false promise of satisfying all manner of material needs in exchange for an illusory security that in the end primarily benefits the criminal oligarchs left free to plunder the real sources of wealth.

Perhaps the most dramatic example of an unexpected historical connection made during the course of research came when Douglas Valentine, an authority on the American government drug complex, identified a respected Chinese American medical doctor named Margaret Chung who had been involved in the transnational opium trade that implicated the KMT and members of the Soong family.[18] By contrast, a biography devoted exclusively to "Mom" Chung Chung recounts the celebrity status she enjoyed within the exclusively "White" world of the Hollywood entertainment business and her special relationship with World War II-era American military brass the likes of Adm. Chester W. Nimitz and Adm. William "Bull" Halsey.[19] As one of the first medical doctors of her gender and ethnicity to gain mainstream social prominence, Chung is portrayed as a proto-feminist role model. Because her biographer is limited by academic liberal-feminist biases, it misses her far more sensational function as a politically connected international intelligence asset.

Following up on this revelation by Valentine, the research sources I obtained uncovered a trail that led to an infamous figure in the history of American organized crime: Benjamin "Bugsy" Siegel.[20] Working closely with Virginia Hill, the flamboyant mistress and business partner of Siegel, Chung was involved with the KMT international dope racket that extended to Soong family bankers at higher levels of the pyramid. From this enhanced perspective that looks at the dark side of history, Chung represents a crucial and direct link between Chinese and Chinese American criminal networks, the American and Southern European mafia, US (and foreign) civilian and military intelligence agencies, and an extensive roster of compromised individuals within the US government, military, and business.

As the research and writing progressed through engaging the work of Seagrave, Trocki, and respected professional journalists, it became clear that the project as originally conceived was fundamentally flawed but for its naivety. Its thesis was that the "color line" – as first articulated by Frederick Douglass (1881) and later invoked by W.E.B. DuBois (1903) – was so indelibly impressed upon race relations in the US that Asian Americans were excluded from illegal forms of business enterprise that have served as the starting point for the political-economic ascent of the Anglo-Saxon establishment and the "White ethnic" groups that followed. That is, by virtue of their non-White racial identity, Asian Americans forever would be denied economic parity, social integration, and cultural representation for having been excluded from primary participation in the hugely profitable illicit economic opportunities that served as a springboard to political power and social legitimacy for a select subset of Irish Americans, Jews, or Italian Americans beginning in the late nineteenth century.

Within the first two years of background research, however, the original thesis had been eroded by the appearance of growing numbers of Asian Americans implicated in high-level criminality. The 2011 conviction of hedge fund founder Raj Rajaratnam for insider trading illustrates that Asian Americans indeed have crossed the color line into key positions that allow for corruption on a scale unimaginable not so long ago. Viewed another way, however, Rajaratnam might be seen as a sacrificial lamb burned as a public spectacle while the bosses of the too-big-to-jail Wall Street firms escaped without penalty while rewarding themselves with hefty bonuses.

Whereas the Sri Lanka-born Rajaratnam led the firm he founded called the Galleon Group, Vikram Pandit (Ph.D. Columbia Business School, finance) was CEO of Citigroup. Pandit therefore was protected by the political clout of the Wall Street giants that in effect has fused with government to execute the transfer of wealth from the middle class to the top one percent. Pandit was one of the first Indian Americans to be hired by a company that once symbolized the hereditary privilege of the WASP white-shoe boys that ran their exclusive club. Pandit and others in his pioneering generation might also be credited for setting off the "quant" boom on Wall Street whereby highly intelligent and ambitious Asian American mathematicians and engineers with little background in business or finance could be relied upon to develop elaborately arcane models that could be sold to institutional investors as snake oil.[21]

Even more sensational is the career of Enron executive Lou Lung Pai. Not long before the politically connected energy conglomerate collapsed, he sold over $250 million in stock and moved to a huge Colorado ranch with a stripper who performed at a local gentlemen's club he frequented with other high rollers.[22] Hawaii-born Wendy Lee Gramm (Ph.D. Northwestern University, economics) held a position with the Commodity Trading Futures Commission during the Reagan administration. From there she was won over by Enron lobbying efforts to gain exemption from regulation. Gramm – wife of Sen. Phil Gramm (R-Texas) – joined the Enron board of directors after leaving the CTFC. Her husband coincidentally was co-sponsor of the Commodity Futures Modernization Act (2000). Public Citizen reported that Enron was his largest corporate contributor at $100,000. Wendy Lee Gramm cashed in her Enron stock for $276,912.[23]

F. Scott Fitzgerald in *The Great Gatsby* (1925) gave fictionalized expression to the perhaps uniquely American story of rising through society starting from undistinguished social origins. The figure "Jay Gatsby" or "Gatz" had made a respectable fortune through his business relationship with "Meyer Wolfsheim," a bootlegger modeled after the notorious Prohibition Era entrepreneur Arnold Rothstein. Nicknamed "The Brain," Rothstein was given imaginative journalistic treatment by Nick Tosches who dubbed him "King of the Jews."[24] Earlier, in a path-breaking book Rich Cohen wrote of Rothstein as part of a larger cohort of "tough Jews" born of immigrant parents.[25] Together, they paved the path to financial solidity and social respectability through their involvement in the often rewarding but unforgiving world of criminal enterprise.

The definitive biography of Rothstein, however, is by popular historian David Pietrusza.[26] Although never prosecuted, it commonly was believed that Rothstein had "fixed" the 1919 World Series. The son of a wealthy and socially prominent businessman who through philanthropy and good works laundered his early reputation as a less-than-respectable wheeler-dealer, Rothstein had a taste for the New York demimonde. He combined his charm, intelligence, vision, and political connections to build a sizeable enterprise that attracted exceptionally talented underworld figures. Such individuals include the above-mentioned Bugsy Siegel, Charles "Lucky" Luciano, Meyer Lansky, and others whose legendary careers are memorialized in the newly opened (2012) world class Mob Museum in Las Vegas, Nevada.

In particular, the visionary Rothstein and company saw an unprecedented business opportunity in the national ban on liquor production, sale, and transport. Historians credit Prohibition with capitalizing the formation and institutionalization of national criminal syndicates. That FBI director J. Edgar Hoover insisted that organized crime did not exist allowed it to further expand and merge with the above ground economy and mainstream political institutions. Independent writer and former BBC producer Anthony Summers has written revealingly of Hoover and his close assistant Clyde Tolson.[27] They were regular guests at the mobbed-up Stork Club in New York and took extended vacations together that included visits to the racetrack, where Hoover could collect on winning bets while not having to cover his losses. Sexual blackmail, according to self-described "mob lawyer" Frank Ragano, was used against Hoover and his lover Tolson to ensure that his clients Jimmy Hoffa, Santos Trafficante, Jr., and Carlos Marcello could operate with minimum interference from the FBI.[28]

As a younger contemporary of Rothstein, by now even academic historians acknowledge the elaborate liquor importation schemes overseen by Joseph P. Kennedy during Prohibition. Wall Street insider trading, stock market manipulation, and clever maneuvers in the movie business further added to the family fortune.[29] Success in these storied endeavors in turn formed the foundation for the political careers of his sons. Two of the Kennedy brothers, however, met their respective deaths as a consequence of what many expert investigators believe to have been criminal conspiracies. Within recent memory, as he began to emerge as redeemer of the family legacy and potential restorer of the American republic, John F. Kennedy, Jr. was killed in the suspicious crash (1999) of the Piper Saratoga II HP he was piloting.[30] The accident also claimed the lives of his wife (rumored to be pregnant with a male child) and sister-in-law.

To place in historical perspective the differential disadvantages imposed on non-White groups such as Japanese Americans, only one year before the publication of this classic American novel by Fitzgerald the US Congress had passed legislation in 1924 that banned further immigration from Asia. The harsh legal-juridical and social sanctions placed upon the Oriental at strategic moments in US national history has been given extensive treatment by a good number of scholars in Asian American Studies. Such work represents a wide selection of academic disciplines ranging from that by the pioneering historian Yuki Ichioka to literary theorist Lisa Lowe and the recent contributions of social historian Mae Ngai.[31] In the social sciences, Michael Omi and Howard Winant wrote the foundational treatise on "racial formation" that establishes the relationship between race-specific legislation, labor market segmentation due to discrimination, and social ideology.[32] The racially defined subordination of Asian Americans, therefore, precluded the founding of family-based financial dynasties the likes of the Forbes, Russell, Rockefeller, DuPont, Astor, or Bundy bloodlines.[33]

Books by independent scholar Kai Bird have been especially useful in providing in-depth scrutiny of the Anglo-Saxon Protestant ethnic elite including McGeorge Bundy and brother

William Bundy.[34] In addition, Bird wrote a critical biography of John J. McCloy that traces his rise from Rockefeller family retainer to chief of the World Bank. His career at the top rung of the American establishment earned him the unofficial title "The Chairman."[35] As it concerns US national history more specifically, McCloy will be remembered as a principal architect of the mass internment and financial dispossession of Japanese Americans by insiders within government (including the US Supreme Court), the military, banking, and newly emerging private surveillance companies such as IBM. Non-academic historian Edwin Black establishes that the IBM data processing system first used to catalog and then round-up Japanese Americans was then employed against holocaust victims under the Third Reich.[36]

By the second decade into the twenty-first century, however, there is a "new" Asian America in the making. It is composed of an ultra-elite stratum of Asian transnationals in possession of exceptionally strong financial ties and international political alliances. As a group, they are poised to break into the ranks of those at the highest reach of society or the "superclass" as David Rothkopf refers to it.[37] A good deal of this book anticipates this historic turnabout. Contenders for this breakthrough bear the family names Murdoch or Zuckerberg. Each of these family lines are led by Asian American women that through strategic matrilineal marriage partnerships provide their spouses with interpersonal and political access to the burgeoning markets of "Greater China." The companies headed by their respective husbands are viewed with distrust by PRC oligarchs and therefore have encountered resistance from doing business in China. Wendy Deng Murdoch assumed responsibility for penetrating the Chinese market with Star TV and appears to making headway.[38] The impact on business based on information that Murdoch and Deng are divorcing remains to be seen.

Mark Zuckerberg also has encountered opposition to setting up Facebook operations in the PRC. That Facebook was exposed in June 2013 along with other US social media and telecom companies as tools of near-universal surveillance (code-named PRISM) via the National Security Agency will not make it an easy sell.[39] His Harvard-educated wife Priscilla Chan holds a medical degree from the University of California, San Francisco.

Her medical specialty in pediatrics and the concern she has expressed for the health of children presents the ideal humanitarian guise for a company whose founder has referred to Facebook users in most disparaging terms.

The opening chapter (since discarded) intended to "prove" the original thesis, concerned the case study of one, Ken Eto.[40] Even in the harshly meritocratic world of organized crime, so the argument went, the Asian American gangster was limited by his non-White racial identity. Among fellow Chicago mobsters on the street Eto was known as "Tokyo Joe" or "Joe the Jap." After being released from wartime internment at Minidoka War Relocation Center, Eto rose to the level of Outfit associate specializing in ethnic-specific gambling pursuits such as the profitable *bolita* numbers game. Despite his demonstrated ability over three decades as a top earner through the reliable and steady management of local rackets, Eto was excluded from top leadership because he was not "White."

After he pleaded guilty to racketeering charges in 1983 it was feared that Eto was going to rat out criminal cohorts to federal government investigators. As a precaution, *caporegime* Vincent A. Solano had Eto brought to him by automobile for a sit-down. En route to the meeting he was shot three times in the head to silence him. Remarkably, Eto survived the attack, testified against his associates, and died of natural causes in 2004 under the name "Joe Tanaka" while under the federal Witness Protection Program (WITSEC). By the time Eto died, however, Asian Americans had achieved a far greater degree of access to corporate, military, academic, and government institutions where higher order criminality can be practiced with impunity. Thus while being of historical interest, the life and times of Eto the small-time hood became less important than investigations into contemporary state-level expressions of Asian American criminality as examined in the present volume.

Chapter Five and Chapter Six revisit the campaign finance scandal that was exposed in 1996 during the Clinton administration. Both Asian Americans and Asian foreign nationals figured prominently in media reportage of the Congressional investigation that ensued. At the outset I assumed (along with his loyalists) that President Bill Clinton had been maligned systematically as part of an ongoing "vast right-wing conspiracy," as asserted in 1998 by First Lady Hillary Rodham Clinton in reference to the sex imbroglio involving Monica Lewinsky.

Despite the usual skepticism and caution exercised where it concerns professional office seekers, I initially held a favorable overall impression of both Bill Clinton and Hillary Rodham. By the time these chapters were completed – having viewed many revealing independent documentary videos such as *The Clinton Chronicles*, sifted through mainstream journalism, and read memoirs by close Clinton former associates such as Larry Nichols and those of partisan detractors – my assessment of the couple changed to that of utter repugnance for the sharp practices and reprehensible deeds they have been accused of committing dating back to their time spent in Arkansas.[41]

This pivotal shift in perception can be credited to books and articles produced by non-corporate, non-academic independent information outlets that proved indispensible in overcoming the parochialism of scholars within the academic community. One of the secondary contributions of the present work, therefore, is its commitment to respecting (while cross-checking and verifying) the reportage of citizen-journalists and non-academic investigators. These important voices went unheard until the advent of podcasts, vidcasts, websites, news aggregators, and e-newsletters that have broken the news and information "media monopoly" identified by Ben Bagdikian decades ago.[42] It was the *Drudge Report*, after all, that broke the Lewinsky story. This in turn forced *Newsweek* magazine – the epitome of corporate dinosaur media – to follow suit after first sitting on the findings of its own investigation into the affair.

Moreover, in researching this book I ignored party lines and eschewed ideological correct perspectives in drawing from diverse sources that run the full spectrum of thought and argumentation. As an example, one of the better books on the Clinton years is the exhaustive, heavily documented *New York Times* bestseller by Rich Lowry, editor of the conservative journal of opinion *National Review*.[43] Another example of the multi-perspective approach I have adopted is the fine investigative work by Charles R. Smith. He has written extensively on national security issues for *WorldNetDaily*, an online conservative website founded in 1997 by Joseph Farah.[44] Based on close to 50,000 US government documents he obtained through the Freedom of Information Act, Smith concludes that the Lewinsky affair was only a sideshow in the Clinton media circus. It distracted from his far more significant involvement with the transfer of US missile and satellite technology to the People's Republic of China. Loral Space & Communications, Ltd. paid a $14 million fine for having made this "mistake." The deeper implications of the "Chinagate" debacle are examined in Chapter Four.

At the "liberal" end of the political spectrum, the respected veteran author David Wise – possibly the first investigative reporter to delve into the shadowy doings of the Central Intelligence Agency and the "invisible government" (1964) – appeared on *Democracy Now!* in 2011 to discuss his book on Chinese spying on the US.[45] In the interview with host Juan Gonzalez, he cites the example of FBI asset Katrina Leung code-named Parlor Maid, who carried on romantic affairs with field agents while passing secrets to the Ministry of State Security for the PRC.[46] He also speaks of the theft of classified information pertaining to the W88 thermonuclear warhead for which Wen Ho Lee was blamed. More immediately, Wise has expressed alarm concerning digital warfare and cyber-espionage waged between the US and China.[47]

The campaign corruption revelations of the mid-1990s taken together represent a political turning point: It was the first time in US political history that Asian Americans had appeared in appreciable numbers on the national stage, albeit in an unflattering light. Guilty or not, their individual and collective involvement represented a political coming-of-age for a group that has been underrepresented historically owing to discriminatory laws, legislation, and social prejudice. The exception to this historical pattern is found in the State of Hawaii because of its large Asian American voting population. Out of this milieu came Nora Lum and her husband Eugene Lum. Through their aggressive support of Democratic Party office holders and candidates, they succeeded in being cut in on complex large-scale business deals both in Hawaii and on the mainland.

The Lum couple figure prominently in the *Frontline* documentary "The Fixers" (1997).[48] Prior to this they were investigated by the Honolulu office of the FBI from the late 1980s to 1993 for political corruption. They pled guilty in 1997 to felony charges for arranging illegal contributions to the 1994 election campaigns of Sen. Edward Kennedy and W. Stuart Price of Oklahoma. More importantly, the Lum pair was linked closely to Democratic Party powerhouse Ronald H. Brown. His role in even more extensive politico-financial machinations will never be known definitively since the Clinton loyalist perished in a plane accident in Croatia (1996) while leading an official trade mission.[49] It has been reported that Brown threatened to bring down the Clintons with him after he was left alone to face multiple government investigations conducted by the FBI, IRS, and Department of Justice. Brown and the Democratic Party had targeted the affluent segment of the post-1965 Asian American population to fund operations and direct the money into the hands of politicians that would look after contributors. DNC operative Melinda Yee left the Organization of Chinese Americans in 1990 to work under Brown. She was charged with the "responsibility of doing outreach to Asian Americans."[50]

I was predisposed to believe that the accusations and disparaging invective that colored the investigation of Asian American figures involved in campaign finance activity was motivated by the historically-rooted fear of a politically mobilized Yellow Peril. Once more, by the time this chapter was completed the self-protective assumptions I held at the outset had been crushed by the weight of evidence. For after having poured over reams of research material, Congressional testimony, published memoirs such as that by Judicial Watch founder and intrepid attorney Larry Klayman, documentary films, and conventional academic scholarship I was forced to accept the conclusion that the principal actors involved in what the press called "Chinagate" were complicit in the systematic attempt to compromise if not subvert the American political process by functioning as bag men for foreign powers seeking to acquire US advanced weapons systems.[51]

The conclusions drawn in the chapters that follow have met resistance from certain quarters within the Asian American establishment and no doubt will inspire negative responses. As an example, I previewed some of the observations and arguments advanced in the present project to a lecturer in ethnic studies and community activist over lunch at a high-end Chinese restaurant of his choosing in Emeryville, California. Aghast, he cut short his feasting and fled before I even had time to pay the check for the exotic dishes that had been ordered in advance of my arrival. But before bolting, he expressed a desire to write about a play about the Larry Wu-tai Chin spy case. Despite confessing to having committed espionage against the US, despite having sold classified documents to Beijing for over thirty years while a CIA employee, my lunch guest asserted that Chin remained true to his adopted country.[52]

This lunchtime encounter with the community activist and Chin defender illustrates that scholarly inquiry into Asian American history and politics has quite a way to go before it overcomes its ethno-nationalist biases and reaches a level of maturity where dark and unsavory doings are acknowledged, investigated, and punished. The objective in these pages is to realize a more nuanced and sophisticated understanding of contemporary Asian Americans within a social and political economic system dependent upon the advanced intellectual skills provided by its scientists, engineers, medical specialists, corporate managers, and allied professionals that function as ethno-specialist support personnel for "postmodern imperialism," as Eric Walberg describes it.[53] The essays in the present volume are intended to point up the centrality of race and ethnicity in the engineering of the postmodern techno-fascist world order.

As a consequence of sifting through countless government documents, depositions, TV and independent documentaries, interview transcripts – in addition to consulting scores of mass market, trade, and academic books – the present work represents a new synthesis that far exceeds the expectations I held at first undertaking this project. To cross check key information and analytical insights, a number of independent researchers were interviewed and consulted in developing the perspectives presented in these pages. (The theoretical underpinnings of the present critique will be outlined in a separate volume.)

These individuals include the prominent barrister the Hon. Matthias Chang, who in addition to being a writer of incomparable courage and passion, formerly served as political secretary to Prime Minister Dr. Mahatir Mohamad of Malaysia.[54] As head of the Perdana Global Peace Foundation, I met with him at his offices in 2011 just after Chang had just escaped a harrowing encounter with the Israeli Navy. While on a ship named in honor of Rachel Corrie that carried humanitarian cargo, the crew somehow managed to run a naval blockade and came within one kilometer of the Gaza Strip coastline before being fired upon and driven back into Egyptian territorial waters.

Recognized authority on Anglo-American and Israeli intelligence Mr. Gordon Thomas was kind enough to invite me into his home outside London to discuss different aspects of the detailed investigative work he has done. I was particularly interested in his reportage concerning PRC intelligence operations within the US. Not long before visiting the prolific author, the partially decomposed body of Gareth Williams, a Government Communications Headquarters code and cyphers expert on secondment to the Secret Intelligence Service ("MI6 "), had been found (August 2010) in a Georgian townhouse (possibly safehouse) in central London only blocks away from headquarters. He had been stuffed into a holdall (gym bag) padlocked on the outside. We also discussed the assassination of Mahmoud Al-Mabhuh of Hamas by Mossad agents carrying fake or fraudulently obtained passports from several different European countries.

What brought me to visit Thomas, however, was his assertion in one of his many well-researched books that both Chinese and Israeli intelligence cooperated in the theft of sensitive data from the Los Alamos National Laboratory for which computer scientist Wen Ho Lee took the blame.[55] More recent publications focusing on the advanced PROMIS software used for surveillance and espionage by Kenn Thomas and Jim Keith, Michael C. Ruppert, and Cheri Seymour have appeared following the trail blazing book on China spy operations by Thomas whose writing career covers over three decades of close professional contacts with members of the CIA, Mossad, SIS (Britain) and the BND (Germany).[56]

Over the past several years I have spoken with innumerable individuals both within and outside the confines of academia at lectures and conferences devoted to advancing the boundaries of knowledge concerning the hydra-headed globally integrated social system known variously as the national security state, shadow government, deep state, corporatist state, or the "new world order" as H. G. Wells decades ago (1940) wrote of it.[57] I have gone to great lengths in attending conferences, lectures, and presentations featuring such noteworthy figures as Peter Dale Scott (UC Berkeley), Jim Marrs (*New York Times* best-selling author), Ian R. Crane (formerly of Schlumberger oilfield services firm), and Peter Phillips and Mickey Huff (Project Censored).[58]

Most of these figures go ignored by the academic establishment, whose research agenda are severely constricted by norms set by the respective disciplines and dictated by extramural funding sources provided by private foundations that serve super-elite families, government agencies, and large corporations. Against such obstacles, credentialed independent researchers, writers, and scholars that operate outside of the university have been highly influential in the development of my thoughts on state-level criminality. Such acknowledged masters of independent scholarship include Edward Jay Epstein (Ph.D. Government, Harvard); John Prados (Ph.D. Political Science, Columbia); and Roger Morris (Ph.D. Government, Harvard).[59] Their individual contributions have made a tremendous impact on my grasp of the "deep politics" (Peter Dale Scott) that undergirds the ceremonial governmental superstructure.[60]

Over one memorable weekend in October 2010, I had the opportunity to attend an eight-hour presentation by the British writer David Icke at the Marin Center in San Rafael, California. The capacity crowd included younger "alternative" types, the aging Bay Area counterculture cohort, New Age dabblers, raw food enthusiasts, neo-pagans, café hipsters, and spiritual seekers. Attendees were about ninety percent "White," which might have accounted for my having been seated by ushers conspicuously close to front row center.

A former BBC presenter who once was shunned for his prematurely prescient analysis of the deep state, Icke has since held forth at no less than the Oxford Union Debating Society (2008) and in 2012 addressed an international audience via the internet from a packed Wembley Arena. The range of his socio-political analysis and thoughts on spiritual matters has placed him at the top rank of public intellectuals. His non-standing within academia notwithstanding, having lectured in twenty-five countries and published several books translated into a dozen languages, Icke might possibly be the most widely recognized thinker within contemporary popular culture.[61]

The very next day found me eighty miles to the south on the historic Santa Cruz boardwalk at the Cocoanut Grove to witness a stirring lecture to a capacity crowd by alternative media innovator Alex Jones. Beginning as host of a cable access program about nineteen years ago, Austin-based Jones has built an audience for his *Infowars* daily program that far outnumbers that of the conglomerate-media franchises like CNN or MSNBC. He also has directed and produced a number of masterful film documentaries that have done much to stimulate mass recognition of the social and political forces behind an emerging "technetronic" (Brzezinski) controlled world system whose endgame is the radical reduction of the human population rendered obsolete by advances in science and engineering.[62] During the June 2013 meeting of the ultra-secretive private Bilderberg Group held in Watford, England, both Icke and Jones joined forces with grass roots opponents of new world order predations. Acclaimed for his incisive and engaged reportage, Jones also was the first documentary filmmaker to peal back the mask worn by Barack Hussein Obama to reveal the banker-led globalist tyranny he was brought forth to impose.[63] Among 130 attendees of the conference was an international contingent of politicians, top corporate executives, and royalty convened to decide the fate of the world and its inhabitants.

Within this technetronic control grid, Asian Americans have been slotted into a defined function as "servitors" – neither masters nor servants – of an emerging totalitarian world system that has been warned against consistently since the end of World War II. Philip K. Dick, John le Carré, Thomas Pynchon, Don DeLillo, Umberto Eco, and many other brilliant minds in the world of arts and letters have delved into the secret world of political intrigue, conspiracy, and assassination. Diverse as they are in genre, style, and audience, the one underlying theme these artists express in common is alarm for the abstracted yet hyper-rationalized systems of control and contempt for the select incestuous few that sit at its apex. It is hoped that the separate but linked studies collected in the present volume offer insights and observations sufficient to sound the alarm for common defense against the accelerating deathly encroachment of the meticulously engineered, decades-in-the-making, globally integrated, centralized supra-state such as that being imposed by anti-democratic corporatist entities to complete the enslavement of free and sovereign humanity.

Endnotes

1) Ko-lin Chin, *Heijin: Organized Crime, Business, and Politics in Taiwan* (Armonk, NY: M. E. Sharpe, 2003).

2) T. J. English, *The Westies: Inside the Hell's Kitchen Iris Mob* (New York: Putnam, 1990); *Born To Kill: America's Most Notorious Vietnames Gang and the Changing Face of Organized Crime* (New York: William Morrow, 1995); *Havana Nocturne: How the Mob Owned Cuba and Then Lost It to the Revolution* (New York: William Morrow Paperbacks, 2009).

3) Robert I. Friedman, *Red Mafiya: How the Russian Mob Has Invaded America* (Boston: Little, Brown, 2000).

4) Anna Politkovskaya, *Putin's Russia: Life in a Failing Democracy* (New York: Owl Books, 2007).

5) Misha Glenny, *McMafia: A Journey Through the Global Criminal Underworld* (New York: Knopf, 2008).

6) Nicholas Pileggi, *Wiseguy: Life in a Mafia Family* (New York: Simon & Schuster, 1985); George De Stefano, *An Offer We Can't Refuse: The Mafia in the Mind of America* (New York: Faber and Faber, 2006).

7) Gay Talese, *Honor Thy Father* (New York: Harper Perennial, 2009).

8) Wayne Barrett, *Rudy!: An Investigative Biography of Rudy Giuliani* (New York: Basic Books, 2001).

9) Selwyn Raab, *Five Families: The Rise, Decline, and Resurgence of America's Most Powerful Mafia Empires* (New York: St. Martin's Griffin, 2006).

10) William Cran & Ben Loeterman, *Frontline*: "Who Was Lee Harvey Oswald?" WGBH Educational Foundation, 2003. Http://www.pbs.org/wgbh/pages/frontline/shows/oswald/etc/credits.html.

11) Charles Bowden, *Murder City: Ciudad Juarez and the Global Economy's New Killing Fields* (New York: Nation Books, 2010).

12) Aimee Rawlins, "Mexico's Drug War." Council on Foreign Relations 11 Jan. 2013. Http://www.cfr.org/mexico/mexicos-drug-war/p13689.

13) Carl A. Trocki, *Opium, Empire, and the Global Political Economy: A Study in the Asian Opium Trade, 1750-1950* (London: Routledge, 1999).

14) Sterling Seagrave, *The Soong Dynasty* (New York: Harper & Row, 1985).

15) Karen J. Leong, *The China Mystique: Pearl S. Buck, Anna May Wong, Mayling Soong, and the Transformation of American Orientalism* (Berkeley & Los Angeles: University of California Press, 2005), 160-61.

16) Mike Allen, "'America's First Pacific President.'" *Politico* 13 Nov. 2009. Http://www.politico.com/news/stories/1109/29511.html.

17) Alex Jones & Aaron Dykes, "Bombshell: Barack Obama Conclusively Outed as CIA Creation." *Infowars* 18 Aug. 2010. Http://www.infowars.com/bombshell-barack-obama-conclusively-outed-as-cia-creation/.

18) Douglas Valentine, *The Strength of the Wolf: The Secret History of America's War on Drugs* (New York: Verso, 2004), 72.

19) Judy Tzu-Chun Wu, *Doctor Mom Chung of the Fair-Haired Bastards: The Life of a Wartime Celebrity* (Berkeley and Los Angeles: University of California Press, 2005).

20) Ed Reid, *The Mistress and the Mafia: The Virginia Hill Story* (New York: Bantam Books, 1972).

21) Scott Patterson, *The Quants: How A Small Band of Math Wizards Took Over Wall St. and Nearly Destroyed It* (New York: Crown, 2910).

22) Robert Bryce, *Pipe Dreams: Greed, Ego, and the Death of Enron* (New York: Public Affairs, 2003), 205-09.

23) Nomad, "Friends of Rick Perry: Mr. and Mrs. Gramm 3/4." *Political Gates* 12 Nov. 2011. Http://politicalgates.blogspot.com/2011/11/friends-of-rick-perry-mr-and-mrs-gramm_12.html.

24) Nick Tosches, *King of the Jews: The Greatest Mob Story Never Told* (New York: Harper Perennial, 2006).

25) Rich Cohen, *Tough Jews: Fathers, Sons, and Gangster Dreams* (New York: Vintage, 1999).

26) David Pietrusza, *Rothstein: The Life, Times, and Murder of the Criminal Genius Who Fixed the 1919 World Series*, 2nd ed. (New York: Basic Books, 2011).

27) Anthony Summers, *Official and Confidential: The Secret Life of J. Edgar Hoover* (New York: Pocket Books, 1994).

28) Frank Ragano and Selwyn Raab, *Mob Lawyer* (New York: Scribners, 1994).

29) Ted Schwartz, *Joseph P. Kennedy: The Mogul, the Mob, the Statesman, and the Making of an American Myth* (Hoboken, New Jersey: Wiley, 2003).

30) John Hankey, dir. *The Assassination of JFK Jr.: Murder By Manchurian Candidate* (DVD). Alice in Arms, 2006.

31) Yuji Ichioka, *The Issei: The World of the First Generation Japanese Immigrants, 1885-1924* (New York: Free Press, 1988); Lisa Lowe, *Immigrant Acts: On Asian American Cultural Politics* (Durham, North Carolina: Duke University Press, 1996); Mae M. Ngai, *Impossible Subjects: Illegal Aliens and the Making of Modern America* (Princeton, New Jersey: Princeton University Press, 2004).

32) Michael Omi & Howard Winant, *Racial Formation in the United States: From the 1960s to the 1990s* (New York: Routledge, 1994).

33) Fritz Springmeier, *Bloodlines of the Illuminati*, 3rd ed. (Portland, Oregon: Pentracks Publications, 2007).

34) Kai Bird, *The Color of Truth: McGeorge Bundy and William Bundy: Brother in Arms* (New York: Touchstone, 2000).

35) Kai Bird, *The Chairman: John J. McCloy and the Making of the American Establishment* (New York: Simon & Schuster, 1992).

36) Edwin Black, *IBM and the Holocaust: The Strategic Alliance Between Nazi Germany and America's Most Powerful Corporation* (New York: Three Rivers Press, 2002).

37) David J. Rothkopf, *Superclass: The Global Power Elite and the World They Are Making* (New York: Farrar, Straus and Giroux, 2008).

38) Bruce Dover, *Rupert Murdoch's China Adventures: How the World's Most Powerful Media Mogul Lost a Fortune and Found a Wife* (Rutland, Vermont: Tuttle Publishing, 2008).

39) Steve Nolan, "Revealed: Google and Facebook DID Allow NSA Access to Data and Were In Talks to Set Up 'Spying Rooms' Despite Denials by Zuckerberg and Page Over PRISM Project." *Daily Mail* 08 Jun. 2013. Http://www.dailymail.co.uk/news/article-2337863/PRISM-Google-Facebook-DID-allow-NSA-access-data-talks-set-spying-rooms-despite-denials-Zuckerberg-Page-controversial-project.html.

40) William F. Roemer, Jr., *The Enforcer: Spilotro: The Chicago Mob's Man Over Las Vegas* (New York: Ivy Books, 1995), 249-51.

41) Patrick Mastriciana, *The Clinton Chronicles: An Investigation Into the Alleged Criminal Activities of Bill* Clinton (video). Citizens Video Press, 1994; David M. Bresnahan, *The Larry Nichols Story: Damage Control: How to Get Caught With Your Pants Down and Still Get Elected President* (Midvale, Utah: Camden Court, 1998).

42) Ben H. Bagdikian, *The Media Monopoly*, 6th ed. (Boston: Beacon Press, 2000).

43) Rich Lowry, *Legacy: Paying the Price for the Clinton Years* (Washington, DC: Regnery Publishing, 2003).

44) Charles R. Smith, *Deception: How Clinton Sold America Out to the Chinese Military* (La Porte, Indiana: Pine Lake Media Group, 2004).

45) David Wise and Thomas B. Ross, *The Invisible Government* (New York: Random House, 1964).

46) Juan Gonzalez, "As Biden Visits China, Author David Wise on 'Tiger Trap: America's Secret Spy War with China.'" *Democracy Now!* 18 Aug. 2011. Http://www.democracynow.org/2011/8/18/as_biden_visits_china_author_david; Michael Kirk, dir. *Frontline: From China With Love*. WGBH Educational Foundation, 2003. Http://www.pbs.org/wgbh/pages/frontline/shows/spy/.

47) David Wise, *Tiger Trap: America's Secret Spy War with China* (Boston & New York: Houghton Mifflin Harcourt, 2011).

48) Michael Kirk, dir. *Frontline: The Fixers*. WGBH Educational Foundation, 1997. Http://www.pbs.org/wgbh/pages/frontline/shows/fixers/.

49) Jack Cashill, *Ron Brown's Body: How One Man's Death Saved the Clinton Presidency and Hillary's Future* (Nashville, Tennessee: WND Books, 2004).

50) Steven A. Holmes, *Ron Brown: An Uncommon Life* (New York: John Wiley & Sons, Inc., 2000), 228.

51) Larry Klayman, *Whores: Why and How I Came to Fight the Establishment* (Sarasota, Florida: New Chapter Publisher, 2009).

52) Todd Hoffman, *The Spy Within: Larry Chin and China's Penetration of the CIA* (Hanover, New Hampshire: Steerforth Press, 2006).

53) Eric Walberg, *Postmodern Imperialism: Geopolitics and the Great Games* (Atlanta, Georgia: Clarity Press, 2011).

54) Matthias Chang, *Brainwashed For War: Programmed To Kill* (Washington, DC: American Free Press, 2006).

55) Gordon Thomas, *Seeds of Fire: China and the Story Behind the Attack on America* (Tempe, Arizona: Dandelion Books, 2001).

56) Kenn Thomas & Jim Keith, *The Octopus: Secret Government and the Death of Danny Casolaro*, rev. ed. (Los Angeles, California: Feral House, 2004); Michael C. Ruppert, *Crossing the Rubicon: The Decline of American Empire at the End of the Age of Oil* (Gabriola Island, British Columbia: New Society Publishers, 2004); Cheri Seymour, *The Last Circle: Danny Casolaro's Investigation Into the Octopus and the PROMIS Software Scandal* (Walterville, Oregon: Trine Day, 2010); Gordon Thomas, *Gideon's Spies: The Secret History of the Mossad*, rev. ed. (New York: Thomas Dunne Books, 2009).

57) H. G. Wells, *The New World Order: Whether It Is Attainable, How It Can Be Attained, and What Sort a World a World At Peace Will Have To Be* (New York: Alfred A. Knopf, 1940).

58) Peter Dale Scott, *The Road to 9/11: Wealth, Empire, and the Future of America* (Berkeley and Los Angeles: University of California Press, 2008); Jim Marrs, *The Rise of the Fourth Reich: The Secret Societies That Threaten to Take Over America* (New York: William Morrow, 2008); Ian R. Crane, *BP: Population Reduction & The End of An Age* (DVD), IanRcrane.co.uk, 2010; Mickey Huff, Peter Phillips, and Project Censored, eds., *Censored 2011: The Top Censored Stories of 2009-10* (New York: Seven Stories Press, 2010).

59) Edward Jay Epstein, *Agency of Fear: Opiates and Political Power in America*, rev. ed. (London: Verso, 1990); John Prados, *Presidents' Secret Wars: CIA and Pentagon Covert Operations Since World War II* (New York: William Morrow and Company, Inc., 1986); John Prados, *Safe For Democracy: The Secret Wars of the CIA* (Chicago: Ivan R. Dee, 2006); Roger Morris, *Partners in Power: The Clintons and Their America* (New York: Henry Holt and Company, 1996).

60) Peter Dale Scott, *Deep Politics and the Death of JFK* (Berkeley: University of California Press, 1993).

61) David Icke, *Radical Truth: Knowledge and Revolution* (DVD). Sacred Mysteries, USA, 2011; *Remember Who You Are: Remember 'Where' You Are and Where You 'Come'From* (Ryde, Isle of Wight, United Kingdom: David Icke Books, 2010).

62) Alex Jones. *Endgame: Blueprint for Global Enslavement* (DVD). Jones Productions, 2007; Zbigniew Brzezinski, *Between Two Ages: America's Role in the Technetronic Era* (New York: Viking Press, 1970).

63) Alex Jones, dir. *The Obama Deception: The Mask Comes Off* (DVD). Jones Productions, 2009.

CHAPTER ONE

ASIAN AMERICANS AND THE NEW WORLD ORDER SYSTEM

Twice-Told Tales

The overriding intention of *Servitors of Empire* is to move beyond outworn popular narratives and orthodox academic studies that describe and explain Asian American history almost exclusively through the lens of racial oppression, economic exploitation, and lingering regressive social attitudes that are claimed to limit access to the higher reaches of mainstream institutional power whether in business, the military, politics, or representation in the larger popular culture. These are major tropes in Asian American Studies, an academic enterprise that as currently constituted appears to be at odds with the defined population and the discipline it purports to represent. For if a recent Pew Research Center report on "Social & Demographic Trends" is to be believed, US Asians (most do not even accept the designation "Asian American") are overwhelmingly content with their position within American society and have great expectations for the future.

According to "The Rise of Asian Americans" (2012), this fastest-growing demographic group – outpacing even "Hispanics" – when compared to the general populace is characterized by advanced levels of education, enjoys a significantly higher median annual household income, and exhibits apparent ease in structural assimilation as seen in the prevalence (almost thirty percent) of marriage to non-Asians. With almost three-quarters of its population born overseas, Asian Americans reportedly are optimistic about their prospects in America and are confident that their goals can be reached by dint of hard work.[1]

The chapters that follow, however, also demonstrate why such optimism not only is misplaced but dangerously blinds Asian

Americans – even top-echelon adepts among the science, corporate, military, academic, and administrative super-class – to the exactingly planned installation of an unimaginably harsh comprehensive new world order system born of both ancient and contemporary totalitarian states but brought into fully-realized form through hyper-advanced technology that will supplant the vast majority of humanity irrespective of race and nationality. The most prominent proponent of this worldview is conceptual genius and creative innovator Ray Kurzweil, who advances a vision of man and machine merging in what he came to call "The Singularity."[2] Against Kurzweil stands Bill Joy – chief scientist and co-founder of Sun Microsystems – who in his essay "Why the Future Doesn't Need Us" (2000) sounded the alarm against the danger to humanity posed by developments in robotics, genetic engineering, and nanotechnology.[3]

As will be argued consistently in these pages, Asian Americans as a defined population have been recruited and positioned by the globalist overlords to assist in the planning and implementation of what Obama shadow-advisor Zbigniew Brzezinski in 1970 dubbed the "technetronic era."[4] Today, this blueprint authored by the co-founder of the Rockefeller-funded Trilateral Commission, member of the globalist Anglo-American Council on Foreign Relations (CFR), and former National Security Advisor (1977-81) to President Jimmy Carter includes the biological sciences, engineering, information technology, physics, and mathematics.

In addition, branches of the social sciences including economics, psychology, sociology, and anthropology have been staffed by appreciable numbers of Asian Americans to facilitate both the ringing in of the comprehensive new world order system and then to manage those held captive to it. Compartmentalized, specialized technical labor such as this is paralleled by a select class of Asian American intellectual labor placed at the highest levels within business, the military, and politics.

The one defining characteristic these super-managers share is a demonstrated commitment to the emerging new world order political-economic structure otherwise known in popular and academic discourse as "globalization." Indra Krishnamurthy Nooyi, chairman and CEO of PepsiCo by way of Yale School of Management, is ranked by *Forbes* magazine as sixth on its list of the

"World's 100 Most Powerful Women" along with four others born in India.[5] But Nooyi ranked #2 on its list of "powerful women" in the business world.[6] As Americans grow more aware of the dangers associated with the consumption of aspartame in so-called diet beverages and the use of MSG in snack food, the huge market in the exploited "developing" world has become crucial to Pepsi-Co, Inc.'s quarterly profits. With its historical connections to the American intelligence community, PepsiCo is among major corporations, the US military, federal government agencies, wealthy individuals, and private foundations pouring massive resources into the medico-pharmaceutical industry.[7]

As a political appointee, prior to her insertion as US labor secretary (2001-09) under George W. Bush, Elaine Lan Chao served on the board of directors of an insurance company co-owned by a subsidiary of the Lippo Group. The Hong Kong-based subsidiary, China Resources Holdings Co., is reportedly "an intelligence-gathering front company for China's People's Liberation Army."[8] The Lippo Group headed by the powerful Riady family of Indonesia was at the center of the campaign finance scandal that broke in 1996. The imbroglio helped subvert the political advance of Asian Americans as a group by smearing them with accusations of foreign influence and manipulation owing to illegal campaign contributions to US political candidates that were at bottom orchestrated and executed by foreign nationals and select numbers of highly placed officials such as Taiwan-born Chao.[9]

The daughter of James S. C. Chao, who founded a successful company in the shipping industry (Foremost Maritime, Corp.), Chao married into the American political system in 1993 by joining in holy matrimony with Sen. Addison Mitchell "Mitch" McConnell, Jr. (R-Kentucky). As a US senator, McConnell enjoyed campaign contributions and honoraria from intelligence-connected insurance giant American International Group, Inc. (AIG), headed by the legendary Maurice "Hank" Greenberg. Not coincidentally, AIG was the first foreign insurance firm granted approval to sell their services in China.

Elite family connections helped Chao pass through institutional filters into talent pools such as the conservative Heritage Foundation, where she served as chair of the Asian Studies Center Advisory Council formed in 1983 "in recognition of the dynamic

Asia-Pacific region's growing importance to U.S. interests."[10] In truth, Chao was paid an annual salary of $200,000 "to open doors in China for Heritage's corporate donors."[11] After stints as "deputy maritime administrator" with the US Department of Transportation and chair of the Federal Maritime Commission, she was tapped to head the ostensibly humanitarian Peace Corps. (1991-1992). She next moved over to the United Way of America (1992-1996) to help repair the public relations disaster caused by reports by the *Washington Post* of an organization plagued by "financial improprieties, mismanagement, and abuse ... "[12]

The corporate media, distracted by such an impressive record of public service, was silent about the close ties enjoyed by the Chao family with leaders at the highest level of government in China. Former PRC president Jiang Zemin (1993-2003), for example, formed a lifelong friendship at college with James S. C. Chao although he later fled to Taiwan in 1949. Conservative news organ *WorldNetDaily* claimed that both Elaine Chao and her father maintained "regular" and "deep" contact with President Jiang.[13] Yet on the website maintained by the appropriately named Horatio Alger Association, the elder Chao is characterized as the son of "subsistence farmers" although his father served as "principal of the village elementary school."[14]

The late Sherman H. Skolnick, an investigative journalist and court reformer based in the notoriously corrupt city of Chicago, went even further by writing of Chao and McConnell as a "husband and wife team" that are "reportedly fronts for the Beijing government in Washington." Writes Skolnick: "European and American intelligence sources assert that Elaine L. Chao's reputed links to the Red Chinese Secret Policy, together could easily fill a good-sized book or magazine article."[15]

Lest his work be dismissed as the ravings of an Internet conspiracy pundit, it should be noted that investigative reportage by Skolnick has been instrumental in exposing and checking the proliferation of judicial corruption and governmental criminality. Kenneth A. Manaster, former Assistant Attorney General of Illinois and currently Presidential Professor of Ethics and the Common Good at Santa Clara University School of Law, places Skolnick at the center of exposing a classic example of official corruption in *Illinois Justice* (2001) and lauds his contribution to rooting out the misdeeds of political insiders.[16]

Ultra-elite connections notwithstanding, as head of the $60 billion Department of Labor, Chao delivered the *coup de grâce* to the American working class by pressuring fat-cat labor union leaders to disclose the financial dealings of their respective organizations. She was not interested in eradicating union corruption as such. Rather, Chao used the threat of public exposure and possible criminal investigation to further induce well-compensated union leaders to cooperate with the master plan of sending heavy industrial manufacturing jobs to China, which had been designated by the international banking establishment as the means for realizing its vision of a post-industrial America.[17] From the time China was admitted to the World Trade Organization in 2001, the relocation of approximately 26,000 manufacturing plants overseas has spelled the loss of over 5.5 million jobs in the US.[18]

India, too, was brought in to crush the service sector and undercut even highly trained computer and information technology specialists. "Post-colonial" types like S. Gopalakrishnan and Nandan Nilekani were instrumental in facilitating the demise of the American economy through the multinational organization they co-founded with others in 1981, Infosys Technologies, Ltd.[19] Neither was specialized MBA-level intellectual labor shielded from the regulatory, tax, and profit benefits of moving such jobs outside the US. Athul Vashistha and Avinash Vashistha breathlessly tout the transfer of junior analyst jobs by Wall Street brokerage firms to "Bombay to do research functions" as the "booming hedge fund industry also jumped on the bandwagon and is offshoring everything from research to fund accounting."[20]

Keeping company with legions of unemployed American blue collar workers is an entire generation of young people that otherwise would have joined the educated middle class in productive professions that not long ago required only undergraduate degree credentials for entry. According to the *Associated Press*, fully half of recent college graduates were either without jobs or underemployed.[21] The goal of globalist mega-banks such as Bank of America, JP Morgan Chase, Citibank, and Goldman Sachs was to undermine the US economy by sending its formerly world-class manufacturing base overseas while reducing the once vibrant middle class to a state of perpetual debt bondage and eliminating what little remains of independent producers and small businesses unable to compete in the Wal-Mart economy. China was positioned by globalist planners to bring about this new economy of radically reduced circumstances for the majority of Americans who in turn would have no recourse but to utterly depend upon centralized government "social welfare" programs. By the end of 2012, almost fifty million Americans were receiving federal food-stamp disbursements.[22]

Having done her part by putting a Chinese American face on the global corporatist agenda of using China and India to decimate the working class while holding back middle class real income growth, Chao proved to be the best US Secretary of Labor that investment banks could ever have hoped for. While a thin stratum of politically connected business people in the People's Republic of China will reap massive financial benefits, James Petras daringly defies conventional wisdom in soberly predicting that its national economy will "become a territorial outpost for foreign controlled and operated banks and multinational corporations."[23] Meanwhile, at Foxconn assembly plants that manufacture Apple products, suicides, riots, and abuse by supervisors are endemic to these "teeming facilities" staffed by workers siphoned into industrial centers from the countryside.[24]

The Chao family, although successful in having staked a seemingly secure claim in the US system, are only mid-level players among contemporary Asian transnationals. At the highest reaches are heads of state that have been scrupulously cultivated, brought to power, and then burned after having outlived their usefulness. One of the better examples is the ultimate power couple, Ferdinand E. Marcos and Imelda Romualdez-Marcos. The illegitimate son of a Chinese-Filipino law student at the University of the Philippines who later rose to power as a judge, Ferdinand Chua, Marcos and his extended family benefitted from the patronage of his biological father and namesake.[25]

Having fabricated a tale of his being a resistance fighter against Imperial Japan during its three-year occupation of the Philippines, beginning in 1946 Marcos advanced through a succession of elective offices until he was tapped by American operatives to head a US puppet state that a the time was unrivaled in its political corruption and murderous police-state tactics that kept him in power as president from 1965 to 1986. Conditions had deteriorated so badly in the

Philippines that Marcos and his wife were forced to flee Malacañan Palace and were allowed by the US government to take up residency in Hawaii. Over the course of his US-sponsored reign, "Transparency International estimated that Marcos looted between $5 billion and $10 billon during his time in power."[26] The current generation of Marcos political leadership is characteristic of Asian transnational royalty, having been educated overseas while maintaining residences and secure bank accounts outside their home country.

Fantastic stories of political corruption, purloined wealth, and hidden treasure are not the only legacy of the US-Philippines relationship that dates to 1898. Alfred W. McCoy in *Policing America's Empire* (2009) argues convincingly that what began as a colonial police state established by the US in the Philippines gradually took root in the imperial core society were a "distinctively American system of public and private surveillance persisted in various forms for the next fifty years as an omnipresent, sub rosa matrix that honeycombed U.S. society with active informers, secretive civilian organizations, and government counterintelligence agencies."[27] That is, the national security state that grew to enslave ordinary Americans of the present was first rolled out in inchoate form overseas throughout Southeast Asia – the Philippines, Indonesia, Thailand, Vietnam, Cambodia, Laos – and brutally beta-tested on its civilian population before being implemented in the US homeland against American citizens with mounting intensity from the 1950s to the post-9/11 paramilitary takeover. According to John Prados of the National Security Archives in Washington, the Far East Division of the CIA at its peak during the 1960s "became the largest component of the clandestine service."[28]

After the US extricated its military from Vietnam, "frontline counterinsurgents" turned their attention to Latin America where the process was repeated using similar tactics and often employing the same shadow figures that were engaged in covert operations in Southeast Asia.[29] The production of opium, cocaine, or cannabis transshipment to the US, and money laundering by large banking institutions were the common denominator in Southeast Asia and Latin America, as in the case of Afghanistan today.

Perhaps even more significant than the obvious examples of ongoing political repression and official violence against its citizens, the Philippines since the early twentieth century has been one of the preferred test sites for medical experimentation and racial domination by the US government under the guise of "public health" research into tropical disease. This medico-social apparatus in turn was exported to the US mainland thanks to "colonial health officers" stationed in the Philippines that were "among the first advocates of what came to be known in the United States as the new public health."[30] As in the Philippines, non-Whites – particularly African Americans in the South – were targeted for the hygienic regime favored by the private Rockefeller Foundation and other mainline organizations that shared a philosophical and social commitment to eugenics.

Medical and scientific research along the lines pioneered by the international modern medical science establishment was given wide public exposure with the revelations at the Nuremberg Trials held after World War II. This did not, however, cause such experimentation and implementation to cease. Rather, a wealth of literature published in the decades after World War II documents that inhuman medical research has only accelerated and intensified. Highly sophisticated methods of crippling and culling the human population have been developed at the behest of the globalist elite that have advanced this agenda through their supra-sovereign bodies such as the United Nations and its World Health Organization.

Whereas historically the colonial powers including Japan have conducted inhuman scientific research through much of Asia, today Asian American research specialists predominate in the very endeavors that continue to sicken, deform, and kill massive numbers of human being without discrimination by race or nationality. There is genetic engineer Anada Mohan Chakrabarty, who set a disturbing precedent by prevailing in a landmark US Supreme Court case (1980) that cleared the way for him to become the first person to patent a genetically modified microorganism he developed while employed by General Electric.[31] There is Shyh-Ching Lo, who, as senior researcher at the Armed Forces Institute of Pathology, isolated and patented a pathogenic mycoplasma taken from an AIDS patient for use in bio-warfare and the creation of a host of illnesses that have run rampant despite ever-increasing funding for medical research. Diseases on the increase since the 1970s include chronic fatigue syndrome, Parkinson's disease, Crohn's colitis, multiple sclerosis, and fibromyalgia.[32]

Most prominent of all is David Da-i Ho, a hard-charging and ambitious medical doctor recruited to stand in as the public relations face of the campaign against AIDS. Having arrived in the US at age twelve without the ability to speak English, at the tender age of thirty-seven Ho was hand picked from the meticulously cultivated contemporary crop of Asian American bioscience workers to head The Aaron Diamond AIDS Research Center affiliated with Rockefeller University. As George Dyson compellingly recounts in *Turing's Cathedral*, the Rockefeller family early on reinvested substantial sums drawn from its ill-gotten wealth into science and technology research conducted by brilliant foreign-born intellectuals such as John von Neumann, Kurt Gödel, Edward Teller, and Albert Einstein.[33] It was Rockefeller money that transformed the medical profession in the US and wed it permanently to the pharmaceutical industry. The enormous profit this generated only added to family wealth that was shielded from taxation through its foundations.[34]

In an effort reminiscent of past campaigns run by the controlled corporate press, *Time* magazine named Ho as its "Man of the Year" of 1996 for his presumed contribution to ending the scourge of AIDS. Not all, however, were convinced of his achievement. Celia Farber writes in *Serious Adverse Events* (2006) that she embarked on her study of AIDS research largely accepting of the public relations story line crafted to win public sympathy and apply political pressure for more aggressive government funding.[35] She devotes an entire chapter to Ho and profiles the major figures competing with one another to make the breakthrough that would guarantee their respective reputations. What she expected to be a sympathetic inquiry into the AIDS saga instead left Farber deeply skeptical of the entire enterprise. A number of respected scientists including molecular and cell biologist Peter H. Duesberg at UC Berkeley and Nobel laureate Kary Mullis earlier had expressed disagreement with keepers of the AIDS orthodoxy. In the case of Duesberg, his previously thriving career slowed considerably for daring to raise legitimate objections among the community of retrovirus specialists.[36]

Orientals For Hire

Providing intellectual ballast and *ex post facto* ideological justification for the postwar triumph of Anglo-American political-economic corporatism on a near-universal scale is the likes of Yoshi-hiro Francis Fukuyama, the grandson of a hardware store owner in Little Tokyo, Los Angeles. Part of his family was interned during World War II in a US concentration camp although his own parents managed to avoid the same fate.[37] His maternal grandfather, Kawata Shirō, studied in Germany with one of the giants in sociological theory, Werner Sombart, whose library he acquired and took back to Japan with him.[38] Kawata Shirō founded the economics department of the esteemed institution today known as Kyoto University.

As an undergraduate at Cornell University, Fukuyama studied with Allan Bloom, who himself was to be thrust into the public arena with the much-discussed *The Closing of the American Mind* (1988). As a graduate student at Yale University, Fukuyama began as an acolyte of Jacques Derrida, Roland Barthes, and related figures responsible for the rise of philosophically-inflected "Theory" that overcame academic life after the demise of the political Left and dissolution of the counter-culture. It did not take him long to decide that this was not the path to follow. He then switched from literary studies at Yale to political science at Harvard, where he encountered the estimable Samuel P. Huntington. Not yet out of his twenties, Fukuyama wormed his way into foreign policy research at the RAND Corporation. This was his entrée to the world of full-time idea mongers that conceived of themselves as a managerial elite that would preside over the affairs of humankind.

With permission granted by RAND and given free access to its archives, author Alex Abella rendered a highly disturbing portrait of social science technocrats guided by "rational choice" theory. According to Abella, the shared ambition of his coterie of quirky and utterly mad intellectuals was to manage every aspect of life under an envisioned one-world government order led by the US.[39] Stanley Kubrick, who had connections to high-level insiders within the national security establishment that allowed him to realize the landmark film *2001: A Space Odyssey* (1968), lampooned the hubris of this collection of yahoos housed at RAND in *Dr. Strangelove* (1964). After dramatizing too accurately in *Eyes Wide Shut* (1999) the Saturnian occult sex-magick underground that thrives in plain view of blinkered humanity, Kubrick died suddenly only days after nervously screening his edit of the film to displeased Warner Bros. executives.[40]

Fukuyama might have languished in obscurity at the RAND Corporation in picturesque Santa Monica, California at the Pacific edge of mainland American empire had it not been for the publication of his often-cited essay "The End of History?" (1989). The article launched his career among neoconservative policy intellectuals that helped usher in the new world order or what they called "The New American Century." His timing could not have been better: The essay provided the sense of meta-historical destiny needed by his neoconservative adoptive family for their successful *putsch* launched during the Bush II administration.

After he belatedly realized that ideas have consequences, when they were used by his PNAC cronies to help set the stage for the US military invasion of Afghanistan in October 2001, Fukuyama tried to distance himself from the neo-con cabal. With the publication of *America at the Crossroads* (2006) and apparent climb-down from end-of-history triumphalism, his fate was sealed.[41] Fukuyama was cast out of Eden; shunned by those that had embraced him as an ideological brother. Charles Krauthammer, *Washington Post* columnist and promoter of the American-led "unipolar world," was particularly bitter over the apostasy of Fukuyama whom he cattily referred to as the "world's most celebrated neo-conservative."[42] Neo-conservative or not, the Fukuyama vision persists long after Bush departed from office. For his successor President Barack Hussein Obama has gone much further in violently imposing the "New American Century" upon countries such as Iraq, Syria, and Iran that remain holdouts to the new global regime.

Owing to his preternatural ability to morph physically and intellectually into seemingly every major historical turning point over the past three decades, Fukuyama might well be considered the "Zelig" of Anglo-American policy experts.[43] *Zelig* (1983) is the mockumentary directed by Woody Allen that traced the life of the fictional Leonard Zelig, who magically found himself among famous figures and major historical events during the 1920s and 1930s. In this, Zelig was the grandfather to Forrest Gump, who had uncanny dumb luck in altering the course of history from the immediate postwar years through the turbulent 1960s and into the Reagan era when Fukuyama was beginning to emerge.

The analogy drawn between *Zelig, Forrest Gump* (1994), and Fukuyama the historical chameleon is not at all strained. For in a Zeligian/Gumpian moment he once had the ear of none other than Libyan dictator Muammar Gaddafi. Fukuyama for a time had worked for a private consultancy group based in Cambridge, Massachusetts that held a $3 million contract to polish the image of Gaddafi for public consumption. Perhaps it is simple coincidence that only a few years later Libya was destabilized, Gaddafi deposed, and then murdered in 2011.[44]

After spending twenty-two years in Washington, DC as a policy intellectual during perhaps the most decisive moment in postwar world history, Fukuyama and his wife pulled up stakes and moved into a "beautiful house" located in "one of the most expensive zip codes in America."[45] This would be the zip code for Palo Alto, California; home to Stanford University and its famed foundation-funded think tank (Hoover Institution) that pays him to ponder deep questions concerning political systems, governance, and human civilization; classic themes brought together in his sweepingly magisterial *The Origins of Political Order* (2011).[46] Not bad for one of the founding members of the Project for the New American Century (PNAC) and signatory to perhaps the seminal document of the Anglo-American unipolar new world order endgame, *Rebuilding America's Defenses* (2000). As Fukuyama luxuriates in the California Dream situated in the heart of Pentagon Valley, the ideas he crafted in the deceptively measured cadence and tonality of serious social science has led to the blood sacrifice of countless lives lost to the end of history and the beginning of the new world order.[47]

Post-Sovereignty Illusion

The storied split between Fukuyama and the neo-conservative movement (whose founding members were internationalists of the controlled Left in their former devotion to Trotsky), however, is more apparent than real. For like his former political bedfellows, Fukuyama remains an ardent globalist who seeks a solution to largely engineered conflicts by invoking the suicidal concept of "shared sovereignty."[48] Neither is promotion of the one-world unitary power center agenda unique to past and present neo-cons alone. Left-liberal jargon-mongers are equally as guilty. The fuzzy vision of centralized supra-national governance is very much in vogue within contemporary academic orthodoxy, even among those that otherwise are repulsed by PNAC-derived foreign policy. Seemingly beneficent, humanistic, and caring concepts such as "flexible citizenship," "global citizenship," "cultural citizenship," or "borderless economics" sound warm, welcoming, expansive, inclusionary, and therefore highly appealing and saleable on an emotional level.[49]

These same concepts, however, also imply the abolition of US national sovereignty and demolition of the nation-state that, despite its unsavory history of systemic corruption, economic exploitation, and structured inequality, still stands as a firewall against predatory foreign mega-banks controlled by the supranational hereditary ruling caste that desires to bring down the United States of America financially and reduce its people to the condition of neo-feudal servants to the new world order. Those that trifle with clever-sounding formulations like "transnational citizenship" leave the door wide open for foreign nations to compromise political decision-making in the US. This was seen to be true despite the rhetorical evasions and denials of Asian American professional ethno-nationalists in the "Chinagate" scandal that launched a Congressional investigation during the Clinton presidency.[50]

The "Israel lobby," as John J. Mearsheimer and Stephen M. Walt refer to the constellation of institutions, organizations, and sponsored intellectuals like Fukuyama that have come to dictate US foreign policy over the past five decades, is a living example of the subversive influence that a foreign government can have on the American political system.[51] At the same time, sympathy for the plight of Palestinians subjected to Israeli oppression does not necessarily imply that Arab nations and Muslim theocracies are hapless victims of Anglo-American hegemony.[52]

While perhaps not as influential as the Israel lobby, the House of Saud exercises formidable political, financial, and cultural influence in the US due to its calculating deployment of petro-dollars across a wide swath of institutions and among a network of individual movers and shakers.[53] At the highest level, such individuals represent American dynasties such as the Bush family. Russ Baker in *Family of Secrets* reveals the unsavory history of the "Bush dynasty" by tracing its pattern of wealth acquisition through alliances with totalitarian governments, fascist political interests, and terrorist groups including those that use religion to cloak their decidedly earthly doings.[54]

The former Saudi ambassador to the US (1983-2005) was so close to the Bush family that he was called affectionately "Bandar

Bush." The love affair, however, was not to last. Prince Bandar bin Sultan met his death in July 2012 at the hand of an assassin, possibly because he was "wise to Washington's plot against the Saudi royal regime and sought a future in which Washington was no longer Saudi Arabia's superpower patron."[55]

Prior to the spectacular launch of Fukuyama into the elite intellectual firmament one would be hard pressed to find an Asian American thinker paid so much attention or conferred such an appreciable degree of political influence. Similarly, in a volume of essays (2010) that expands upon his concept of "inverted totalitarianism," the eminent political theorist Sheldon S. Wolin devotes more than a few paragraphs in an entire chapter on anti-democratic "intellectual elites" to Fareed Zakaria, the seemingly omnipresent Pakistani American opinion machine who writes a column for *Time* magazine and hosts his own program on CNN while pumping out books that simultaneously celebrate the wonders of his adopted homeland while promoting the dubious notion of the "post-American world." Interestingly, Wolin takes Zakaria – the privileged scion of an elite family that enjoys close acquaintance to such titans of global industry as Ratan Naval Tata – with the utmost seriousness.

As a protégé of Samuel P. Huntington with a whiff of Straussian elitism thrown in, Zakaria is viewed as emblematic of elite intellectuals that today put their formidable gifts to the service of state.[56] If his oily opportunistic hucksterism was not obvious enough to viewers of "Fareed Zakaria GPS" on CNN, in August 2012 it was found that a column he wrote for *Time* magazine "had passages lifted almost entirely" from an article by historian Jill Lepore that appeared in the April issue of *The New Yorker*.[57] He did receive a slap on the wrist by being suspended from both *Time* and CNN. His "public affairs" program, however, barely missed a beat and Zakaria continued with his Sunday morning fawning face-time sessions with such noteworthy figures such as Zbigniew Brzezinski, David Miliband, Hillary Clinton, Niall Ferguson, Timothy Geithner, Paul Krugman, George Soros, Bill Gates, Wen Jiabao, Thomas Friedman, Henry Kissinger, Condoleezza Rice, Jeffrey Sachs, Tony Blair, Al Gore, Madeleine Albright, Hamid Karzai, Robert Gates, and an all-star roster of other new world order types with an occasional Barbara Ehrenreich or Dalai Lama thrown in for the sake of variety.

Fattening Frogs For Snakes

The most clever trap currently being set for Asian Americans to divest them of their patrimony of individual liberty and accumulated community wealth is baited with flattery, praise, and accolades. This time around, the liberal multicultural revolution has paved the way for hand-picked Asian American specialists and brilliant minds from a variety of fields – ranging from the hard sciences, social sciences, and arts and letters – to participate in the planning and implementation of their own demise. Bringing this introduction full circle to the seemingly laudatory report issued by the Pew Research Center, "The Rise of Asian Americans," it would be wise to take the lessons of history seriously by harkening back to the illicit origins of Pew family wealth. Although the origins of Rockefeller wealth and power are fairly well known, Joseph Newton Pew was a key figure in the petroleum revolution as well. Having founded Sun Oil, the company grew multifold under his son and successor Joseph Howard Pew (1882-1971).

J. Howard Pew benefitted royally from insider access and near-monopoly control in oil and shipbuilding through two world wars. For most of the postwar period, Pew companies were notorious for the extraction of energy resources in Latin America and ruthlessly putting down resistance by "near-genocidal massacres of indigenous peoples."[58] With part of the proceeds from such massive, state-level criminality the Pew Family Charitable Trust was founded to protect its fictive legal status from taxation while funding a panoply of right-wing organizations ranging from the National Association of Manufacturers to arch-conservative think tanks including the American Enterprise Institute, Heritage Foundation, and Manhattan Institute for Policy Research.

Given the centrality of the Pew family enterprise to the corporatist power structure, the question arises as to why its intelligence arm (Pew Research Center) would be interested in Asian Americans as an object of investigation. The answer is obvious: Even more so than military might, information collection, research and development, and intelligence gathering combined with long-range planning has been the signal strength of ruling oligarchs in the West. It makes perfect sense for contemporary elite families such as Pew to commission studies on the different groups that it seeks to control (Pew Hispanic Center founded

2001) or those that might present a threat to its current and future fortunes.

Moreover, analytical assessment reports such as "The Rise of Asian Americans" serve as an entry point for the eventual financial dispossession of this identifiable US ethnic group with low-hanging assets ripe for the plucking. If this scenario seems far-fetched, a look back historically to the precipitous rise in the economic fortunes of Japanese Americans over the decades prior to World War II should serve as a warning. Through their US-born progeny and other means, this heavily studied group – seeded with co-ethnic informants and self-aggrandizing opportunists in business, the clergy, civic organizations, and education – was marked for the theft of its accumulated financial assets and real property.

Historian of American criminality Gus Russo perceptively likens this cooperative effort between elite mobsters ("Supermob") and US government insiders to the "Aryanization" of Jewish-owned property in Germany under the Third Reich. Under the auspices of the US Department of Justice, speculators with direct contacts in government succeeded in absconding with prime parcels of *Nisei*-owned agricultural land. "But for speculators with deep pockets," Russo writes, "the real bargains were in houses, undeveloped Nisei land, and commercial property such as stores, warehouses, and hotels."[59]

Beyond this and other innumerable examples of dispossession on the American continent alone, the rise, maintenance, and expansion of powerful central governing bodies controlled by the banking establishment is a universal pattern in history, parallel with the rise and expansion of the centralized nation-state. The process has reached its zenith in the contemporary US economy where now it is the entire middle class – irrespective of race or ethnicity – that is being dispossessed not only of its property and what is left of its devalued savings. Government reports state "middle income families have seen nearly 40 percent of their net worth go up in smoke since 2007."[60] Moreover, with the proud assistance of noteworthy Asian American scholars of law such as John Choon Yoo ("torture memos") and Viet Dong Phung Dinh ("USA Patriot Act") US citizens have been stripped of the personal liberty and individual freedom that are the preconditions of general economic prosperity.

The academic career marked out by Yoo and its disastrous consequences for the American republic is given extended treatment by Pulitzer Prize recipient Charlie Savage in an exemplary study of the political "takeover" executed via the unlawful and unconstitutional elevation of the US presidency to that of "imperial" chief executive. In devising scholarly arguments presented at symposia and published in law journals that undermined constitutionally specified congressional power, Yoo won the favor and support of the ultra-rightwing Federalist Society for Law and Public Policy. On the fateful day of September 11, 2001 the thirty-four-year old Yoo was in place with the Office of Legal Counsel attached to the White House to provide legal opinions justifying unchecked presidential power that bypassed Congress altogether. A confidential memorandum issued on September 25 makes this argument, "Yoo cited his own academic writing six times in thirty-two footnotes."[61] Thanks to the academic scholarship and memoranda issued by Yoo – known to former Atty. Gen. John Ashcroft as "Dr. Yes" in an allusion to the Oriental villain crafted by author and British intelligence hand Ian Fleming – the Bush administration was given legal cover to engage in all manner of horrific evil in the name of prosecuting the War on Terror.[62]

Harold Hongju Koh, his former professor at Yale Law School and an international-law authority on human rights, was critical of Yoo and his questionable arguments in support of limitless power for the commander-in-chief. Yet in 2009 Koh accepted a position as senior legal advisor to Secretary of State Hilary Clinton and turned from a harsh critic of "extrajudicial killings" to its most visible, ardent, and intellectually formidable proponent of the "official process of placing people on a death list" while providing "legal justification for the program."[63] Koh did his protégé Yoo one better by supporting the practice of so-called "targeting killing" and the use of what the Pentagon calls "unmanned aerial vehicles" (UAVs) in waging war against al Qaeda, the Taliban, and other so-called "non-state actors."[64]

The privileged son of a former South Korean diplomat and carefully groomed product of the transnational elite class, Koh has been complicit in an open conspiracy whereby the Mujahideen, al Qaeda, the Taliban, and lesser militant organizations were created, financed, and controlled by American intelligence with direct participation of foreign governments such as Pakistan and its Inter-Services Intelligence (ISI).[65] Such groups have been employed by the Anglo-American alliance to destabilize resistant regimes in Central Asia and the Near East; at the same time providing the pretext to place the US and its irrationally frightened inhabitants under lockdown, in anticipation of widespread rebellion against dispossession and the engineered economic crisis, to push what remains of the free republic into full corporatist tyranny.

This cynical war of maneuver has been acknowledged by establishment figures including foreign policy insider Selig Harrison, Rockefeller *consigliere* Zbigniew Brzezinski, and even Secretary of State Clinton herself in an interview (2012) with Greta Van Susteren on Fox News Channel.[66] Closer to home, through his public advocacy of targeted assassination Koh has opened the door for the domestic deployment of US military aerial drones against the American people.[67] At an annual meeting (2010) of the American Society of International Law, Koh representing US Secretary of State Hillary Clinton presented legalistic rationalizations for all manner of official violence including the "precision targeting of specific high-level belligerent leaders" which he claims does not violate "domestic law."[68]

The underlying argument of his presentation had it that the US was in full accord with so-called international law. In truth, as used by Koh and his sympathetic audience of legal specialists, "international law" is little more than a code-phrase for global centralized jurisprudence that undermines US national sovereignty against the predations of the foreign banking families that are determined to bring America to its knees. This alarming turn of events reveals the "endgame" of the foreign hereditary financial elite that has assumed control over the US economy over time to place it under military lockdown in anticipation of widespread social chaos and political rebellion of the sort bursting forth through much of Western Europe.[69]

Boiling Frogs

Now that the "frogs" have been "fattened" to the maximum by the US laboring classes over several decades of wealth-generation and technological advance unprecedented in world history, the "snake" families among the globalist financial dictatorship have swallowed the national economy whole and spat it out on the People's Republic of China where the process is already being repeated.[70] The Chinese Communist Party (CCP), however, according to a CNN "senior China analyst," is preparing for an anticipated double-cross by strengthening its existing military and making official statements about the possibility of war with the US. State Council think-tank associate Tong Gang has been quoted as saying that the US-led Iraq War is the first stage in the desire of American leaders to "build a new world order under U.S. domination."[71]

Tellingly, the *Financial Times* reports that a PRC expatriate who has been living in the US since 1994 has published a book that has become a best seller in China (200,000 copies sold; 400,000 estimated pirated editions) and read at "senior levels of government and business."[72] Song Hongbing, author of *Currency Wars* (2007) discovered to his surprise that the US Federal Reserve is in truth a privately held central bank and warns of the potentially disastrous implications for the Chinese economy should its financial system be exposed to outside global oligarchs. It is the central banks, such as the non-governmental US Federal Reserve and International Monetary Fund (IMF) established by international finance oligarchs via stealth, assassination, disinformation, and munificent pay-offs, that function as the dynamo of the new world order political-economic system.[73]

Although the present study runs the risk of incurring renewed suspicion and hostility against Asian Americans who historically have been politically contained and culturally constrained by members of the dominant society and its institutions, it is clear that an open and honest look at its crimes, misdemeanors, and misprisions is long overdue. Thanks to the equality revolution of the 1960s, an expanded social space has been created and related opportunity structures set in place that have allowed Asian Americans a markedly better shot at achieving the full and substantive equality that undergirds the promise of a constitutional republic and its liberal democratic political culture that is being undermined by the corporatist terror state installed by domestic and foreign offshore banking oligarchs. In America, the privately owned US Federal Reserve Bank and its income tax scheme stands at the center of a political-economic order that is undergoing a controlled collapse.

Such measurable progress over the past forty years, however, cannot ignore the reality that certain segments of the contemporary Asian American population have filled this newly created social space with their own brand of cynically driven exploitation, opportunism, and power mongering. One of the important lessons derived from the present wide-ranging and often dark account, is that the concepts of "race" "ethnicity," and "class" that were once held at the margins of scholarly inquiry are now benign and taken-for-granted categories of observation, description, and explanation. The danger lies in the fact that what was once a radically innovative contribution to the theory and method of understanding the social world has become not just domesticated but turned against the very groups that brought these once-incisive analytical concepts to the fore.

"Race" and "ethnicity" as social categories and organizing concepts have been appropriated by the contemporary globalist planners and propaganda agents for cynical use in the political sphere. The political apotheosis of Barack Hussein Obama is perhaps the best example of this twisted race-logic that leads to the totalitarian endgame presided over by the banking elite that seeks to bring America to its knees by making the economy scream until its dramatically devalued assets are snapped up for pennies on the dollar.

Meanwhile, as those in the social sciences and humanities dicker over race/class/ethnicity/gender, advances in human genomics science have seen "race" being weaponized in corporate, government, and university research laboratories for current and future use in the disease creation medico-pharmaceutical industry established by Rockefeller agent and "master talent scout" Simon Flexner (1863-1946) early in the twentieth century.[74] This is clearly stated in "Rebuilding America's Defenses" wherein its PNAC-affiliated authors allow for "advanced forms of biological warfare that can "'target' specific genotypes" to realize its bleakly Satanic vision of the world. The contemporary cohort of Asian Americans in white lab coats installed at the finest, prestigious research institutions across the land have been recruited at home and abroad to help realize this system of total scientific control as first articulated both in fiction and essay form by British giants of arts & letters such as H.G. Wells (1866-1946), Aldous Huxley (1894-1963), and George Orwell [Eric Arthur Blair] (1903-1950).

Contrary to orthodox literary criticism taught at school and the university, their works of fiction were not warnings of a dystopic, totalitarian future. Rather, such popular entertainments were public announcements (predictive programming) of the shape of things to come as articulated as far back as the reign of Elizabeth I (1558-1603) when promising forays into the "new world" inspired her advisor and magus Dr. John Dee (1527-1608) to advance the argument (*Brytannicae reipublicae synopsis* (1570) for a global "Britannia."[75]

That the likes of Yoshihiro Francis Fukuyama was signatory to this foundational document of Anglo-American globalized evil that has led to endless foreign wars and domestic police-military repression is possibly the most extreme example of the perverse success that select Asian Americans now enjoy within the larger US society.[76] By his insistence that centralized and concentrated power is required to allow the state to function properly, Fukuyama has provided ideological legitimacy to the rapidly evolving Brzezinskian-Kurzweilian hyper-efficient technetronic-managed corporatist Über-State that will cause widespread material deprivation and human suffering that will engulf all save the hereditary banking monarchs and a limited number of the "super-class" (as referred to by former managing director of Kissinger Associates David Rothkopf) to oversee the totalitarian system.[77]

For the rest of us left above ground and outside the blast door to fend for ourselves, the liveried crypto-classicist intellectual Fukuyama can revel in the historical irony that his work has laid the ideological foundation for a global gulag, far more extensive than that which his interned relatives were forced to endure under the "New Deal" regime, staffed by globalists like John J. McCloy (who proved his mettle to his superiors by orchestrating the internment of Japanese Americans during World War II and then advanced to the highest level of corporate and governmental positions) and other unelected architects of the new world order. The final double-irony for Fukuyama, however, is that the grand ideas he has wrapped in the rhetoric of classical liberalism has been appropriated and put to practical use by nefarious elements to justify the imposition of an absolutist leviathan supra-state that condemns his progeny to a chaotic present and a dismal future.

Endnotes

1) Paul Taylor, ed., "The Rise of Asian Americans." Washington, DC: Pew Research Center 19 Jun. 2012.

2) Ray Kurzweil, *The Singularity Is Near: When Humans Transcend Biology* (New York: Penguin Books, 2006).

3) Bill Joy, "Why The Future Doesn't Need Us." *Wired* (Apr. 2000). Http://www.wired.com/wired/archive/8.04/joy.html.

4) Zbigniew Brzezinski, *Between Two Ages: America's Role in the Technetronic Era* (New York: Viking Press, 1970).

5) "Indra Nooyi, Chandra Kochar in Forbes Most Powerful Women List." *Zeebiz.com* 22 Aug. 2012. Http://zeenews.india.com/business/news/companies-/indra-nooyi-chanda-kochhar-in-forbes-most-powerful-women-list_58652.html.

6) Jenna Goudreau, "The World's Most Powerful Women In Business 2012." *Forbes.com* 22 Aug. 2012. Http://www.forbes.com/sites/jennagoudreau/2012/08/22/worlds-most-powerful-women-in-business-indra-nooyi-sheryl-sandberg-meg-whitman/.

7) Mike Adams, "NaturalNews Exposes Secret Vaccine Industry Ties and Military Involvement with Institute of Medicine, Reveals Fatal Conflicts of Interest at IoM." *NaturalNews.com* 29 Aug. 2011. Http://www.naturalnews.com/033455_Institute_of_Medicine_vaccines.html.

8) Paul Sperry, "Chao Has Biz Ties to Lippo." *WorldNetDaily.com*, 01 Jan. 2001. Http://www.wnd.com/2001/01/7869/.

9) Larry Klayman and Thomas Fitton, *The Judicial Watch 2002 "State of the Union" Report: Bush Administration Ethics Enforcement "A Failure of Leadership"* 01 Feb. 2002. Http://www.judicialwatch.org/archive/ois/specials/bushenforce.htm.

10) *The Heritage Foundation* website. Http://www.heritage.org/about/staff/departments/asian-studies-center.

11) Paul Sperry, "Heritage Raised 'Several Million' in Hong Kong," *WorldNetDaily* 29 Jun. 2001. Http://www.wnd.com/2001/06/9830/.

12) *ElaineLChao.com*. Http://www.elainelchao.com/united-way/.

13) John Dougherty, "Elaine Chao's Ties to Chinese Leader." *WorldNetDaily* 13 Jan. 2001. Http://www.wnd.com/2001/01/7823/.

14) *Horatio Alger Association* website. Http://www.horatioalger.org/member_info.cfm?memberid=cha09.

15) Sherman H. Skolnick, "Red Chinese Get Big Bucks in Secret Hostage Deals." *Skolnick's Report* 11 Apr. 2001. Http://www.skolnicksreport.com/rcshdeals.html.

16) Kenneth A. Manaster, *Illinois Justice: The Scandal of 1969 and the Rise of John Paul Stevens* (Chicago: University of Chicago Press, 2001).

17) Whitney Black, "The Last One Standing." *The Weekly Standard* 15 Jan. 2001. Http://staging.weeklystandard.com/Content/Public/Articles/000/000/013/148kdjsl.asp.

18) Dustin Ensinger, "Trade Deficit With China Could Cost Half-a-Million Jobs." *Economy In Crisis* 04 Oct. 2010. Http://economyincrisis.org/content/trade-deficit-china-could-cost-half-million-jobs.

19) Al Saracevic et al., "Pioneer in the Field of Global Outsourcing." *San Francisco Chronicle* 29 Jun. 2008. Http://sfgate.com/cgi-bin/article.cgi?f=/c/a/2008/06/29/BUFS11EDL1.DTL *SFGate.com*.

20) Atul Vashistha and Avinash Vashistha, *The Offshore Nation: Strategies for Success in Global Outsourcing and Offshoring* (New York: McGraw-Hill, 2006), 42-43.

21) Hope Yen, "Half of Recent College Grads Underemployed or Jobless, Analysis Says."

Associated Press 23 Apr. 2012. Http://www.cleveland.com/business/index.ssf/2012/04/half_of_recent_college_grads_u.html.

22) Alan Bjerga, "Food-Stamp Use Climbs to Record, Reviving Campaign Issue." *Bloomberg* 04 Sep. 2012. Http://www.bloomberg.com/news/2012-09-04/food-stamp-use-climbed-to-record-46-7-million-in-june-u-s-says.html.

23) James Petras, *Rulers and Ruled in the US Empire: Bankers, Zionists, Militants* (Atlanta, Georgia: Clarity Press, 2007), 162.

24) Jay Greene, "Riots, Suicides, and Other Issues in Foxconn's iPhone Factories." *CNET* 25 Sep. 2012. Http://news.cnet.com/8301-13579_3-57515968-37/riots-suicides-and-other-issues-in-foxconns-iphone-factories/.

25) Sterling Seagrave, *The Marcos Dynasty* (New York: Harper & Row, Publishers, 1988), 22-24.

26) Michael Woodiwiss, *Gangster Capitalism: The United States and the Global Rise of Organized Power* (New York: Carroll & Graf Publishers, 2005), 172.

27) Alfred W. McCoy, *Policing America's Empire: The United States, the Philippines, and the Rise of the Surveillance State* (Madison, Wisconsin: The University of Wisconsin Press, 2009), 521.

28) John Prados, *Lost Crusader: The Secret Wars of CIA Director William Colby* (New York: Oxford University Press, 2003), 158.

29) Greg Grandin, *Empire's Workshop: Latin America, the United States, and the Rise of the New Imperialism* (New York: Owl Books, 2007), 111.

30) Warwick Anderson, *Colonial Pathologies: American Tropical Medicine, Race, and Hygiene in the Philippines* (Durham, North Carolina: Duke University Press, 2006), 96-97.

31) "Gene Patents and Global Competition Issues." *Genetic Engineering & Biotechnology News* 01 Jan. 2006 (Vol. 26, No. 1). Http://www.genengnews.com/articles/chitem.aspx?aid=1163&chid=0.

32) Lawrence K. Altman, MD, "The Doctor's World; Unusual Microbe, Once Dismissed, Is Not Taken More Seriously." *New York Times* 16 Jan. 1990. Https://www.nytimes.com/1990/01/16/science/the-doctor-s-world-unusual-microbe-once-dismissed-is-not-taken-more-seriously.html.

33) George Dyson, *Turing's Castle: The Origins of the Digital Universe* (New York: Pantheon, 2012.)

34) Gary Allen, "The Power of Foundations." *Educate-Yourself* (1976). Http://educate-yourself.org/ga/RF4chap1976.shtml.

35) Celia Farber, *Serious Adverse Events: An Uncensored History of AIDS* (Brooklyn, New York: Melville House, 2006).

36) *House of Numbers: Anatomy of an Epidemic*. Brent W. Leung, dir. Knowledge Matters (2009).

37) Ben Wattenberg, *Think Tank* 07 Oct. 1999. Http://www.pbs.org/thinktank/transcript914.html.

38) Fred Halliday, "An Encounter With Fukuyama." *New Left Review* I/193 (May-June 1992), 89-95.

39) Alex Abella, *Soldiers of Reason: The RAND Corporation and the Rise of the American Empire* (Orland, Florida: Harcourt, Inc., 2008).

40) Jay Weidner, "Kubrick's Odyssey: The Brotherhood of Saturn and the Clash of Civilizations. *Red Ice Radio* 06 Mar. 2011. Http://www.redicemembers.com/secure/radio/program.php?id=453. Weidner notes that the altered orgy scene was filmed at mansion (Mentmore Towers) outside London built by Baron Mayer de Rothschild.

41) Francis Fukuyama, *America at the Crossroads: Democracy, Power, and the Neocon-*

servative Legacy (New Haven: Yale University Press, 2006).

42) Charles Krauthammer, "Fukuyama's Fantasy." *Washington Post* 28 Mar. 2006. Http://www.washingtonpost.com/wp-dyn/content/article/2006/03/27/AR2006032701298.html

43) According to the late Carroll Quigley (cited publicly as an intellectual influence by President [and Rhodes scholar] Bill Clinton) of Georgetown University, the British and American alliance was cemented by the early 1900s via a close-knit group empire builders centered on Cecil Rhodes and then Alfred Milner. The alliance to the present day is at the center of what is referred to in these pages as the new world order. See Carroll Quigley, *The Anglo-American Establishment: From Rhodes to Cliveden* (San Pedro, California: GSG & Associates, 1981).

44) Ed Pilkington, US Firm Monitor Group Admits Mistakes Over $3m Gaddafi Deal." *The Guardian* 03 Mar. 2011. Http://www.guardian.co.uk/world/2011/mar/04/monitor-group-us-libya-gaddafi.

45) Andrew Bast, "The Beginning of History." *The Daily Beast* 10 Apr. 2011. Http://www.thedailybeast.com/newsweek/2011/04/10/the-beginning-of-history.html.

46) Francis Fukuyama, *The Origins of Political Order: From Prehuman Times to the French Revolution* (New York: Farrar, Straus and Giroux, 2011).

47) "Over One Million Iraqi Deaths Caused by US Occupation." *Project Censored* 30 Apr. 2010. Http://www.projectcensored.org/top-stories/articles/1-over-one-million-iraqi-deaths-caused-by-us-occupation/.

48) Fukuyama (2006), 179-80.

49) See Aihwa Ong, *Flexible Citizenship: The Cultural Logics of Transnationality* (Durham, North Carolina: Duke University Press, 1999); April Carter, *The Political Theory of Global Citizenship* (New York: Routledge, 2001).

50) Michael Chang, *Racial Politics in an Era of Transnational Citizenship: The 1996 "Asian Donorgate" Controversy in Perspective* (Lanham, Maryland: Lexington Books, 2004).

51) John J. Mearsheimer and Stephen M. Walt, *The Israel Lobby and U.S. Foreign Policy* (New York: Farrar, Straus and Giroux, 2007).

52) John R. MacArthur, "The Vast Power of the Saudi Lobby." *The Providence Journal* 16 Apr. 2007. Http://spme.net/cgi-bin/articles.cgi?ID=2134.

53) The Center for Public Integrity, "Saudis Drop Big Bucks For Washington Influence." *Publicintegrity.org* 22 Sep. 2004. Http://www.publicintegrity.org/2004/09/22/5961/saudis-drop-big-bucks-washington-influence.

54) Russ Baker, *Family of Secrets: The Bush Dynasty, The Powerful Forces That Put It In the White House, and What Their Influence Means For America* (New York: Bloomsbury Press, 2009).

55) Saman Mohammadi, "Did Washington Kill Its Favourite Saudi Prince, Bandar Bush?" *Infowars.com* 01 Aug. 2012. Http://www.infowars.com/did-washington-kill-its-favourite-saudi-prince-bandar-bush/.

56) Sheldon S. Wolin, *Democracy Incorporated: Managed Democracy and the Specter of Inverted Totalitarianism* (Princeton, New Jersey: Princeton University Press, 2010), 174-78.

57) Christine Haughney, "A Media Personality, Suffering a Blow to His Image, Ponders a Lesson." *New York Times* 19 Aug. 2012. Http://www.nytimes.com/2012/08/20/business/media/scandal-threatens-fareed-zakarias-image-as-media-star.html?_r=2&pagewanted=all&.

58) Richard Sanders, "J. Howard Pew (1882-1971)." *Press for Conversion!* March 2004. Http://coat.ncf.ca/our_magazine/links/53/pew.html.

59) Gus Russo, *Supermob: How Sidney Korshak and His Criminal Associates Became America's Hidden Power Brokers* (New York: Bloomsbury, 2007), 105.

60) Mike Whitney, "Welcome to the Lousiest Recovery of All Time." Http://www.counterpunch.org/2012/11/16/welcome-to-the-lousiest-recovery-of-all-time/.

61) Charlie Savage, *Takeover: The Return of the Imperial Presidency and the Subversion of American Democracy* (New York: Back Bay Books, 2008), 82.

62) David Cole, *Justice At War: The Men and Ideas That Shaped America's War on Terror* (New York: New York Review Books, 2008), *xix.*

63) Tara McKelvey, "Interview With Harold Koh, Obama's Defender of Drone Strikes." *The Daily Beast* 08 Apr. 2012. Http://www.thedailybeast.com/articles/2012/04/08/interview-with-harold-koh-obama-s-defender-of-drone-strikes.html.

64) Renee Dopplick, "ASIL Keynote Highlight: US Legal Adviser Harold Koh Asserts Drone Warfare Is Lawful Self-Defense Under International Law." *Inside Justice* 26 Mar. 2010. Http://insidejustice.com/law/index.php/intl/2010/03/26/asil_koh_drone_war_law.

65) Washington's Blog, "Sleeping With the Devil: How U.S. and Saudi Backing of Al Qaeda Led to 9/11." *Global Research* 05 Sep. 2010. Http://www.globalresearch.ca/sleeping-with-the-devil-how-u-s-and-saudi-backing-of-al-qaeda-led-to-911/5303313.

66) *Global Research TV*, "Hillary Clinton Admits the U.S. Government Created al-Qaeda" 22 May 2012. Http://tv.globalresearch.ca/2012/05/hillary-clinton-admits-us-government-created-al-qaeda.

67) Jennifer Lynch, "Newly Released Drone Records Reveal Extensive Military Flights in US. *Electronic Frontier Foundation* 05 Dec. 2012. Https://www.eff.org/deeplinks/2012/12/newly-released-drone-records-reveal-extensive-military-flights-us.

68) Harold Hongju Koh, "The Obama Administration and International Law." Annual Meeting of the American Society of International Law." Washington, DC (March 25, 2010). Http://www.state.gov/s/l/releases/remarks/139119.htm.

69) Alex Jones, *Endgame: Blueprint For Global Enslavement* (DVD). Disinformation, 2007.

70) Ma Nan, "Rothschilds and Rockefellers Team Up, Target Rich Chinese." *Morning Whistle.com* 01 Jun. 2012. Http://www.morningwhistle.com/html/2012/FinanceMarkets_0601/212496.html.

71) Willy Wo-Lap Lam, "China Preparing For Future Fight With US." *Rense.com* 27 Jun. 2003. Http://rense.com/general38/conflict.htm.

72) Richard McGregor, "Chinese Buy Into Conspiracy Theory." *Financial Times* 25 Sep. 2007. Http://www.ft.com/cms/s/0/70f2a23c-6b83-11dc-863b-0000779fd2ac.html.

73) *America: Freedom to Fascism*. Aaron Russo, dir. Aaron Russo Productions, 2006; G. Edward Griffin, *The Creature From Jekyll Island: A Second Look at the Federal Reserve*, 4th ed. (Westlake Village, California: American Media, 2002).

74) Ron Chernow, *Titan: The Life of John D. Rockefeller, Sr.* (New York: Vintage Books, 2004), 477.

75) William H. Sherman, *John Dee: The Politics of Reading and Writing in the English Renaissance* (Amherst, Massachusetts: University of Massachusetts Press, 1995), 128-147.

76) Paul Joseph Watson, "Leaked U.S. Army Document Outlines Plan For Re-Education Camps In America." *Infowars.com* 03 May 2012. Http://www.infowars.com/leaked-u-s-army-document-outlines-plan-for-re-education-camps-in-america/; *Police State 4: The Rise of FEMA*. Alex Jones, Rob Dew, Jason Douglass, dirs. (Infowars.com, 2010).

77) David Rothkopf, *Superclass: The Global Power Elite and the World They Are Making* (New York: Farrar, Straus and Giroux, 2009).

Charles Soong (ca 1882-86)

CHAPTER TWO

First Family: Soong Clan and Asian American Political Power

Bottom Up Bias

Much of the scholarship concerning Asian America reflects certain methodological biases that, although yielding important insights and broadening the knowledge base of the field, remain biases nonetheless. One of the more salient of such biases has been the tendency to focus upon the Asian American working class historical experience. This is understandable since historically this group represented the vast majority of the immigrant population going back to mid-nineteenth century America. Less obvious from the vantage point of the present, however, is that pioneering examples of scholarship that self-consciously identified as "Asian American Studies" coincided with the New Social History that enjoyed prominence in academia during the late 1960s prior to the importation of "theory" from continental Europe.

This bottom-up approach to understanding culture, society, and historical forces was the academic complement to the larger, more encompassing political ferment centered around the emergence of radical politics of diverse sectarian expressions after a period of Cold War dormancy. This form of academic and political practice has been placed under the rubric of the "New Left," to which many volumes of popular and scholarly attention has been devoted. This second complementary development yielded another bias within the scholarship that obtains in much research in Asian American studies being done today: The epistemological conceit of an actually-existing majority left-liberal-progressive Asian American population. The result is an odd and unacknowledged disjuncture between a largely left-liberal academic cohort that has contributed the bulk of literature and a majority politically conservative Asian American population that includes not only individuals with a multi-generational family presence in the US but those of more recent immigrant or refugee origins. Much of this has to do with American academia itself, which as critics like former leftist David Horowitz and others have observed, at minimum leans toward a liberal welfare state politics while maintaining a laissez-faire cultural worldview.

It is risky offering generalizations regarding contemporary Asian American attitudes and opinions. As alluded to above, there is ample literature that documents – almost to the point of romanticizing – the left-liberal legacy of historical Asian America.[1] By contrast, there is a paucity of inquiry into the right wing and fascist politics that have been an integral aspect of the respective Asian American groups albeit expressed in different ways. Under-examined within much of the history and social science scholarship dedicated to the study of Japanese Americans, for example, is the not insignificant core of ultranationalists among *Issei* and *Kibei Nisei* that in general or more specific terms supported the notion of *Dai Nippon* or the imperial political economic subjugation of Asian populations as ruled through military dictatorship. The rightwing cohort within the mainland Japanese American immigrant population was put in greater relief once it was forced into close quarters with fellow internees in internment camps that did not share its pro-imperial Japan politics. The study by Eichiro Azuma, *Between Two Empires* (2005) touches upon the Japanese American Right, but its emphasis is more broadly on the *Nikkei* population as a whole being squeezed into an untenable, unresolved, vulnerable middle position suspended between Imperial Japan and imperial USA.[2]

According to a 2008 "National Asian American Survey" fifty-three percent of Vietnamese Americans polled indicated support for John McCain as president of the United States.[3] Apparently, his admirers were not offended by his off-hand reference to his intense dislike of "gooks" owing to his experience as a prisoner of war. The current battle over power and leadership between the generations among myriad factions within the Vietnamese American community as seen in the documentary *Saigon, U.S.A.* (2008) or the widely publicized Madison Nguyen recall campaign in San

Jose, California requires a rethinking of a "refugee" model within Asian American Studies that does not deal squarely with strong right-wing political forces within the different communities.[4] In "Little Saigon" Orange County, California business owner Truong Van Tran threw the community into an uproar after he put up a poster of Ho Chi Minh and draped the national flag of Vietnam in his store.[5] After being accused by detractors of being a communist sympathizer, San Jose, California city councilperson Nguyen managed to hold on to her job by surviving a special recall election in 2009.[6]

There are signs, however, that the rightwing political current within Asian American history is beginning to be addressed in the scholarly literature; albeit in a tentative and almost apologetic fashion so. For example, the singular and perhaps defining importance of a strong anti-Communist political stance maintained by Hmong American community leaders is given extended treatment in an essay by Chia Youyee Vang.[7] Still, this historical survey conveys little awareness of the "deep politics" underlying the employment and then abandonment of Hmong mercenary forces by the US government as it conducted its covert operations on behalf of the international drug and banking cartel, as detailed in work by such writers as Alfred W. McCoy, Jonathan Marshall, Peter Dale Scott, Carl A. Trocki or even more specific to the Hmong people of Laos, Jane Hamilton-Merritt in *Tragic Mountains*.[8]

As a partial corrective to the liberal pro-worker bias found in Asian American Studies scholarship, it is instructive to delve into what might be considered the First Family of right-wing Asian American history. Historian Sterling Seagrave, who has also written on the incomparably more powerful Yamato imperial family of Japan, dubbed them the "Soong Dynasty."[9] While its founding father was of relatively modest social origins, the descendants of Charlie Soong occupied a privileged position on the world stage, as they have been pivotal in negotiating the shifting relationship between China and the US. In addition, they represent an important aspect of Asian American history that has been given short shrift in academic inquiry due, as stated above, to the institutional emphasis on working class social history.

In the following treatment of the Soong family, it is hoped that an honest acknowledgement and appraisal of right-wing

Asian American politics become part of the contemporary discussion. Hopefully, this will pave the way for understanding such diverse right-wing authoritarian figures of international stature as Nguyen Cao Ky and Vang Pao as being *consistent* with the Asian American historical experience rather than finessed in the literature as idiosyncratic aberrations. Although not nearly successful as the Soong clan in amassing family fortunes based upon wartime sweetheart business deals, international drug dealing, and thoroughgoing political corruption, certain individuals have done quite well within a political economic system otherwise heavily weighted against the respective Asian American groups.

Dynastic Politics

Not long after the American Civil War there arrived in America an ambitious immigrant from Hainan Island in South China who went on to found what became one of the more influential American family dynasties of the Twentieth Century. While there is some dispute over the origins of his various names, the man born as Han Jiaozhun/Chiao-shun (韓教準) but commonly known as Charles Soong has not been given full and proper recognition for the considerable influence he and his family have had in shaping the contours of both US national history and that of China. So important is Soong to the trajectory of world history during the years prior to World War II that noted author Sterling Seagrave devotes an entire volume to the legacy of this earnest young man who came to the US at the height of anti-Chinese hatred yet succeeded in forging crucial personal and institutional alliances that made him both wealthy and powerful; who would one day help organize and finance a political revolution in the land of his birth.[10]

Not only did Soong manage the financial affairs of the political organization headed by Sun Yat-sen (孫逸仙) – a towering figure in the founding of Republican China – his three US-educated daughters and three sons went on to play significant roles on the world-historical stage. The best known of the daughters, Mei-ling Soong (宋美齡), would later become Madame Chiang Kai-shek (蔣夫人) and in this capacity she stood as the most recognizable advocate for the Republic of China among the American public. One of her contemporaries writes in unabashedly admiring tones of her beauty and likened Madame Chiang to a "cinema star" rather than being a mere "political figure."[11] Thanks to the relentless promotion of *Time* magazine publisher Henry R. Luce – son of Presbyterian missionaries in China – the Chiang duo enjoyed heroic status among many Americans. Luce and his stable of propagandists kept his readership ignorant of the corrupt doings of the Nationalist government that claimed to represent the political interests of "China" in total. The fiction of the Kuomintang and the legitimate government representing all of China was maintained well into the Cold War until trade relations between the Peoples Republic of China were established in the early 1970s followed by formal diplomatic recognition in December 1978 during the presidency of Jimmy Carter, a hand-picked minion of the Trilateral Commission founded in 1972 by David Rockefeller and whose family had extensive financial interests in pre-Communist China.

Harvard-educated T. V. (Tzu-wen) Soong (宋子文) rode the wave of family fortune in the years leading to World War II, occupying a variety of government positions including governor of the Central Bank of China (1928-31) and then finance minister (1932-33). He was known to have had a direct hand in the opium market, which helped keep the fledgling Republic of China afloat financially while adding to the already substantial Soong family wealth.[12] The transnational upbringing pioneered by his father allowed Soong to move easily amongst both Chinese and American power families. He has been described as "that quintessentially Shanghaiese breed of businessmen that knew East-West dealings from both sides, and from which most of these bankers were descended."[13]

Once the Kuomintang finally buckled under the superior fighting forces of the People's Liberation Army and popular support of the peasantry commanded by the Communist Party led by Mao Zedong (毛泽东), T. V. Soong left for the US and lived in New York until his death in 1971 at age seventy-seven. While comfortably ensconced in his Long Island estate, the Chinese American tycoon worked diligently at amassing even greater wealth and enjoyed behind-the-scenes political clout among such establishment figures as W. Averell Harriman, whose own family name bespoke wealth, power, privilege, and the political access that comes with it. At street level, Song was close to local *tong* allies who protected him from calumny by detractors within the Chinese American community that were put off by KMT corruption and the "extravagant lifestyle of the high-class refugees" living in Washington, DC or New York.[14]

Younger brother T. A. Soong (Soong Tse-an, 子安), a graduate of Harvard University, also exerted a presence in the financial world by serving as chairman of the board for the Bank of Canton in San Francisco. An announcement published in *Time* magazine of his engagement to the daughter of the prominent military leader who controlled Manchuria during the "warlord period" referred to his brother T. V. Soong as "China's Mellon"; an allusion to one of the wealthiest individuals of the day, financier Andrew W. Mellon.[15] His father-in-law Marshal Chang Hsueh-liang/Zhang Xueliang (張學良) later ran afoul of both the Communist Party and the Kuomintang and was to spend half of his life under house arrest as a political prisoner. Only after the death of Chiang Ching-kuo in 1990 was Chang released. In 1993, he immigrated to Honolulu, Hawaii where he lived until his death in 2001 after reaching the age of one hundred years. His son-in-law T. A. Soong predeceased him by a few decades, having died in the British crown colony of Hong Kong in 1969.[16]

T. L. Soong (Soong Tse-liang, 子良) fell in the middle of the birth order and resided in the US where he could more safely tend to the family wealth put into play by patriarch Charles Soong decades before. Based in New York, T. L. Soong got curiously close to the administrative center of US national wealth by reportedly working as a "secret consultant" to the Department of Treasury.[17] Prior to that shadowy role, he had helped administer the Lend-Lease program that was signed into law by Roosevelt in 1941 and continued until shortly after World War II came to an end. With $1.6 billion worth of American goods and services transferred to Republican China during the war years, it can be safely assumed that T. L. Soong was compensated royally not simply for his financial acumen but due to his closeness to those at the absolute highest reaches of government.

Eldest daughter Soong Ai-ling (宋藹齡) was educated in the US at Wesleyan College in Macon, Georgia. After returning to China, she served as secretary to Sun Yat-sen. In 1914, Soong Ai-ling married the widowed wealthy banker, H. H. (Hsiang-hsi)

Kung (孔祥熙). He was not nearly so savvy as his wife, but like her had extensive experience living in the US––having graduated from Oberlin College and Yale University. Kung served as Minister of Industry and Commerce (1928-1933), Minister of Finance (1933-1944), and governor of the Central Bank of China (1933-1945). In close cooperation with Du Yuesheng (杜月笙) [1887-1951] – the infamous head of the Green Gang triad in Shanghai who had helped bring Chiang Kai-shek (Jiang Jieshi) [蔣介石] to power through money earned by opium trading, gambling, and prostitution – Kung consolidated control over the banking system and financial market while taking care "not to risk confrontation" with the Japanese occupiers.[18] In his hey-day, Kung was reputed to be the richest man in all of China. His working relationship with Rockefeller financial interests through Standard Oil also rewarded him handsomely. With the demise of the Kuomintang, both Kung and wife Soong Ai-ling returned to the US, where she died at the age of eighty-three in New York.

The role of secretary to Sun Yat-sen was passed from Soong Ai-ling to her younger sister Soong Chi'ing-ling (宋慶齡), who in 1915 married the much older man against the wishes of family patriarch Charles Soong. As one of his most ardent financial and political backers, Soong felt that Sun had betrayed him personally and as a consequence did what he could to prevent the marriage. Sun in fact was already married, which offended the selectively applied Christian moral sensibilities of Soong and his wife. Soong determined thereafter to break with Sun Yat-sen both personally and politically. Author Sterling Seagrave suggests that the death of Charles Soong in 1918 occurred under suspicious circumstances; especially since he died suddenly without having suffered serious illness prior to his death. The guardians of Sun Yat-sen's legacy largely wrote Soong out of the official history once he renounced his friendship and political alliance with the "father of the nation" (*guofu* 國父).[19]

Sworn Society

Although typically not conceived of as such by scholars, the Soong family is as much a part of Asian American history as they are central to the history of modern China.

Charles Soong began his rise in the world as the son of a relatively successful Hainan merchant named Han Hongyi/Han

Hung-i (韓鴻翼). As a builder and operator of sea-vessels, the elder Han was a senior member of a *Chiu Chao* (潮州) secret society that tended to the social and economic welfare of the tightly knit regional trading class. Smuggling was a major source of revenue, with opium in particular being crucial to such commercial activity. Among family members were those of Hakka (客家) "guest families" ethnicity who had fled Northern China with the advent of oppressive Manchu rule in 1644. As such, an abiding antipathy toward the Manchu usurpers shared by the displaced Hakka people helped fuel political rebellion in the south culminating in the revolutionary fervor that brought about the birth of the Republic of China (中華民國) in the year 1912.

Through *Chiu Chao* control of opium commerce that in turn bought them political access, they evolved into extensive syndicates that thrived well into the modern era of European colonialism and its continuation through the postwar period of US global dominance. Organizations such as these have occupied a central position in the international drug trade from World War II to the present, with the active involvement of sundry governments including the US. Indeed, much of the history of modern Asia and the larger capitalist world system derives from the power struggles among competing "opium regimes" and the nation-states that benefitted financially and politically through the extraction of hyper-profits from demoralized and demonized drug-addled populations rendered all the more controllable.[20]

Beginning in the 1850s, thousands of young men from Guangdong Province would leave behind political turmoil and poverty to pursue good fortune overseas in the US. In 1878, amidst violently aggressive anti-Chinese immigrant agitation in America, Soong (then "Soon") was only twelve years of age when he arrived in California with a putative uncle (possibly a fictive or "paper" relative).[21] Shortly thereafter, the two relocated to Boston, where his uncle opened a tea and silk shop. Frequent visitors to the establishment were two American-educated countrymen and cousins named Wen Bing-chung (B. C. Wen) and New Shan-chow (S. C. New). Both individuals later were to assume important roles in league with their sworn brothers in subverting the tottering Manchu dynasty to make way for republican rule in China.

In tandem with their political involvement, Wen and New proved to be valuable business associates of Soong in Shanghai, which became the shared base of operations subsequent to their respective stays in the US. Upon returning to China, the three men married into the same prominent Catholic family and became brothers-in-law with the wedding of Soong to Ni Kwei-tseng (倪桂珍) [Katherine Hsu] in 1887. This marriage further solidified their business and political relationship. Importantly, it was Wen and New who brought Soong into the inner sanctum of triad life that dominated almost every aspect of pre-revolutionary Shanghai society including commerce and government.

By the mid-19th century the city had evolved into a major center of the opium trade, which included foreign commercial concerns such as Jardine, Matheson and Company. By the 1920s the Shanghai underworld included 100,000 hoodlums or *liumang*. This large criminal underclass thrived from enormous profits made once opium was banned in 1917. "Virtually all of these underworld elements belonged to small bands of gangsters called *bang* or *hui* that were ruled over by a massive criminal confederation and secret society," writes Frederic Wakeman, "originally organized by Yangzi River boatmen, called the Green Gang (Qingbang)."[22] Of course it was the Green Gang under the leadership of its legendary boss Du Yuesheng (笙馆) that was instrumental in the coming to power of Chiang Kai-shek and the *Kuomintang*.

Christian Charity

B. C. Wen and S. C. New introduced the intellectually receptive Charles Soong to contemporary political thought and a modern world-view to which they had been exposed as students with the Chinese Educational Mission. The two engaged Soong in many an impassioned discussion of politics at his uncle's shop. The necessity of transforming China along the lines of the Western liberal democracies was a key theme that dominated their regular talks. Moreover, through the influence of Wen and New, Soong was encouraged to further his formal education and move beyond the bounds of his immediate social world. Wen, New, Soong, and others of their elite social class who came to the US espoused a cosmopolitan and liberal world-view combined with progressive political thought that in time would liberate the land of their birth from the feudalist dynastic ruling class whose fundamental military weakness had allowed foreign nations to dominate key sectors of the political economy at the expense of the Chinese people.

In defiance of his adoptive uncle, who wanted his young charge to remain at work in the family business, the teenage Soong ran away from home and was shepherded into the Christian faith by a succession of benevolent White men of means who saw missionary potential in the young heathen. The most important of these individuals who set Soong on the path of righteousness was millionaire tobacco magnate, industrialist and banker, Julian S. Carr. Along with the Methodist Church, it was Carr who provided the financial resources that enabled the ambitious young man to attend Trinity College in Durham, North Carolina upon his arrival in 1881. Bright, industrious, driven, and not a little alienated from his White American classmates, Soong graduated in 1883 after only two years of concentrated study.

Christian charity, however, extended only so far: Charles Soong was sent packing from the home of Professor O. W. Carr (cousin of Julian Carr) when it became evident that the Chinese man had become enamored of his daughter, Miss Ella. "It was right and proper for Charlie to fill a role in the fantasy world of missionary endeavor," writes biographer Seagrave. "He was their town Celestial, but they had to draw the line at intimacy between a Chinaman and one of their own daughters."[23] Although Christian theology posited a radical equality among humankind in the abstract, the racial politics of the day practiced by earth-bound adherents to the faith overrode the doctrinal niceties of the Methodist church.

After leaving Durham for Nashville to attend Vanderbilt University, Soong found himself facing similar problems after falling for the daughter of Reverend Thomas Page Ricaud, one of his new white sponsors. The daughter, Rosamond, was sent off to keep her away from the flirtations of Soong. He then, however, became sweet on another local White girl; a certain Eula Bell. This budding love affair also met strenuous opposition from the local elite, given the racial condescension if not outright enmity held toward the Chinese at the time. This held true even where it concerned the relatively well educated, English-speaking Christian convert

Soong. After all, these minor romantic scandals involving Soong took place in 1882; the year that the US Congress passed federal legislation prohibiting – with few exceptions – further immigration from China.

Although hostility toward Chinese immigrants was more overtly oppressive in the Western states, there was a thoroughgoing understanding nationally among the White intelligentsia and religious leadership that their Oriental converts placed lower on the scale of humanity than they. Anti-Chinese sentiment notwithstanding, Soong was granted a theology certificate from the Divinity School at Vanderbilt. A dilemma arose, however, when it came to the matter of ordination. While Soong was allowed to complete his church-sponsored education and learn its catechism (which presumably included the notion of universal brotherhood under Christ) he met an obstacle when it came to full induction into its ministry because of his Chinese racial identity. Although Chinamen were not ordinarily conferred the privilege of entering the clergy, Holland Nimmons McTyeire (one of the founders of the university and a bishop in the Methodist Episcopal Church, South) interceded and Soong was ordained as a Methodist minister in 1885.[24] Individual acts of kindness and intercession, however, do not negate the reality of a more thoroughgoing anti-Chinese prejudice held by the Methodist leadership. Contrary to his wish to remain in the US, at least for a short while, Soong was certified by the church with the intention of sending him "home" to China so he could spread the gospel to the benighted masses there.

Having availed himself of the finest in Methodist higher education and reluctantly agreeing to propagate Christian belief in the land of his nativity, Soong at age nineteen returned to China in January, 1886. He had been absent from his home country for about ten years. His humble duties began at a Southern Methodist School near Shanghai. Although ordained as a minister, it was not long before Soong's bonds with the Methodist Church began to loosen. Within two years of his return overseas, Soong found more worldly and immediate blessings by entering the secret society known as *Hung Pang* (洪幫) or "Red Society" (紅幫). This anti-Manchu brotherhood, along with the *Ching Pang* (清幫) or "Green Society" (青幫), sprang from the failure of the Taiping rebellion against the central Qing government. In these sworn societies, revolutionary politics, religious mysticism, and criminal enterprise came together in the form of parallel institutions that provided for the material needs of those persons otherwise excluded from the benefits, privileges, and perquisites enjoyed by the ruling elite that controlled the ongoing operations of the officially-constituted state. Once having acquired the financial stature and local support through an elaborate system of patronage and sanctions to the point of challenging the very legitimacy of the state, the two entities – the criminal and the government – often would converge at nodes of strategic value to both, thereby blurring the distinction between them. Nor is the interpenetration of criminality and the official organs of governance unique to China. It is a marriage of convenience integral to all societies and political systems including that of the US.

Revolutionary Religion

Both as a man of the cloth and a member of the most formidable triad in Shanghai, Charles Soong proved to be a skilled businessman. By 1904 he had amassed a personal fortune through his involvement with a blend of legitimate business concerns and illicit enterprises. He was involved in noodle production, flour milling, and invested in cotton and tobacco factories. He published both commercial textbooks and religious literature – including Chinese-language editions of the Bible – through his Sino-American Press and Commercial Press of Shanghai. At the same time, subversive political tracts found their way into print through these concealed means. Soong pursued business opportunities characteristic of the comprador all the while working closely both with triad brothers in extra-legal activities and political comrades engaged more specifically in anti-government intrigue. In Charles Soong, the realm of the divine in combination with the profane world of commerce and criminality commingled with that of political revolution. None of it, however, would have been possible had not Soong married into a financially and politically well-connected family with direct ties to organized crime, specifically the *Hung Pang*. His wealth and elevated social status was the result of the "cross-pollination between his missionary career and his new secret life."[25]

Soong was a mere lad when he underwent conversion to Christianity and but nineteen years old when he returned to China. Thrust as he was into the heart of the burgeoning American industrial capitalist order from a wretchedly underdeveloped China in the death-grip of foreign imperialist nations, it is not difficult to understand his being attracted to the lure of the Methodist catechism. For its church-related institutions provided Soong with material benefits and a practical education that he knew would vastly improve his prospects in life. Since Christianity predominated in the commanding nations of the West, it seemed reasonable to infer that modernity itself and the economic might of these world powers might be linked to its religio-philosophical underpinnings. Soong discovered while in America, however, that the Oriental – even if a Christian convert – would be made to occupy a circumscribed, subordinate position within this community of believers.

Christian Fellowship

Had Charles Soong been content to pursue his successful career as a prominent member of the Shanghai comprador class, socially respected Christian minister of the International Settlement, and father to a distinguished brood that came to exert exceptionally high measure of influence in both China and the US, his place in world history would be secure on that basis alone. But Soong was driven by a political vision as well: not in the abstract but as a means of protecting and extending family wealth and privilege beyond existing political constraints.

The embodiment of his desire to bring about a new social order came in the person of a fugitive from the Qing authorities by the name of Sun Wen (孫文) or as he is more commonly known outside China, Sun Yat-sen (孫逸仙). [26] With Soong's vast network of financial and criminal associates operating behind the veil of Christian probity in support of Sun's organizational genius that brought with it a close relationship with the all-important overseas immigrant communities, together these two men helped bring about a fundamental change in the structure of modern Chinese society.

As a fellow Methodist convert and member of the Anglo American-educated Chinese elite who shared progressive ideas concerning the historical destiny of a nation yet unborn, Soong felt an "instant affinity" to Sun. [27] He cast his lot with Soong almost immediately after their first meeting in early 1894. As his money-man, Soong aided Sun in garnering the cash required to help finance the overthrow of the Qing Dynasty. After a successful fund-raising tour of North America during 1905-06, Soong returned to Shanghai with $2 million to fill the coffers of the T'ung-meng Hui (同盟會) [Revolutionary Alliance] led by Sun. Subsequently, Soong was appointed treasurer of this clandestine political organization. Early Soong sponsor Julian S. Carr apparently understood the long-term commercial opportunities in a post-revolutionary China and there is a strong possibility that the multimillionaire invested heavily in the revolutionary enterprise.

Supporters strove to supplant moribund dynastic rule with a republican form of government guided by the sophisticated and well-wrought political philosophy Sun had refined through extensive study and frequent international travel that allowed him to evade agents of the Manchu regime. He looked to Western Europe and Imperial Japan for practical insight into the principles of modern governance while drawing also from the lessons of Chinese history and classical philosophy. Inspired by the growing industrial and military strength brought about by the Meiji oligarchs and to evade arrest in China by the Qing government, from 1897 onward Sun spent a number of years in Japan with sympathizers and co-conspirators. He worked closely with Japanese nationalists who shared his view of Western imperialism as the bane of Asian peoples.

An under-appreciated practical contribution of Sun as a political theorist was his articulation of the relationship between European empire building and White racial supremacy. "Underlying Sun's urgent call for Asian unity against imperialism," write two authorities on the political thought of Sun Yat-sen, "was his fear of western racism."[28] He fully understood that the Western imperial project was bolstered by anti-Asian racism, which in turn justified and perpetuated colonial exploitation.

Sun's bond with Chinese American immigrant communities – experiencing first-hand their unequal treatment within White supremacist society – added greatly to his understanding of ideological racism and its historical roots. He observed first-hand the material link between racism, imperialism, and the exploitation of non-White labor. While in Japan, Sun called for pan-Asian unity to blunt the destructive impact of European colonialism.

His Japanese sponsors supported Sun's mission of overthrowing the imperial Qing government and expelling European colonizers from East Asia, thereby positioning Japan as leader among other Asian nations. The ultra-nationalist *Kokuryūkai* (黑龍會), often translated as "Black Dragon Society," viewed the stated ambitions of Sun as useful to their own expansionist ambitions in Asia and rendered financial assistance to his cause.

Heaven, Earth, Man

Consistent with practices shared with other shapers of history, Soong and Sun drew from the strength, resources, and organizational discipline of outlaw institutions. Both men belonged to the same underground criminal network; the *Sanhehui* (三合會), or "Three Harmonies Society," which was woven within the social fabric of their shared South China origins. These ethnic-primordial ties were put to good use not only within their local orbit in Shanghai but throughout China, the US, and internationally.

Wherever there were communities of *Huáqiáo/hua-ch'iao* (華胞) or "overseas Chinese" to be found, Sun Yat-sen could find refuge and rally varying degrees of support for his progressive political program. On December 13, 1903 at the Maunakea Market Place in Honolulu, for example, Sun succeeded in attracting about one thousand fellow Chinese Americans who came to hear of his plans to bring about the end of Qing rule. In its stead would be founded a democratic republic informed by socialist principles which were later underplayed by the anti-Communist Kuomintang so that they too could lay claim to his potent political legacy.

For all his ambition, exceptional intellect, advanced education, and keen political sense, all would have been for naught had it not been for the direct support of multiple triad affiliations Sun shared with the leadership of Chinese immigrant communities in the US, Canada, and the American territory of Hawaii. Despite the failure of several attempts by the underground T'ung-meng Hui to overthrow the Qing rulers through military force, Sun became a "charismatic figure to the overseas Chinese" and remains so to the present.[29] In the land of his nativity, Sun remains well regarded among the leadership of the Chinese Communist Party for his anti-imperialist politics and the well-articulated "Three Principles of the People" (*Sān Mín Zhyì*) [三民主義] predicated upon nationalist, democratic, and socialist principles.[30]

Without triad assistance at crucial junctures of his career as a professional revolutionary, Sun Yat-sen might have been jailed as a political prisoner, assassinated by Qing agents, or perhaps executed if returned to China. In one spectacular episode that garnered wide attention, Sun was "kidnapped" in London on October 11, 1896 and held in the Chinese Embassy for several days before the Foreign Office secured his release. Further adding to his legend, a well-known episode during his storied life in political exile occurred when political enemies in the Society to Protect the Emperor informed US officials of Sun's attempt to enter the country illegally on April 06, 1904.[31]

Had he been expelled from the US and returned to China, Sun would have faced severe penalties because of his seditious anti-Qing political activities. The politically well-connected Chee Kung Tong in San Francisco came to his assistance by posting bail and hiring a lawyer to represent Sun. By obtaining through less-than-honest means official documents such as a "Certificate of Hawaiian Birth" and collecting bogus sworn statements from several witnesses, Sun and his advisors were able to establish that he had been born at Waimalu, Ewa, Oahu on November 24, 1870.[32] Hence the American nationality of Sun Yat-sen was established by a combination of individual deceit and official corruption; a scenario repeated countless times by far less exalted Asian immigrants to the US over past decades.

The further conjoining of politics and criminality came in the success Sun enjoyed in transforming the Chee Kung Tong "from a Triad mutual aid club into a tightly organized revolutionary party."[33] During much of 1904, Sun traveled throughout the US recruiting with mixed success new members for the Chee Kung Tong while advancing his political goal of realizing a republican China free of foreign domination. He made considerably more progress in co-founding with Song Jiaoren (宋教仁), the T'ung-meng Hui in Tokyo (1905) and then expanding its operations overseas, including the US. In 1909, Lee See Nam founded the Young China Association in San Francisco as a political front for the T'ung-meng Hui to engage university students in the republican cause. In 1907, Lee had cast his lot with Sun while in the British crown colony of Hong Kong.

During the period 1909-1911, Sun stepped up the T'ung-meng Hui organizational drive by forming chapters in New York, Boston, Chicago, Portland, Milwaukee, and smaller cities with large Chinese American populations such as Sacramento, California. The Chee Kung Tong was formally merged with the T'ung-meng Hui in 1911 with a ceremony presided over by Sun himself in San Francisco that attracted about one thousand participants. He formed the *Hongmen Chouxiang Ju* or "Triad Subscription Bureau" as the financial engine of the nascent republic. The bureau was located in the headquarters of the Chee Kung Tong in San Francisco and "began to channel substantial amounts of money to revolutionary groups in China."[34]

Overseas Chinese Connection

As a US territorial possession (i.e. colony), Hawaii became home to countless Chinese immigrants who were recruited to labor on plantations owned by the New England Protestant White oligarchy who had wrested control of the islands from its native inhabitants. Among these men primarily from Guongdong was the elder brother of Sun Yat-sen named Sun Mei (also known as "S. Ahmi"). In 1871, he himself had followed the footsteps of an uncle named Young Mun-nap who found success as a merchant in Honolulu.

Sun Yat-sen, born in the village of Choy Hang, went to live with his prosperous older brother in 1879 at thirteen years of age. Sun Mei started out in Hawaii as a common laborer, but advanced himself as a farmer and then as a merchant. He also profited by recruiting others from his home region as contract laborers to work the vast sugar plantations held by White settler families who had imposed their legal-juridical system of privately held land tenure on the native people.

The superior intellectual ability of Sun was demonstrated while a student at the exclusive Iolani School from 1879 to 1882: a private preparatory institution founded by the Anglican Church of Hawaii. Although having only native Chinese-language ability when he arrived in Hawaii, his rapid mastery of English earned him an award bestowed by King David Kalakaua himself. The following year, Sun continued his studies at Oahu College (later Punahou). The school was established by Congregationalist missionaries to educate their own children and maintains its elite status to the present day. As he gravitated ever closer to Christian belief, in July 1883 his disapproving brother Sun Mei sent him home before full religious conversion could occur.

Sun Yat-sen, however, became a Christian convert soon enough. While attending school in Hong Kong, he was baptized in 1884 by an American missionary. It was the Congregationalist clergyman Dr. Charles Hager who anointed his protégé "I-Hsien" ("daily renewal") or "Yat-sen" (日新) as pronounced in Cantonese. One authority on the political thought of Sun speculated that the "mainspring of his revolutionary personality" might be attributed to a "Christian faith based on rebellion."[35] More likely – as in the case of fellow convert Charles Soong – it was as much a matter of the practical material advantage of being aligned with a religious institution that had proven its earthly martial and political efficacy that lured Sun and others of his generation to the Christian faith. Religious conversion was a means of social and political advancement for the colonial subject clever enough to bring theology to earth.

The Hawaii Chinese History Center published in 1999 a monograph that positions

Sun Yat-sen more fully as a distinctively American political thinker and revolutionary. Hawaii is claimed as the "cradle of Chinese revolution" because it was there that the Hsing Chung Hui (興中會) "Revive China Society," was founded by a band of little more than 100 Chinese Americans who conspired to challenge the Qing state.[36] The organization was founded after the ignominious 1894 defeat of China by the militarily superior forces of Imperial Japan. In October of that same year, Sun returned to Hawaii to found the Hsing Chung Hui. By then, he was a successful doctor of medicine who had earned his professional degree in Hong Kong.

From the date of his return and through the following year, Sun and his followers recruited over 100 workers, intellectuals, and petit bourgeois merchants (including Sun Mei, whose wealth enabled him to finance the education of his younger brother) who dedicated themselves to toppling the Qing government and enacting envisioned political reforms. An engaged revolutionary, Sun stood at the center of at least ten failed armed coup attempts between 1895-1911. He and his allies finally succeeded with the Wuchang Uprising (武昌起義) of October 10, 1911 which precipitated the Xinhai Revolution (辛亥革命). Sun learned of the rebellion while in the US soliciting financial support from Chinese Americans who believed they had a vested interest in the anti-imperial struggle. Indeed, about eighty percent of the money used to fund the ten failed insurrections came from overseas Chinese.[37] And so was founded the Republic of China; the first nation in Asia to embody democratic and socialist ideals aligned against the vestiges of hereditary monarchal rule.

As an ardent internationalist, Sun traveled for fully sixteen years through the US, Canada, England, Japan, and Southeast Asia to unite overseas Chinese communities in support of his revolutionary ambitions. The organizational activity of Sun and those of his generation – including politically-invested overseas Chinese living in the Americas – can properly be placed within the context of other world-historical early twentieth century revolutionary social movements that attempted to refigure the contested power relationship between the state and its subjects.

Marriages of Convenience

With the death of a Sun Yat-sen in 1925, any number of contenders stepped up to fill the political void he left including Wang Jingwei (汪精衛) and Hu Hanmin (胡漢民). It was Chiang Kai-shek, however, who prevailed. Troops loyal to Chiang had out-fought warlords resistant to Kuomintang (中國國民黨) governance while out-maneuvering the various cliques and internal political rivals such as Wang and Hu. His Communist challengers were dealt with in similar fashion. The purge of KMT leftists and the Communists by Chiang precipitated the Nanchang Uprising (南昌起義) on August 1, 1927; a date which also marks the birth of the People's Liberations Army (中國人民解放軍) and the onset of a civil war that was to end in military victory over the Kuomintang and founding in 1949 of the People's Republic of China (中華人民共和國).

Long before his military defeat and retreat to the island of Taiwan, Chiang had gone to great lengths in bringing together the foundational legacy of Sun Yat-sen with Soong family wealth and the armed strength he commanded by benefit of having served as the first principal of the Whampoa Military Academy (黃埔軍校). Founded in 1924 with Soviet assistance, the academy and its officer corps gave martial strength and backing to a fledgling state struggling for survival amidst contending power centers.

Chiang consolidated his power-base by marrying into the Soong family against the strenuous objections of matriarch Ni Kwei-tseng. As a devout Christian she recoiled at the thought of bringing a non-believer into the blessed circle of bourgeois Chinese in Shanghai. Nor did the fact that Chiang was already married while angling to join forces with Soong interests necessarily endear him to his future mother-in-law. His promised conversion to Christianity, however, calmed her doubts and smoothed his way to full entry into joint politico-familial dynastic rule.

The wife he later shed in favor of Soong Mei-ling was all of thirteen years old when Chiang, at the worldly age of 32, tried to seduce the innocent child who had roused him to the point of near-obsession. As a Green Gang soldier and close friend of Shanghai boss "Big-Eared" Du Yueh-sheng (1887-1951), he had already earned the reputation among authorities as "an alleged murderer, extortionist, and armed robber."[38]

Having first tried to force himself on the Ch'en Chieh-ju (Ah Feng) or "Jennie Chen" in 1919, Chiang persisted in making the woman-child his own against the strenuous defense erected by her justifiably protective mother. In time, the death of her father and subsequent fall in family fortunes led to permission being granted for the union to take place. Ch'en was fifteen years old when the couple was married in a civil ceremony on December 5, 1921 at the Great Eastern Hotel in Shanghai before fifty distinguished guests comprising business associates, political allies, triad brothers, and family members.

The survival of the Kuomintang was being threatened by a left-coalition during the Northern Expedition of 1926-27 when Soong Ailing (Mme. H. H. Kung) came forth with a proposal to Chiang, whom she foresaw as the ultimate victor in the contest. According to a credibly perspicacious account based on notes written by Ch'en during her marriage to Chiang but not published until 1993, the exceedingly ambitious Soong Ailing proposed that

Chiang appoint her husband as prime minister and install her brother T. V. Soong as minister of finance. To cement the deal between two power-entities, her younger sister Soong Mei-ling would be interposed as his wife.[39] In orchestrating this grand opera, Soong Ailing would realize the goal of placing her family at the very center of the newly evolving Chinese state with Chiang at the apex of power. In her memoirs, Ch'en refers to these opportunistic machinations as the "Great Intrigue." It was an offer Chiang could not refuse, for it linked him directly to the legacy of Sun Yat-sen, backed by the solid financial base composed of Shanghai bankers and businessmen who would in turn benefit by their calculatingly close relationship to the regime.

To clear the way for his power-marriage to Mei-ling Soong, Chiang hatched a plan to send his wife Ch'en overseas to the US. After a tearful parting in Shanghai, she boarded the steamship *S.S. President Jackson* with her party of attendants bound for America. While landing in San Francisco Ch'en learned from the local newspapers of the assertion by Chiang that the woman aboard the ocean liner was not his wife. He claimed that the story originated with political rivals who were intent on embarrassing him. She was driven to such a state of despondency by the time she reached New York that only the intervention of a kindly stranger kept Jennie from throwing herself into the Hudson River.

With Ch'en out of the picture, the coming together of Chiang with the cosmopolitan English-speaking Mei-ling Soong – well-acquainted with the ways of the Christian White folk from whom she had received her formal education at Wellesley College – became the personification of China itself in the eyes of an adoring American public whose perception of the couple had been crafted as carefully as that of the Hollywood stars with whom they sometimes were compared by journalists.

The story of Jennie Chen and her relationship with Chiang Kai-shek remained hidden for decades. Working from diaries she had kept during their marriage, she began writing her memoirs during the 1950s with the expectation that monies received from a publishing contract would ease her financial burden. According to a detailed account rendered by the editor of her autobiography, noted historian of China Lloyd E. Eastman, writes of a KMT "elder" living in New Jersey named Ch'en Li-Fu who caught wind of the project and "implored Jennie to keep her memories to herself."[40] Upon completion of the manuscript in early 1964, friends of Chen helped her seek out an American literary agent to negotiate publication of a title that certainly would have found an eager audience. As president of the nationalist government that had relocated to Taiwan in 1949, Chiang Kai-shek was still a figure of international prominence as he exercised autocratic rule over an island nation that maintained the fiction of its sovereign claim over all of China. Similarly, Mme. Chiang Kai-shek and her rise to power would be subject to possibly unflattering critical scrutiny by the very woman who had been unceremoniously pushed aside to make way for the most politically ambitious of the Soong sisters to assume the world-historical center stage.

An agent named Lawrence Epps Hill succeeded in placing the Chen manuscript with Doubleday publishers in April 1964. By early the following year, however, the deal fell through. There is evidence, according to Eastman, that individuals close to the government of Taiwan had a hand in scuttling the plans for publication. Ch'en Li-Fu teamed up with Mme. H. H. Kung (Soong Ai-Ling) – both of who lived near New York City – and threatened Hill with legal action if the book were to be released. In turn, Doubleday withdrew its offer in fear of being drawn into a lawsuit for libel.

Censored By Death

Ch'en Li-Fu (陈立夫) was a particularly nasty piece of work. Eastman neglects to mention that it was he and his brother Ch'en Guofu who headed the influential so-called "CC Clique" that was integral to the early success of Chiang Kai-shek and the KMT. Moreover, Ch'en Li-Fu had served as his "personal secretary and confidante" in addition to having held the post of secretary general with the KMT.[41] It was he who pressed Chiang to exterminate their Communist rivals and bragged about it in a feature article that appeared in the May 26, 1947 issue of *Time* magazine. Its cover featured a handsome portrait of Ch'en. Coyly alluding to the MS degree he was awarded by the School of Mines at the University of Pittsburgh he said, "I had planned to go underground for coal. Instead, I went underground for Communists."[42] Leaders of the Nanjing government had viewed the Communists as a greater threat than the Japanese invaders and in keeping with this duality Chiang Kai-shek articulated the policy of *"xian annei, hou rangwai"* or "first internal pacification, then external resistance."[43]

In March 1928, Ch'en became head of the KMT secret police body known as the Organization Department. It was he who also established the notorious Central Bureau of Investigation and Statistics (Zhongtong) that allowed Dai Li – valued henchman of the autocratic Chiang Kai-shek – to develop his fearsome reputation as the "Himmler" of China. His biographer Frederick Wakeman, Jr. portrays Dai Li as "at once a simulacrum of fascist terrorism, an embodiment of the modern police state, an enforcer of stern Confucian ideals, and ... the fiercely ambitious heir of storied medieval strategists who traditionally emerged when Chinese empires quivered and fell."[44]

His sadistic *métier* involved kidnapping, assassination, torture, and maintaining a system of concentration camps that helped the Kuomintang suppress political dissent and vanquish its political rivals. General Dai Li, however, never lived to see the founding of the People's Republic of China nor the retreat of his beloved leader and the Kuomintang to the island of Taiwan. The widely hated enforcer was to die in a plane accident near Nanjing on March 17, 1946 under circumstances that appeared to be an assassination according to more than a few commentators.

Through repressive state institutions such as those devised and managed by the likes of Dai Li, Chiang and his son-successor Chiang Ching-kuo enforced authoritarian discipline among ROC subjects both within Taiwan and overseas on sovereign US soil. Trusted Kuomintang officials were stationed in the US; some even electing to settle in the US. (Noted media personality Constance "Connie" Yu-hwa Chung, for example, is the daughter of former KMT intelligence officer William Ling Ching Chung, who was based in the Washington, DC area.) Ch'en used the KMT secret police to squelch political dissent expressed by students, journalists, graduate students, academics, and others who did not hew to the orthodoxy of the repressive one-party autocracy supported by the US government that ruled Taiwan without interruption for over fifty years until the election of Chen Shui-bian (陳水扁) in 2000.

Given the intimidating background of Ch'en Li-Fu and his demonstrated willingness to do whatever was necessary to protect the interests of the ruling KMT government, combined with the political pull exercised by the Soong-Chiang-Kung family in the US, it is remarkable that those involved with getting the memoirs of Jennie Chen published prevailed in the end. The task, however, was not without its dangers. For his efforts the literary agent Hill was beaten up more than once and received menacing phone calls. Both his hotel room and office were burglarized a few times. When anonymous warnings and physical intimidation did not suffice, Hill was threatened with lawsuits by two New York City law firms in addition to having the FBI set on him.[45] By 1965, Chen and her representatives came to terms with the realization that her manuscript would never see publication. They accepted a $170,000 pay-off from an attorney by the name of Eugene Kiang in exchange for what he believed were all extant copies of the contested manuscript and accompanying photographs.

Years later, in 1983, the grandson of Jennie Chen, Ch'en Chung-jen, announced that he would deliver to the world the story that had been suppressed. Again, pressure from unfriendly Taiwanese sources was exerted upon Ch'en the grandson, living in Hong Kong, with a warning to exercise discretion. But it was the October 15, 1984 assassination of journalist Henry Liu (who wrote under the name Chiang Nan) at his home in Daly City, California that convinced Ch'en that defying the wishes of the KMT leadership would be harmful to his physical well being.

Liu had written a biography critical of Chiang Ching-kuo – eldest son and successor to Chiang Kai-shek – and the killers were dispatched to eliminate him. Out of a sense of patriotic duty the leader of Bamboo United (Chu Lien Pang 竹聯幫) himself, aided by two accomplices, murdered Liu. One of the hit men, Tung Kuei-sen, admitted to shooting in the belief "that he was killing a traitor on orders from the Taiwanese Government."[46] Tung was convicted of murder on March 17, 1988 and imprisoned at Lewisburg Federal Penitentiary before dying from wounds suffered in a knifing. Chen served time in a Taiwan prison for his involvement in the plot, but fled to Cambodia in 1996. There he lived at his mansion in Phnom Penh before his death in 2007 and a posthumous return to his homeland for a fabulous funeral "fit for a national celebrity" in Taiwan.[47]

Fortunately, a separate copy of the manuscript by Jennie Chen found its way to the Hoover Institution archives at Stanford University. It was discovered among the papers bequeathed by Chang Hsin-hai, a deceased KMT official. The Hoover copy in turn served as the basis for publication of the contested memoirs in serial form by two different Taiwan journals in 1992 and collected in book form. Ailing Soong died in 1973 at the age of eighty-four while Ch'en Li-Fu lived to age 100. The Asian American dynasty carried forth by these siblings at long last was paid tribute by the Hong Kong-produced feature film *The Soong Sisters* (1997) directed by Mabel Cheung and starring the beautiful trio of Maggie Cheung, Michelle Yeoh, and Vivian Wu in the title roles. Mme. Chiang, Mei-ling Soong, lived for several years after the film debuted. She lived in New York to the grand age of 105, dying on October 23, 2003 in the land where her father laid the foundation for the family dynasty.

Endnotes

1) William Wei, *The Asian American Movement* (Philadelphia: Temple University Press, 1993); Robert G. Lee, "The Hidden World of Asian Immigrant Radicalism" in Paul Buhle and Dan Georgakas, eds., *The Immigrant Left in the United States* (Albany, New York: State University of New York Press, 1996), 256-288."

2) Azuma, Eiichiro. *Between Two Empires: Race, History, and Transnationalism in Japanese America* (New York: Oxford University Press, 2005).

3) Deepa Bharath, "Little Saigon Dedicates Campaign Office to McCain. *Orange County Register* 24 Oct. 2008. Http://www.ocregister.com/articles/mccain-vietnamese-nguyen-2205722-war-vietnam#.

4) Lindsey Jang and Robert C. Winn, dirs. *Saigon U.S.A.* KOCE-TV.

5) Mary Vuong, "Documentary Prompts Vietnamese Immigrants to Re-Examine Roots." *Chron.com* 26 Apr. 2004. Http://www.chron.com/entertainment/movies/article/Documentary-prompts-Vietnamese-immigrants-to-1972024.php.

6) Ira Glass, "Turncoat." *This American Life* 22 May 2009. Http://www.thisamericanlife.org/radio-archives/episode/381/transcript.

7) Chia Youyee Vang, "Hmong Anti-Communism at Home and Abroad" in Ieva Zake, ed. *Anti-Communist Minorities in the U.S.: Political Activism of Ethnic Refugees* (New York: Palgrave Macmillan, 2009), 211-231.

8) Jane Hamilton-Merritt, *Tragic Mountains: The Hmong, the Americans, and the Secret Wars for Laos, 1942-1992* (Bloomington and Indianapolis: Indiana University Press, 1999). See Alfred W. McCoy, *The Politics of Heroin: CIA Complicity in the Global Drug Trade*, 2nd rev. ed. (Chicago, Illinois: Lawrence Hill Books, 2003); Jonathan Marshall, *Drug Wars: Corruption, Counterinsurgency and Covert Operations in the Third World* (Forestville, California: Cohan & Cohen Publishers, 1991); Peter Dale Scott, *Drugs, Oil, and War: The United States in Afghanistan, Colombia, and Indochina* (Lanham, Maryland: Rowman & Littlefield Publishers, Inc., 2003); Carl A. Trocki, *Opium, Empire and the Global Political Economy: A Study of the Asian Opium Trade 1750-1950* (London and New York: 1999).

9) Sterling Seagrave and Peggy Seagrave, *The Yamato Dynasty: The Secret History of Japan's Imperial Family* (New York: Broadway Books, 2001).

10) Sterling Seagrave, *The Soong Dynasty* (New York: Perennial Library, 1986).

11) Emily Hahn, *The Soong Sisters* (New York: e-reads, 2003 [1941]), 63.

12) Martin Booth, *Opium: A History* (New York: St. Martin's Press, 1998), 166.

13) Pan Ling, *Old Shanghai: Gangsters in Paradise* (Kowloon, Hong Kong: Heinemann Educational Books, 1984), 69-70.

14) Renqui Yu, *To Save China, To Save Ourselves: The Chinese Hand Laundry Alliance of New York* (Philadelphia: Temple University Press, 1992), 169.

15) *Time*, "Milestones" 12 Jan. 1931. http://www.time.com/time/magazine/article/0,9171,930307,00.html.

16) T. A. Soong is resurrected in a memoir by Gus Lee, *Chasing Hepburn: A Memoir of Shanghai, Hollywood, and a Chinese Family's Fight For Freedom* (New York: Three Rivers Press, 2004).

17) Seagrave, 454.

18) Pan Ling, *Old Shanghai: Gangsters in Paradise* (Hong Kong: Heinemann Asia, 1984), 72.

19) Seagrave, 142-3.

20) Timothy Brook and Bob Tadashi Wakabayashi, eds. *Opium Regimes: China, Britain, and Japan, 1839-1952* (Berkeley and Los Angeles: University of California Press, 2000).

21) For a first-person account of the practice of exploiting fictive family ties see Tung Pok Chin with Winifred C. Chin, *Paper Son: One Man's Story* (Philadelphia: Temple University Press, 2000).

22) Frederic Wakeman, Jr., *Policing Shanghai 1927-1937.* (Berkeley and Los Angeles: University of California Press, 1995), 25.

23) Seagrave, 36.

24) "The School for China's Daughters." *Shanghai Daily News* 20 Jun. 05. Http://english.eastday.com/eastday/englishedition/node20665/node20667/node22808/node45576/node45577/userobject1ai1194357.html.

25) Seagrave, 58.

26) As a political exile in Japan Sun was known as Nakayama Shō 中山樵. In China, he is known as Sūn Zhōngshān (孫中山).

27) Stella Dong, *Shanghai: The Rise and Fall of a Decadent City* (New York: Perennial, 2001), 103.

28) Sidney H. Chang & Leonard H. D. Gordon, *All Under Heaven: Sun Yat-sen and His Revolutionary Thought* (Stanford, California: Hoover Institution Press, 1991), 87.

29) Jonathan D. Spence, *The Search for Modern China* (New York: W. W. Norton & Company, 1990), 262.

30) His reputation within the CCP was solidified further by his widow Ch'ing-ling, who, as the second-born Soong sister, rose to a high position within the government of the People's Republic of China. An implacable foe of her brother-in-law Chiang Kai-shek, she denounced his Kuomintang government as a military dictatorship.

31) Marie-Claire Bergère, *Sun Yat-sen*, trans. Janet Lloyd (Stanford: Stanford University Press, 1998), 125.

32) Copies of the documents and historically-significant photographs may be viewed on the *Dr. Sun Yat-sen Hawaii Foundation* website. Http://www.sunyatsenhawaii.org/english/visits/fifth/index.html.

33) Shih-Shan Henry Tsai, *The Chinese Experience in* America (Bloomington and Illinois: Indiana University Press, 1986), 94.

34) Tsai, 95.

35) Audrey Wells, *The Political Thought of Sun Yat-sen* (New York: Palgrave, 2001), 2.

36) Yangsheng Ma and Raymond Mun Kong Lum, *Sun Yat-sen in Hawaii: Activities and Supporters* (Honolulu: Hawaii Chinese History Center, 1999), xv.

37) Yansheng Ma Lum and Raymond Mun Kong Lum, "Sun Yat-sen in Hawaii: Activities and Suporters." Http://www.sunyatsenhawaii.org/english/research/yatsen8.html.

38) Martin Booth, *The Triads: The Chinese Criminal Fraternity* (New York: St. Martin's Press, 1990), 77.

39) Chieh-ju Ch'en, *Chiang Kai-Shek's Secret Past: The Memoir of His Second Wife*, Lloyd E. Eastman, ed. (Boulder, Colorado: Westview Press, 1993), 236-243.

40) Ibid, *xvi-xvii*.

41) *Asian Political News*, "Fervent Anticommunist KMT Elder Chen Li-fu Dies At 100" 12 Feb. 2001. Http://findarticles.com/p/articles/mi_m0WDQ/is_2001_Feb_12/ai_70506808/pg_1.

42) "Chih-k'o on Roller Skates," *Time* 26 May 1947. Http://www.time.com/time/magazine/article/0,9171,793720-4,00.html.

43) So Wai Chor, "The Making of the Guomindang's Japan Policy, 1932-1937: The Roles of Chiang Kai-shek and Wang Jingwei" in *Modern China*, Vol. 28, No. 2 (Apr. 2002), 213-252. Http://links.jstor.org/sici?sici=0097-7004(200204)28%3A2%3C213%3AT-MOTGJ%3E2.0.CO%3B2-L.

44) Frederic Wakeman, Jr., *Spymaster: Dai Li and the Chinese Secret Service* (Berkeley and Los Angeles: University of California Press, 2003), 365.

45) Ch'en, *xvi*.

46) "Taiwan Gangster Convicted of Killing Writer." *New York Times* 17 Mar. 1988. Http://query.nytimes.com/gst/fullpage.html?res=940DEFD7113FF934A-25750C0A96E948260.

47) Mark Oneill, "King Duck Goes to His Taiwanese Reward." *Asian Sentinel* 24 Oct. 2007. Http://www.asiasentinel.com/index.php?option=com_content&task=view&id=793&Itemid=386.

President Johnson signing Immigration
Act of 1965 on Liberty Island, New York.

CHAPTER THREE

Tactical Immigration: Contemporary Asian American Scientists and Engineers in the Arsenal of Empire

Strategy of Inclusion

Standard interpretations of the immigration from Asia credit the Hart-Celler Act of 1965 for "remaking" the contemporary Asian American population on the whole.[1] While not untrue, most such accounts minimize or ignore the underlying cynicism of what was at bottom an expedient political decision. That is, a tactical immigration strategy to tap overseas Asian intellectual labor to fuel growth in the high technology sector, intensify military weapons capability, and provide workers for the burgeoning medico-pharmaceutical complex that underlies the healthcare insurance-industrial monopoly. Handsome profits for the Wall Street banking establishment would result from this vital admixture of highly trained foreign-born science and technology workers combined with research and development funded largely at public expense for private corporate profit.

By contrast, in her review of historian Oscar Handlin and the reigning ideology of "liberal nationalism" that informed this critical piece of legislation, Mae M. Ngai more accurately emphasizes "Asian immigration was conceived almost entirely from the vantage point of U.S. Cold War foreign policy interests."[2] As such, the sentiment of an aggrieved already existing Asian American community did not figure into the calculations of policy makers, legislators, or public intellectuals like Handlin. That is, the objective of the Immigration Act of 1965 was not necessarily to remedy race-based immigration quotas that had placed Asians at a disadvantage vis-à-vis those from European countries. Rather, its intention was to exploit a ready source of labor that would fuel the permanently militarized post-industrial society that had been envisioned by globalist-funded social planners as the foundation of postwar US political and economic supremacy. Extending this observation, the present sub-regime of the Asian American Scientific-Technological Elite owes its existence first and foremost to the political-economic imperatives of the US postwar world order but wrapped in the seemingly benign rhetoric of liberal nationalism. This selfsame science and engineering Asian immigrant subpopulation, however, entered *en masse* a society historically hostile toward Orientals irrespective of social status or professional affiliation.

Viewed another way, the Immigration Act of 1965 was part of the larger Cold War "strategy of containment" (Kennan) achieved through, ironically, what might be called here a "strategy of inclusion"; the latter involving the systematic tactical recruitment of Asian immigrants with qualifying specialized skills and education that could be put into the service of the military-industrial complex. Project Paperclip had proven that foreign-born intellectual talent from Nazi Germany could contribute a great deal to the advancement of science and technology. With daring scholarship such non-academic researchers as Joseph P. Farrell have written extensively on ultra-sophisticated innovation in aviation, space travel, and energy generation made possible by Nazi scientists brought to the US for top secret research projects.[3]

Similarly, biological warfare research and results gleaned from human experimentation confiscated by US authorities from Japanese science investigators proved a boon to their American and German counterparts housed in such notorious facilities as Camp Detrick (later Ft. Detrick) in Maryland. Their Japanese brethren in science would go unpunished for well-documented criminal acts as discussed in a sizable body of scholarship, documentary films, and journalistic accounts.[4] Meanwhile, scientists in the US developed techniques for producing all manner of biological agents. Today, private, military, and university laboratories are staffed heavily with Asian American technicians and researchers ostensibly performing research for the benefit of humanity.

Similar to the influx of expatriates and immigrants from Europe during the interwar years, the Cold War period opened the door to Asian intellectual talent that staffed the laboratories and research institutions sustained and therefore controlled by federal, corporate, and military dollars directed to science and technology development. Currently, in the early years of the twenty-first century, Asian immigrants figure prominently in cutting-edge research that while imaginatively spectacular is fraught with immediate and long-term threats to social freedom and individual autonomy as the basis of life itself is re-engineered for private profit and political control. Even a casual reading of *Wired*, the monthly journal of techno-wow owned by Condé Nast Publications, yields many an Asian name attached to leading research universities and companies committed to cracking the secrets of the physical universe so that its components can be reassembled as both value-added saleable commodities for the civilian sector while functioning as devastatingly effective tools of command and control in weaponized form for police-military applications.[5]

As an example, an article in *Wired* gushes over the promising progress of a crackerjack research team led by "neuroscientist" Ed Boyden attached to the MIT Media Lab, itself a creation of US intelligence. As "principal investigator" with the Synthetic Neurobiology Group, Boyden relies upon ill-compensated, temporarily employed post-doctoral fellows such as Xue Han to perform the tasks basic to larger research enterprise. He claims to have found a use for lasers in refiguring neurons in primates.

These investigators tout the potential therapeutic applications of their discovery in the treatment of Parkinson's disease, epilepsy, depression, and a spectrum of psychiatric disorders. The risks posed by such neurological intervention go unmentioned.[6] A 2010 group photograph of individuals attached to the Synthetic Neurobiology Group shows that nine or ten of the twenty-one researchers are Asian American. Another set of thumbnails – sixty in total – reveals about one-third of postdoctoral fellows, graduate and medical students, visiting scientists and students, undergraduate researchers, and senior lab members to be either Asian or Asian American.[7]

Scientific-Technological Elite

In the oft-cited Farewell Address to the republic on January 17, 1961, where President Dwight D. Eisenhower warned of the perils posed by the "military-industrial complex," he spoke also of the "danger" represented by the "scientific-technological elite" that would govern it. Eisenhower occupied a privileged vantage point from which to issue his cautionary observations concerning not only the armed forces but also the expanded scope of the federal government and its compromised relationship to corporate power. Prior to serving as president for two terms, he had a distinguished career in the military that spanned two world wars culminating in his appointment as Supreme Commander of Allied Forces in the European theater during World War II. He also got a preview of the coming globalist order by serving as the first supreme commander of NATO.

Almost fifty years after Eisenhower's words of warning, total defense-related expenditures stood close to $1 trillion in support of a gargantuan military-corporate infrastructure put in place for the consolidation and enforcement of what the political leadership has openly announced as the "new world order."[8] Today, the financial influence and lethal culture of the Pentagon reaches every corner of society. The political-economic clout of institutions dependent upon Department of Defense largesse and the pervasive militarist culture it has spawned has violated the ideals of a constitutional republic and turned the United States of America into a corporatist dictatorship intent on maintaining its unipolar power and extending its control grid domestically and abroad with long-term imperial projects the world over.

The university, averred Eisenhower in the same speech, already had become an integral part of the military-industrial complex. He had served, after all, as president of Columbia University for several years prior to his election as chief executive. By the time he delivered his cautionary words, the "free university" as the "fountainhead of free ideas and scientific discovery" already was on its way to becoming dependent primarily upon the "government contract" as "virtually a substitute for intellectual curiosity."

First wave science-conceptualists such as Vannevar Bush, J. Robert Oppenheimer, John von Neumann, and Ernest O. Lawrence laid the foundation for the concentration of state-military power that began with the coordinated total war effort during the 1940s that in turn expanded and intensified to become the dynamo of an American-led world techno-order. In 1941, Bush was appointed by

President Franklin D. Roosevelt as head of technology with the Office of Scientific Research and Development (OSRD). For much of his career he pushed for the integration of scientists and engineers with senior military personnel into high-level discussions and planning, going so far as to propose the formation of a specialized governing committee that he presumably would head. The techno-fascism of the present was on its way to becoming realized.

War Street

The merging of corporate, military, and government institutions during World War II and the Cold War brought to prominence the inchoate scientific elite. "For prophets of technocracy," writes former *Wall Street Journal* writer and Bush biographer G. Pascal Zachary, "the war seemed to redeem their faith in engineers and scientists as decisive social actors."[9] Their collective exploits were lauded by the press and dramatized in certain Hollywood movies to the point where the "atom" by the end of the war attained totemic significance within American popular culture.[10] With much of the world still in ruins, the National Security Act of 1947 had sealed the fateful commitment to the permanent warfare corporatist state. With the passage of this Congressional bill, according to a sympathetic historical account provided by Douglas T. Stuart, the "leading institutions of the US national security bureaucracy" were set in place.[11]

For its deep influence and fundamental reshaping of American society, Stuart ranks this example of federal legislation as equal in importance to the Civil Rights Act of 1964. Also critical to this act of Congress was the genesis, outlined "in six short and sketchy paragraphs" writes *New York Times* national security reporter Tim Weiner, of the Central Intelligence Agency.[12] The scientific-technological complex and US intelligence have been conjoined formally ever since. Wall Street was integral to this Cold War strategic partnership. The rise of IT conurbations known as "Route 28" and "Silicon Valley" are extensions of the corporatist national security state rather than expressions of capitalist entrepreneurial genius alone. After all, more than a few founding fathers ("The Old Boys") of the American shadow government – Allen W. Dulles and William J. Donovan are prominent examples – were Wall Street attorneys with elite firms as well as directors of US intelligence agencies.[13]

The relationship between spy-craft, high finance, and IT was to reach its logical endpoint by the formation during the late 1990s of IN-Q-TEL as the financial investment arm of the CIA.[14]

Appropriately enough, the first head of IN-Q-TEL was a Chinese American videogame expert named Gilman Louie. Under his visionary leadership, Louie developed a civilian surveillance technology that today is in wide use: Google Earth. He resigned from the top spot at IN-Q-TEL not long after his appointment to become a fulltime venture capitalist under his own banner as the story goes.[15] It is more likely that Louie has been "sheep dipped" and functions in the guise of a civilian entrepreneur while remaining close to government intelligence-IT entities.

At the moment before he was to retire from public life, Eisenhower voiced the need for "disarmament" or else risk a new kind of war that would "utterly destroy" civilization as it has evolved over millennia. Although he brought about an armistice in July 1953 that ended the military stalemate on the Korean peninsula, the US presence in Vietnam after the defeat of France began to mount during the Eisenhower administration. His successor President John F. Kennedy, according to some historians, had intended to reduce troop levels in Vietnam against the wishes of civilian and military advisors representing the corporate elite.[16] Even more threatening to the national banking establishment that his own father had served loyally to his personal profit, Kennedy on June 4, 1963 had signed Executive Order 11110 that would have struck at the heart of its system of monetary legerdemain whose locus since 1913 had been the privately-held Federal Reserve System.[17]

With Kennedy dead, this non-governmental entity allowed the financial oligarchs to control the form and substance of the American national (and world) economy through the exercise of its illegitimate political power.[18] The politics of its ownership was anti-democratic in its essence and open in its admiration for fascist forms of government. Moreover, its core membership earlier had plotted the assassination of another president they considered a traitor to their plutocratic social class, Franklin D. Roosevelt. The heroism and patriotism of Maj. Gen. Smedley D. Butler, however, foiled the plot to murder the architect of the New Deal.[19]

With the assassination of Kennedy in Dallas, Texas on November 22, 1963, less than six months after signing E.O. 11110, those manifold and intertwined interests that in common constitute the military-industrial complex scored the coup that definitively secured its political fortunes. Kennedy, after all, had fired Allen Dulles in 1961 after the Bay of Pigs fiasco and famously vowed to "shred the CIA into a thousand pieces and scatter them to the four winds." To an audience of the American Newspaper Publishers Association in April 1961, he had spoken of "secrecy" as being "repugnant in a free and open society" and that "we are as a people inherently and historically opposed to secret societies, to secret oaths and to secret proceedings." Lyndon B. Johnson, whose amorality as an individual and ruthlessness as a politician far exceeded even that of the most opportunistic of his professional peers has been underscored by his biographers, reversed the course set by Kennedy almost immediately upon assuming the office of the presidency.[20]

Yet it was as President of the United States that Johnson – seen in an iconic photograph staged on Liberty Island, New York with lower Manhattan in the background – who signed the Immigration and Nationality Act on October 03, 1965. Among dignitaries assembled to witness the historic event was Sen. Daniel K. Inouye, a long-standing friend of the military-industrial complex that has richly rewarded his home state of Hawaii. "Throughout the 1990s, largely through the efforts of Senator Daniel Inouye," writes an expert on the latest generation of "directed energy" weaponry, "high technology exploded and Maui became home to the USAF Maui High Performance Computing Center (located in Kihei), and the ambitious Maui Space Surveillance Complex ..."[21] The author bemoans the paucity of home-grown talent in the physical sciences to supply the intellectual labor to advance high-energy laser (HEL) weapons technology. In the shadow of the Statue of Liberty, on that landmark day in October 1965 that was to fundamentally reform the size and composition of the Asian American population, Inouye bore witness to one of the largest mass transfers of foreign-born scientists and engineers to the US since Project Paperclip.

Project Rice-Paperclip

A military-industrial state of the size and scope envisioned by its ambitious architects required a trained cadre of science and engineering specialists that could help conceptualize an integrated system of defense and then put in place a national security infrastructure that promised to shield the US from threats – real or illusory – posed by its enemies.[22] Enormous profits generated by large corporations in league with Wall Street investment banks would be reaped under the pretense of halting the advance of international communism. The federal government and the military could continue its simultaneous expansion, concentration, and centralization of power made possible by the costly and complex bureaucratic processes required in non-stop preparation for total war. A "permanent war economy" would result.[23] With this cynical postwar world-view in its ascendancy and facing a need for techno-intellectual labor to help realize it, the Office of Strategic Services (OSS) coordinated Project Paperclip beginning in 1946 that brought thousands of prominent researchers from the defeated Third Reich to the US.

The Paperclip scientists and technicians ex-filtrated to the US were charged with the task of advancing research in aeronautics, medical science, electronics, communications, and related technical fields in which German world-class intellectual talent excelled.[24] The most high profile of those secreted into the US was Wernher von Braun. He was to become a pivotal figure in the development of advanced weapons systems. As head of the National Aeronautic Space Administration (NASA), von Braun was an effective promoter of space exploration.

Holder of a doctorate in physics from the University of Berlin, von Braun had been a member of the National Socialist German Workers Party (Nazi) and held the rank of *Sturmbannführer* (major) in the *Waffen-Schutztstaffel* (SS) led by *Reichs*führer-SS Heinrich Himmler, an occult theorist who help set the religio-philosophical foundations of Nazism.[25] The esteemed von Braun admitted to direct knowledge of the slave labor system deployed in the production of the V-2 (for *Vergeltungswaffe* or vengeance) ballistic missile launched against British civilians in retaliation for the fire-bombing of German cities by the allies.

While von Braun the grand visionary and towering intellect gained the highest distinction in his profession and was showered with accolades by the end of a long career in the US, an émigré scientist named Tsien Hsue-Shen whose research specialty was also in the field of rocketry did not fare nearly as well. Tsien was among a cohort of students from China whose education in the US was underwritten by the Boxer Rebellion Indemnity Scholarship Program formalized in 1909 during the administration of Theodore Roosevelt.[26] After having studied mechanical engineering at the Massachusetts Institute of Technology, Tsien received a doctorate in 1939 under the tutelage of Theodore von Kármán at the California Institute of Technology.[27]

In 1943, Tsien and colleagues at Caltech were determined to meet the offensive military challenge presented by the innovative V-2 by designing similarly sophisticated weapons of their own. He was among the core group that founded the Jet Propulsion Laboratory for the express purpose of perfecting long-range ballistic missiles. Among this select circle of JPL founders was homegrown genius Jack Parsons, whose work was consistent with his pursuit of occult knowledge that developed along lines similar to that of Nazi theorists such as Heinrich Himmler.[28]

These intertwined threads of the Gnostic philosophical tradition, sacred magick, and ritual sex, was at the core of the belief system that extended to the US military space exploration program thanks to the expatriate Nazi scientific-technological elite.[29] Parsons was a devotee of Aleister Crowley, the notorious British magus known as "The Great Beast." Although his name is cited numerous times in major biographies of Parsons, there is no hint that Tsien was dedicated to the Luciferian metaphysic that appears to have guided the work of the postwar science and technology dictatorship.[30]

During the opening phase of the Cold War In 1949, as the international armaments race commenced, Tsien applied for US citizenship. As the result of an intelligence investigation into his background, however, the research scientist was accused of harboring communist sympathies based on past personal associations with friends and colleagues in Pasadena known to espouse such political beliefs. So began years of government persecution. Tsien was kept under surveillance and prevented from working in the field that had benefited by his singular genius. The professional quarantine was imposed even though his mentor von Kármán had recommended that Tsien be appointed inaugural director of the Guggenheim Jet Propulsion Center at Caltech. It was not until

1955 that Tsien, his wife, and two American-born children were permitted to leave for the People's Republic of China as he had requested years before. In all, close to 100 other Chinese scientists that had received advanced training at American universities were also released by the US Department of State through negotiations with the government of China. The transfer of these bearers of specialized knowledge enabled the PRC to develop its own complement of nuclear weapons capable of defense against attack by either the US or the Soviet Union.

In the eyes of an American public sold on the romance of space exploration, Wernher von Braun rose to the status of heroic Cold War man of science while Tsien had his career ruined by having been deemed politically suspect. Ironically, Tsien along with von Kármán and other US military investigators had gone overseas to interview von Braun as he was being readied for surreptitious admission to America as part of Project Paperclip. Once resettled in the land of his birth, Tsien trained a new generation of research scientists that helped elevate China to the status of "nuclear weapons state" by 1964.

As a scientist, Tsien remained an active contributor for decades thereafter as seen by the "Silkworm" missiles of his design used by both sides of the Iran-Iraq War during the 1980s. Even after relations between the US and PRC were normalized thanks to the backchannel doings of Henry Kissinger in his capacity as National Security Advisor, Tsien declined repeated invitations to visit America. Subsequent to the Nixon-Kissinger diplomatic breakthrough, however, China began making intelligence inroads into nuclear weapons research institutions such as Los Alamos and acquired information on advanced weapons technology.[31]

The Tsien Hsue-Shen affair was given book length treatment by Iris Chang in *Thread of the Silkworm* (1996). The author reviews the much written about anti-communist mood of the 1950s, when countless lives were ruined by the government-led inquisition and purge of those deemed disloyal to the US. Chang acknowledges the "quiet suffering" that Tsien endured at the hands of American authorities. Chang, however, accuses Tsien as having "betrayed his own principles" for having "bought into the system after he returned to China." She argues that Tsien had become his own "worst enemy" by becoming the "very kind of rigid, unquestioning bureaucrat that he had once so despised within the INS and the U.S. government during the McCarthy era."[32] By this judgment of Tsien, Chang draws a line between the communist regime on whose behalf he worked and that of the postwar cohort of scientists and engineers brought from the joint Kuomintang-US dictatorship of Taiwan that were no less "rigid" and "unquestioning" in their obedience to the demands made of them at US military-industrial research centers, corporations, and universities that began recruiting them in large numbers during the 1960s.

The system of higher education under KMT government rule in Taiwan was tightly controlled, from the classroom and research to supervision of social activities.[33] With such intense socialization and rigorous academic preparation, the scientific-technological elite culled from Taiwan was ideally suited to functioning in an American institutional setting, and more broadly within the burgeoning national security state, wherein hyper-specialized and compartmentalized knowledge could be used to tighten the grip of the emerging new world order system by bringing free and sovereign humanity under increasing measures of biochemical bondage, IT surveillance, and genetically engineered population reduction schemes.[34]

With the appreciable loss of intellectual capital represented by Tsien and other outstanding intellectuals that cast their lot with the new communist nation headed by Mao Zedong (who received US support during his rise to dictatorial power), that left the Cold War client Republic of China (ROC) to supply the bulk of scientists and engineers to support the expansion of the US national security state. The direct promotion of science and technology by government agencies in Taiwan, such as the Ministry of Economic Affairs, began in 1965, according to J. Megan Greene in her penetrating study of this East Asian "developmental state." Throughout the 1960s – largely through the efforts of the foreign and domestic "intellectual community" on one end and "US aid agencies" at the other – Taiwan began aggressively promoting science and technology (S&T) as the engine of economic development.[35] By the mid-1970s, the political leadership, for its own pragmatic reasons (to maintain its legitimacy), supported the emphasis on academic research and science education that in turn elevated Taiwan

87

to world-class status as a high technology manufacturing center. For its part, American strategic interests in East Asia were served by massive economic assistance and political support of the Kuomintang establishment while massaging public opinion of US-Taiwan relations through CIA front organizations such as the Asia Foundation. High-level CIA officer Ray S. Cline looms large in this dark history, along with more familiar and infamous names that appear often in the extensive literature concerning the secrets of the national security state: figures such as Richard Helms, John Singlaub, and E. Howard Hunt.[36]

Greene mentions in passing the "brain drain" from Taiwan that resulted from pouring of private and public resources into S&T-related endeavors. Unexamined by Greene, however, are the extrinsic political-economic demands and foreign policy calculations of the US government, private industry, and academia in admitting large numbers of those from "Free China" who would be given advanced graduate training at government-funded institutions such as the University of Illinois or the University of California. Once trained and properly socialized, they could then be put to work afresh as immigrant workers to build up the initial phase of the "post-industrial" society as outlined by its chief publicist Daniel Bell (1973).[37]

With the passage of the Immigration and Nationality Act in 1965, the national origins criterion that in effect had denied Asians entry since 1924 was modified radically to meet the demands of the new technology-driven, elite-led, corporate-state social system popularized for public consumption by early British futurists and globalists such as H.G. Wells, Bertrand Russell, Aldous Huxley, followed by the Americans B. F. Skinner, Alvin Toffler, John Naisbitt, and more recently Ray Kurzweil and venture capitalist Peter Thiel.[38]

Pentagon Valley

Venture capital marketing expert Steve Blank maintains an intriguing website where he has compiled and synthesized a body of mostly academic literature and first-person accounts devoted to the history of a region in Northern California synonymous with technical innovation and what others have called the "new economy."[39] He traces the origins of what today is known the world over as "Silicon Valley" to the war years, when the federal government prevailed upon private industry to tackle the formidable problems presented by German air defense against Allied bombing raids during World War II. Blank gives a good deal of individual credit to Frederick Terman, named dean of the School of Engineering at Stanford University in 1944, for devising the research and development model in use today. The R&D of the Stanford-Wall Street model combines the resources, funding, and intellectual labor of the university itself, sub-units within the military, the corporation, investment banks, and the federal government, to drive the economy and provide advanced technology for the defense and domestic surveillance establishment.

It was Terman who helped thrust Stanford into the first rank of science and engineering research universities by molding it into an institutional intake mechanism designed to convert the massive infusion of defense-designated government money into research and development projects that would have direct military application while producing marketable spin-offs for civilian use that made such technology appear "friendly" to devoted consumers awaiting the latest iteration of the smart phone track-and-trace surveillance tool.

The cult of MacIntosh spread by Hawaii-born marketing expert and "Chief Evangelist" Guy Kawasaki (not coincidentally, a graduate of Stanford) exemplifies the latter-day manifestation of the occult belief system that suffuses the Apple brand.[40] Its almost universally recognized logo of the Edenic fruit of knowledge with a bite taken out of it was linked to the occultist Isaac Newton (1642-1727), who as every child knows "discovered" the law of gravity when an apple fell on his head. This godfather of modern science was guided by his Freemasonic oaths and remained a lifelong alchemist.[41] The "Newton" was the name given to the personal digital assistant developed by Apple: one of its early failures.

Once the investment of social resources was demonstrated to have profit potential, East Coast investors began showing interest beginning in the late 1950s. Out of this formed a milieu of entrepreneurial capitalism led by the scientific-technological elite earlier envisioned by Vannevar Bush and financed by Wall Street banking houses wed to the military-industrial complex as its wealth-creation dynamo. The demand for skilled labor trained in science lured the best minds from around the world to engage in innovative research that would fuel what was touted as the second industrial revolution. Added to indigenous talent drawn from MIT, Stanford, and UC Berkeley was the large pool of Asian intellectual workers from countries such as India, or disputed political entities like Taiwan, whose respective governments had invested substantial social capital in math and science education as a state-led strategy of economic development.[42]

Within a relatively short time after US-China diplomatic ties were negotiated during the 1970s, graduate students from the PRC filled the pipeline with a fresh supply of advanced-knowledge workers for the Tofflerian "Third Wave" post-industrial globalist economy.[43] Currently, their large numbers in graduate and research institutions financed by the enormous US dollar-debt held by the PRC are laying the foundation of fields such as synthetic biology and by extension the new "life sciences economy" that institutional investors and venture capitalists are betting will be even bigger than the IT boom of the late twentieth century.[44]

Blank and the academic sources from which he draws deftly tell of the military-corporate-university foundation of Silicon Valley while celebrating its select visionaries and the grand institutions that helped construct it. Explicit in his account is a sense of pride in the larger national security state apparatus and Pentagon rule that has taken control of the American republic in the period following World War II. Primary explanatory emphasis is placed on the determinate role of science and technology in its formation and the Great Men who brought together a myriad of competing interests and strong personalities who nonetheless shared a common hyper-rationalist scientific cosmo-vision; individuals the likes of William R. Hewlett and David Packard (students of Terman at Stanford), Charles V. Litton, Sr., and William B. Shockley.

Consistent with the Will To Power of the scientific-technological elite, each of these luminaries are involved in the larger eugenics population-reduction agenda. It is not an accident that Stanford University was home to the so-called birth control pill developed by the Austrian American chemist Carl Djerrasi. One of his less known peers was China-born biologist Min Chueh Chang, an expert on mammalian reproduction, whose work formed the basis for *in vitro* fertilization and who more recently has come to be recognized as the "co-founder of the Pill."[45]

Hyper-hype

Complementing the "Great Men" heroic narrative, Amy Chua in *Day of Empire: How Hyperpowers Rise to Global Dominance and Why They Fall* (2007) foregrounds "human capital" as responsible for US economic supremacy, particularly in the form of immigrants from Asia that historically had been barred from settling in America, beginning in the late nineteenth century, until 1965. Beginning with the stock "America-as-nation-of-immigrants" narrative, Chua credits the willing acceptance and absorption of diverse groups for the "transformation from ragtag colony to continental power to superpower and finally to hyperpower."[46] The storybook quality of this narrative surpasses even the most self-flattering historical accounts. Left unmentioned is a well-documented national history of the unremitting and ruthless subjugation and exploitation of peoples both domestically and overseas from colonial times to present. With specific reference to Asian immigrants and refugees, each respective group has been subjected to harsh regimes of control and containment.

Chua slips into an orthodox paean to the American immigrant in a sustained tribute to Eugene Kleiner, whom she credits with setting off the venture capitalism boom with his success of Fairchild Semiconductor.[47] She, however, omits a basic bit of industry lore. Kleiner was a member of what the legendary physicist and Nobel Laureate inventor of the point contact transistor William B. Shockley, Jr. called the "traitorous eight."

More importantly, Shockley later in his career devoted much energy and resources to an updated version of eugenics that came in reaction to the advances wrought by the Civil Rights Movement. Ironically, Silicon Valley became home to a large population of Asian immigrants, while Stanford University was to become noteworthy for its overrepresentation of Asian American undergraduates and exceptionally talented graduate students from Asian countries, even though the institution has a well-documented history of formal research devoted to demonstrating the superior intelligence of the Anglo-Saxon group.

In her invocation of a well-worn American storyline, the pathway to achieving success in Silicon Valley is unobstructed by racial discrimination, religious bigotry, or national origins. At least for one individual, however, gender remains a barrier to equality in the workplace. Ellen K. Pao, a partner at Kleiner Perkins Caulfield & Byers filed a sexual harassment and gender discrimination lawsuit against her employer of seven years in May 2012. Pao claimed to have been subjected to unwanted sexual advances and being left out of the loop in the "clubby, male-dominated world" of venture capitalists.[48] Since 2007, Pao has been married to Alphonse "Buddy" Fletcher, Jr., a wealthy Wall Street "asset manager" and resident of the famed Dakota apartment building. In early 2011, Fletcher sued the co-op board of the Dakota – whose residents have included John Lennon, Leonard Bernstein, and Lauren Bacall – for racial discrimination.[49] The African American product of an elite education, "Buddy" Fletcher worked as an equity trader with Kidder Peabody before suing them in 1991 for employment discrimination based on race. The power couple both are connected to one of the premier globalist organizations, the Aspen Institute, founded to advance the political economic agenda of the Anglo-American alliance.

The one identifiable group of Asian immigrants that might fit the romanticized historical narrative presented by Chua is the highly educated science and engineering elite brought in ever-increasing numbers to the US beginning in the 1950s and enlisted to build the infrastructure of the national security state and technology-based post-industrial society. Perhaps this historiographic myopia is owed to her origins in this relatively privileged subset within the larger Asian American population. Although she was too modest to mention him in *Day of Empire*, her father Leon Ong Chua is a world-renowned professor emeritus of electrical engineering at the University of California, Berkeley. From a family of Hokkien-speaking Han Chinese in the Philippines, Chua came to the US for graduate study at MIT and then the University of Illinois. His namesake "Chua's Circuit" introduced in 1983 has yielded applications of the sort that have contributed to a variety of related fields and more generally to the rise of industry in the Silicon Valley.

As argued by his daughter, individual genius such as that of Leon O. Chua, and others like him, was the necessary but not sufficient cause of "hyperpower" status enjoyed by the US. As an attorney with a Wall Street firm prior to her academic career and current position as John M. Duff, Jr. Professor of Law at Yale, Chua is faced with reconciling the dilemma of serving as an advocate for "free market" global capitalism but also as one troubled by the unconscionable excesses of its corporate perpetrators and the widespread human misery wrought by the predator pursuit of private profit backed by the violence of a massive and sophisticated war-making machine. In her previous book, *World On Fire: How Exporting Free Market Democracy Breeds Ethnic Hatred and Global Instability* (2002), Chua attempts to explain away the violence inherent in corporatist capitalism: "Market-dominant minorities" such as Chinese in Southeast Asia "turn(s) free market democracy into an engine of ethnic conflagration."[50] This question as formulated, however, is flawed at its core since the notion of the "free market" economy is patently a fiction. At the same time, the Anglo-American exportation of "democracy" as the linchpin of US foreign policy in practice promotes authoritarian rule or outright dictatorial regimes among its allies and client states. This includes the Philippines, whence her family originates.

Targeting its avowed enemies – immediate and long-term – a futuristic DARPA arsenal of weaponry that defies imagination stands at the ready to preserve the allied Anglo-American "free market," which in truth is but a jealously guarded monopoly. The war-making research and development programs of Asian American "geeks of war" such as mechanical and aerospace engineer Loc Vu-Quoc at the University of Florida; electrical and computer engineer Amit Lal at Cornell University; mechanical engineer at the University of Delaware Sunil K. Agrawal; Prem Kumar at the McCormick School of Engineering and Applied Science at Northwestern University; electrical and computer engineer Horace Yuen; and professor of bioengineering at UC San Diego Sangeeta N. Bhatia demonstrate that DARPA is the enforcement arm of US "hyperpower" thanks to fat research contracts granted by the US Department of Defense with its black budget.[51]

Because of her *a priori* professional commitment to the myth of "free market democracy" that has helped excuse all manner of sophisticated high-level corporate thievery and dispossession since the Reagan era, Chua cannot understand the rise of the US as a hyperpower as anything other than the realization of twice-told tales repeated by the dominant conservative-liberal orthodoxy both within academia and among its public popularizers including Paul Krugman, Thomas Friedman, and their many imitators.

By contrast, political economist of social-democratic bent Ha-Joon Chang at the University of Cambridge attributes the supremacy of American capitalism to "an alliance of rich country governments led by the US and mediated by the 'Unholy Trinity'" of the International Monetary Fund, World Bank, and World Trade Organization as coercive instruments wielded against resource-rich nations placed under permanent bondage through the enforcement of neo-liberal economic policy.[52] Silicon Valley and the IT industry developed in the region, despite its bust on Wall Street beginning in 2000, remains in both the scholarly literature and popular imagination as the product of individual genius given free reign by free market principles.

While Asian immigrant "human capital" was tapped to create this historically unprecedented structured agglomeration of enterprises with its geographic footprint in Northern California, the economic infrastructure was supplied by the Pentagon and intelligence agencies via partially-funded subsidiaries and wholly-owned proprietary companies that bear New Age/neo-Pagan (popular among Bay Area technorati) names like Oracle or more deceptively playful hippie-tech designations such as Google; thereby disguising their integral position within the corporatist power-control grid.[53]

As seen in the mistitled documentary *Triumph of the Nerds* (1996), Oracle head Larry Ellison lives like a *shōgun* in a Japanese-style home featuring a *koi* pond with the interior adorned with samurai antique amour.[54] Interviewing Ellison – known for his bluster, arrogance, and wealth – is an unctuous Robert X. Cringely, who was among the first journalists to chronicle the Silicon Valley phenomenon and therefore shape public perception of the region and its key players who even today are seen as lovable unwashed underdogs who succeeded in beating The System. In truth, the mega-success enjoyed by Ellison was made possible by his first customer, the CIA.[55]

In particular the "nerd" image belies the truly cynical, manipulative, and power-mad traits shared by the likes of Ellison, Bill Gates, the late Steve Jobs, and more recent additions such as Larry Page and Sergei Brin of Google, which itself is an intelligence-gathering arm of the US national security state in the guise of a highly-efficient search engine and mapping grid for the masses. Neither is Silicon Valley and the information technology industry an "accidental empire" as dubbed by Cringely.[56] Rather, it is a sprawling web of national security state institutions engineered into being just as surely as the network of roads that allowed Rome at the height of it imperial greatness to extend its political-economic influence and project military power to the farthest reaches of the empire before the barbarian incursions helped accelerate its internal decadent ruin.

A volume of perceptive essays that variously examine the emergence of Silicon Valley has it that the region and the technology-forward companies that were established there was rooted in the massive infusion of government funding, private capital, and intellectual labor that came together as part of the larger Cold War effort. "So it may not be too much of an exaggeration to say that the Department of Defense was the original 'angel' of Silicon Valley," writes one observer.[57] Historian without portfolio and IT industry insider Steve Blank in a talk given before, fittingly perhaps, an assembly of Google employees, states more directly that "Silicon Valley was, and in some cases still is, the heart and mind of NSA; CIA innovation."[58]

Given the origins of Silicon Valley in the postwar national security state and its continued control of the bedrock technology of the IT revolution, it matters little that Santa Clara County, as one prominent Asian American promoter of "national innovation" expresses it, "might be considered a poster child for diversity."[59] The concentration of people from South Asia, Vietnam, and Taiwan that helped establish the region as a world leader in the development of advanced technology remain subordinate to the hereditary ruling families and its banking cartels that are the ultimate beneficiaries of the second industrial revolution.

Having reached its maturity, Pentagon Valley has served its intended purpose in generating vast wealth for the respective monarchs and huge paydays for their high-level representatives on Wall Street and the City of London. More importantly, however, the conception, engineering, and realization of a controlled "technotronic" society will ensure that a constitutional republic governed by free and sovereign individuals – unfettered by hereditary privilege and lorded over by monarchs – will never recover a hard-won revolutionary heritage that brought untold prosperity and personal freedom to its diverse peoples.

To be sure, it is a national history fraught with brutality, exploitation, and mass murder. The possibility of transcending such ugliness was promised by the "scientific dictatorship" lauded by Aldous Huxley and a host of globalist social engineers. By the first decade of the twenty-first century, the postwar cohort of Asian American techno-labor has helped make his vision of the new world order a reality.

The economic crisis signaled by the housing market bust, massive government bailouts of failed financial institutions, and the selective showcase prosecution of Wall Street crooks such as Bernie Madoff and Sri Lankan American inside trader Raj Rajaratnam have overshadowed the less dramatic dispossession of established Silicon Valley engineers that already are being undercut by their highly trained counterparts in overseas tech hubs such as Bengaluru (Bangalore). The late Steve Jobs of Apple, when asked by President Barack Obama what it would take to have their products made in the US, told him bluntly, "Those jobs aren't coming back."[60] While an elite sub-segment of Asian American finance wizards and super-technocrats have proven adept in exploiting the social space cleared by the US postwar racial and gender equality movements, the rest of the population is seeing its collective future being foreclosed on.

Endnotes

1) Bill Ong Hing, *Making and Remaking Asian American Through Immigration Policy, 1850-1990* (Stanford, California: Stanford University Press, 1993).

2) Mae M. Ngai, "The Unlovely Residue of Outworn Prejudices: the Hart-Cellar Act and the Politics of Immigration Reform, 1945-1965," in Michael Kazin & Joseph A. McCartin, eds. *Americanism: New Perspectives on the History of an Ideal* (Chapel Hill, North Carolina: University of North Carolina Press, 2006), 117.

3) Joseph P. Farrell, *Reich of the Black Sun: Nazi Secret Weapons & the Cold War Allied Legend* (Kempton, Illinois: Adventures Unlimited Press, 2005).

4) Sheldon H. Harris, *Factories of Death: Japanese Biological Warfare, 1932-45 and the American Cover-Up*, rev. ed., (New York: Routledge, 2002).

5) An initial financial backer of *Wired* was Nicholas Negroponte, the founder and former head of the MIT Media Lab, which continues to receive positive publicity from *Wired*. He is the younger brother of John Negroponte, who boasts an extensive resumé as a spook under diplomatic cover and high-level national security state functionary. He was the first Director of National Intelligence. MIT historically has enjoyed a close relationship with the CIA.

6) Lizzie Buchen, "Laser-Controlled Humans Closer to Reality." *Wired* 29 Apr. 2009. Http://www.wired.com/wiredscience/2009/04/lasercontrolledhumans/.

7) *Synthetic Neurobiology Group* website. Http://spie.org/x10.xml?WT.svl=tn7. Accessed 12 Aug. 2010.

8) Robert Higgs, "The Trillion-Dollar Defense Budge Is Already Here." *The Independent Institute* 15 Mar. 2007. Http://www.independent.org/newsroom/article.asp?id=1941.

9) G. Pascal Zachary, *Endless Frontier: Vannevar Bush Engineer of the American Century* (Cambridge, Massachusetts: The MIT Press, 1999), 287.

10) "By 1946, American culture had become so 'atomic' that scores of businesses and dozens of race horses had been named for the atom." H. Bruce Franklin, *War Stars: The Superweapon and the American Imagination* (New York: Oxford University Press, 1988), 157.

11) Douglas T. Stuart, Creating the National Security State: A History of the Law That Transformed America (Princeton and Oxford: Princeton University Press, 2008), 1.

12) Tim Weiner, *Legacy of Ashes: The History of the CIA* (New York: Anchor Books, 2008), 27.

13) Burton Hersh, *The Old Boys: The American Elite and the Origins of the CIA* (St. Petersburg, Florida: Tree Farm Books, 2002).

14) According to its website: "Launched by the CIA in 1999 as an independent, not-for-profit organization, IQT was created to bridge the gap between the technology needs of the Intelligence Community (IC) and new advances in commercial technology." Http://www.iqt.org/.

15) Tim Shorrock, *Spies For Hire: The Secret World of Intelligence Outsourcing* (New York: Simon & Schuster, 2008), 143-147.

16) This turning point is argued strenuously among a panel of contemporary historians in James G. Blight, Janet M. Lang, David A. Welch, *Vietnam If Kennedy Had Lived* (Lanham, Maryland: Rowman & Littlefield Publishers, Inc., 2009).

17) F. William Engdahl, *Gods of Money: Wall Street and the Death of the American Century* (Wiesbaden, Germany: edition.engdahl, 2009), 249-251.

18) Jim Marrs, *Crossfire: The Plot That Killed Kennedy* (New York: Basic Books, 1993).

19) Jules Archer, *The Plot to Seize the White House: The Shocking True Story of the Conspiracy to Overthrow FDR* (New York: Skyhorse Publishing, 2007).

20) Randall B. Woods, *LBJ: Architect of American Ambition* (Cambridge, Massachusetts: Harvard University Press, 2006). See also Phillip F. Nelson, *LBJ: The Mastermind of the JFK Assassination*, 2nd ed. (New York: Skyhorse Publishing, 2011).

21) Doug Beason, Ph.D. *The E-Bomb: How America's New Directed Energy Weapons Will Change the Way Future Wars Will Be Fought* (Cambridge, Massachusetts: Da Capo Press, 2005), 162.

22) Such "ambitious architects" of the Cold War included Dean Acheson, W. Averell Harriman, George F. Kennan, John J. McCloy, and others like Henry Cabot Lodge, Jr., and McGeorge Bundy. See Walter Isaacson and Evan Thomas, *The Wise Men: Six Friends and the World They Made: Acheson, Bohlen, Harriman, Kennan, Lovett, and McCloy* (New York: Simon & Schuster, 1986).

23) The concept of the "permanent war economy" had been articulated in 1944 by radical thinker Edward Sard (a.k.a. Walter J. Oakes) and adapted by two-time president of General Electric and high-level government administrator Charles E. Wilson. See Ernest Haberkern, "Prophets of the 'Permanent War Economy.'" *Monthly Review* May 2009. Http://www.monthlyreview.org/090525haberkern.php. Later, Seymour Melman was to devote much of his career to explicating this prescient insight into the postwar political-economic order. See Seymour Melman, "In the Grip of a Permanent War Economy." *CounterPunch* 15 Mar. 2003.

24) Linda Hunt, *Secret Agenda: The United States Government, Nazi Scientists, and Project Paperclip. 1945-1990* (New York: St. Martin's Press, 1991).

25) Nicholas Goodrick-Clarke, *The Occult Roots of Nazism: Secret Aryan Cults and Their Influence on Nazi Ideology* (London: Tauris Parke Paperbacks, 2004).

26) The motives on the part of American negotiators involved with the indemnity were far from altruistic. See Michael H. Hunt, "The American Remission of the Boxer Indemnity: A Reappraisal." *Journal of Asian Studies* 31.3 (May 1972): 539-559.

27) In addition to Tsien, two other noteworthy Chinese scientists studied under von Kármán, Chia-Chao Lin and Hu Ning. Lin remained in the US and finished his distinguished career at the Massachusetts Institute of Technology, while not long after the civil war Hu returned to his homeland and worked in the physics department at Beijing University.

28) George Pendle, *Strange Angel: The Otherworldly Life of Rocket Scientist John Whiteside Parsons* (New York: Harcourt, 2005).

29) Peter Levenda, *Unholy Alliance: A History of Nazi Involvement With the Occult* (New York: Continuum, 2002).

30) John Carter and Robert Anton Wilson, *Sex and Rockets: The Occult World of Jack Parsons* (Port Townsend, Washington: Feral House, 2005).

31) Shirley A. Kan, "China: Suspected Acquisition of U.S. Nuclear Weapon Secrets." *CRS Report for Congress* 01 Feb. 2006. Congressional Research Service, The Library of Congress. WWW.fas.org/sgp/crs/nuke/RL30143.pdf.

32) Iris Chang, *Thread of the Silkworm* (New York: Basic Books, 1995), 263.

33) "Early in the 1950s the government established the Disciplinary Office (*Xundaochu*) in all Taiwan's universities to monitor and control information and student activities." Linda Chao and Ramon H. Myers, *The First Chinese Democracy: Political Life in the Republic of China on Taiwan* (Baltimore, Maryland: The Johns Hopkins University Press, 1998), 69.

34) *The Report From Iron Mountain on the Possibility and Desirability of Peace* (New York: Dial Press, 1967); "Population and the American Future," Rockefeller Commission Report (1969). Http://www.population-security.org/rockefeller/001_population_growth_and_the_american_future.htm; "Rebuilding America's Defenses: Strategy, Forces and Resources For a New Century," Project For the New American Century (2000). Http://www.newamericancentury.org/defensenationalsecurity2000.htm.

35) J. Megan Greene, *The Origins of the Developmental State in Taiwan: Science Policy and the Quest for Modernization* (Cambridge, Massachusetts: Harvard University Press, 2008).

36) Edward Herman and Gerry O'Sullivan, *The "Terrorism" Industry: The Experts and Institutions That Shape Our View of Terror* (New York: Pantheon Books, 1989), 148.

37) The "Post-Industrial Society" concept might not have originated with Bell. See Terry Nichols Clark, "Who Constructed Post-Industrial Society? An Informal Account of a Paradigm Shift at Columbia, Pre-Daniel Bell." *The American Sociologist* Volume 36, Number 1 (March, 2005): 23-46.

38) Kurzweil is the subject of the documentary film *Transcendent Man* (2011) directed by Barry Ptolemy. Http://transcendentman.com/.

39) Steve Blank, *Secret History of Silicon Valley*. Http://steveblank.com/category/secret-history-of-silicon-valley/.

40) Guy Kawasaki, *Enchantment: The Art of Changing Hearts, Minds, and Actions* (New York: Portfolio/Penguin, 2011).

41) Michael White, *Isaac Newton: The Last Sorcerer* (New York: Basic Books, 1999).

42) Julie Hu and Muriel M. Zhou, *Taiwan: A Study of the Education System of Taiwan and Guide to the Academic Placement of Students in Education Institutions in the United States* (Washington, DC: American Association of Collegiate Registrars and Admissions Officers/NAFSA: Association of International Educators, 2004).

43) Alvin Toffler, *The Third Wave* (New York: Morrow, 1980).

44) Jonathan B. Tucker and Raymond A. Zilinskas, "The Promise and Perils of Synthetic Biology." *The New Atlantis* Spring 2006, 25-45.

45) Roy O. Greep, "Biographical Memoirs: Min Chueh Chang." *National Academies Press*, The National Academy of Sciences. No date. Http://books.nap.edu//html/biomems/mchang.html

46) Amy Chua, *Day of Empire: How Hyperpowers Rise to Global Dominance and Why They Fall* (New York: Doubleday, 2007), 235.

47) Chua (2007), 261-63.

48) Sarah McBride, "Kleiner Partner Sues Firm for Discrimination." *Reuters* 22 May 2012. Http://www.reuters.com/article/2012/05/22/kleiner-discrimination-idUSL1E-8GMAJS20120522.

49) Peter Lattman and Christine Haughney, "Dakota Co-op Board Is Accused of Bias." *New York Times* 01 Feb. 2011. Http://www.nytimes.com/2011/02/02/nyregion/02dakota.html.

50) Amy Chua, *World On Fire: How Exporting Free Market Democracy Breeds Ethnic Hatred and Global Instability* (New York: Anchor Books, 2004), 6.

51) John Edwards, *The Geeks of War: The Secretive Labs and Brilliant Minds Behind Tomorrow's Warfare Technologies* (New York: AMACOM, 2005).

52) Ha-Joon Chang, *Bad Samaritans: The Myth of Free Trade and the Secret History of Capitalism* (New York: Bloomsbury Press, 2008), 13.

53) Lee Gilmore, *Theater In A Crowded Fire: Ritual and Spirituality At Burning Man* (Berkeley and Los Angeles: University of California Press, 2010).

54) Robert X. Cringely, *Triumph of the Nerds* (1996). DVD. John Gau Productions and Oregon Public Broadcasting with RM Associates For Channel 4 and PBS.

55) Todd Wallack, "Oracle's Coziness With Government Goes Back To Its Founding." *San Francisco Chronicle* 20 May 2002. Http://articles.sfgate.com/2002-05-20/news/17546036_1_larry-ellison-robert-miner-homeland-security-government-contracts.

56) Robert X. Cringely, *Accidental Empires: How the Boys of Silicon Valley Make Their Millions, Battle Foreign Competition, and Still Can't Get A Date* (New York: Harper Paperbacks, 1996).

57) Stuart W. Leslie, "The Biggest 'Angel' of Them All: The Military and the Making of Silicon Valley," in Martin Kenney, ed., *Understanding Silicon Valley: The Anatomy of an Entrepreneurial Region* (Stanford, California: Stanford University Press, 2000), 50.

58) Steve Blank, "Hidden In Plain Sight: The Hidden History of Silicon Valley."December 18, 2007. Vidcast lecture. Http://wn.com/Shockley_Semiconductor_Laboratory.

59) John Kao, *Innovation Nation: How America Is Losing Its Innovation Edge, Why It Matters, and What We Can Do to Get It Back* (New York: Free Press, 2007), 229.

60) Charles Duhigg and Keith Bradsher, "How the U.S. Lost Out on iPhone Work." *New York Times* 21 Jan. 2012. Http://www.nytimes.com/2012/01/22/business/apple-america-and-a-squeezed-middle class.html?_r=1&adxnnl=1&pagewanted=all&adxnnlx=1338624562-ElGjzm7FMdvt8Z+sn1Ds9A.

CHAPTER FOUR

DOUBLE SUICIDE: THE DEATHS OF ERNEST HEMINGWAY AND IRIS CHANG RECONSIDERED

Pharmacide

Five decades after his suicide by shotgun, it appears that what had been assumed to be simple paranoia on the part of literary giant Ernest Hemingway was in fact grounded in the reality of his ongoing persecution by certain elements within the US government. Veteran writer A. E. Hotchner, a close friend and author of the classic biography *Papa Hemingway* (1966), recounted the days spent with a demoralized, confused, and frustrated individual who was struggling to complete basic creative tasks central to his work. Hemingway had contacted Hotchner in May 1960 to ask for his help in editing an overly long article that had been commissioned by *Life* magazine. In an article published July 1, 2011 in the *New York Times*, Hotchner now acknowledges the validity of claims made at the time by his harried and depressed friend concerning government surveillance and harassment through wiretaps, tax audits, and pharmacologically induced mind control.[1]

The revelation that Hemingway had been targeted for surveillance by the government intelligence unit headed by J. Edgar Hoover is consistent with a well-documented history of American citizens held under suspicion by the FBI or the scores of other less well-known spy agencies within the government, military, and civilian sectors.[2] There is a bounty of literature that raises disturbing questions about the murder of individuals ranging from community organizers such as Fred Hampton to prominent popular artists such as John Lennon.[3]

Examples of assassination as politics by other means abound: John F. Kennedy, Malcolm X, Martin Luther King, and Robert F. Kennedy. According to opinion polls the overwhelming majority of Americans today do not believe the official findings of the Warren Commission formed to investigate the public killing of President Kennedy on November 22, 1963.[4] Moreover, pioneering JFK assassination investigator Mark Lane in *Last Word* (2011) reviews numerous scenarios whereby witnesses, participants, and others that contradicted the government-sponsored cover story met with suspiciously untimely deaths. Conservative newspaper columnist and popular television personality Dorothy Kilgallen, for example, had written about the Kennedy killing and expressed her determination to bring its true circumstances to public attention. Not long after, she was found dead in her apartment. Although suicide was the presumed manner of death, her husband privately believed that Kilgallen had been murdered.[5]

It is in this historical context that the seemingly paranoid claims made by Iris Chang in the months prior to her death in 2004 must be reconsidered. Chang had become a literary sensation at age twenty-nine with the publication of the gripping study *The Rape of Nanking* (1997).[6] Like Hemingway, Chang also died by her own hand. On November 9, 2004 she was found dead in her car. The 1999 Oldsmobile had been parked on an isolated private road near Los Gatos, California. It was determined that Chang had taken her own life with a pistol she had purchased at a firearms store the day before the incident. She was thirty-six years old.

Former journalism school classmate and personal friend Paula Kamen advanced the notion that the Chang suicide was the result of "mental illness." Initially, she thought the "dark topics" that Chang was writing about had pushed her over the edge. Then she surmised that the professionally ambitious, driven author suffered from "bipolar disorder."[7] In *Finding Iris Chang* (2008), Kamen interprets her friend's demise through the lens of the medico-pharmacological orthodoxy that has come to predominate throughout a society populated by sick and debilitated individuals suffering from an ever-lengthening list of ailments grouped under the heading of "mental illness."[8]

At least one person rejected the characterization by Kamen: Iris Chang's mother. It was Ying-Ying Chang who took care of the severely afflicted author during the final months leading to her death. Inspired by the speculation and misinformation that surrounded the death of her daughter, Chang wrote *The Woman Who Could Not Forget* (2011). She contradicts Kamen by standing her argument on its head. Instead, Chang places the blame squarely on the experimental anti-psychotic drugs prescribed to her daughter by a succession of psychiatrists. The side effects attributed to the medication led to the downward spiral of a spirited woman who, although emotionally sensitive, had never before exhibited signs of mental illness.[9] There is a wealth of information ranging from the anecdotal to clinical studies concerning the possible catastrophic impact of SSRIs. Pharmaceutical firms aggressively market the product line to compliant medical doctors that form relationships with company representatives early on during their professional training. In practice, medical professionals can be induced to write prescriptions for heavily promoted product by attractive sales representatives that ply them with "warm doughnuts."[10]

Mind Moles

Kamen herself claimed to suffer from chronic pain. As such, the underlying theme of her book on Chang is that the revolution in anti-depressant pharmacology has been a boon to the sad and afflicted masses. Against Kamen, however, there is a sizeable and growing body of literature that traces the less-than-altruistic origins of psychopharmacology to the mind-control human experiments conducted by the CIA beginning in the 1950s. Based upon documents that saw limited release due to pressure from the US Congress and its Church Committee investigation, *The Search For The "Manchurian Candidate"* (orig. 1979) by John Marks – onetime Foreign Service Officer with the US Department of State – is a good place to start for those ignorant of government initiatives in mind management and political pacification.[11]

Dr. Harold G. Wolff, famed neurologist at Cornell University Medical College in New York, promoted himself to CIA director Allen Dulles as an expert on so-called "brainwashing." As a medical researcher at the highest reaches of the nascent neuroscience sub-discipline, he emerged as a leading figure within what was to become the mind-control establishment. Government-funded projects that fell under the designation MK-ULTRA included "chemical, biological, and radiological materials to be used in clandestine operations and capable of controlling or modifying human behavior."[12] Wolff established the Society for the Investigation of Human Ecology in 1955 with CIA funds. Re-branded the Human Ecology Fund in 1961, the entity allowed the agency to finance advanced studies in the behavioral sciences.

A key figure in the "new religion" of psychiatry was the Canadian medical doctor Ewen D. Cameron, son of a Presbyterian minister born and educated in Scotland.[13] Controversy regarding both the ethics and efficacy of the techniques he pioneered such as "psychic driving" dogged him early in his career. Nonetheless, in Cameron the CIA found an ideal figure through which the new regime of psychiatric control could be imposed upon the entire population under the pretext of neutralizing the formidable specialized skill along similar lines practiced by the communist enemies: China, North Korea, and the Soviet Union. Influenced by the seminal work of Alfred McCoy, recent books by noted Canadian author Naomi Klein and American "human rights consultant" Michael Otterman each connect the MK-ULTRA mind-control experiments to the contemporary torture complex exposed at Abu Ghraib prison in Iraq.[14]

In *A Question of Torture* (2006) McCoy devotes an entire chapter reviewing the sordid history of Canadian-American collaboration in CIA-sponsored medical and psychiatric programs intended to radically alter behavior, "de-pattern" the mind, or cripple normal brain functions through neurosurgery, electroconvulsive therapy, or the forced administration of hallucinogenic drugs.[15] Moreover, McCoy connects the Cold War competition for mind-war supremacy over the Soviet Union and the People's Republic of China with the current "War on Terror."

In this most recent manifestation of the US torture complex, however, its perpetrators and executors operate under the full sanction and approval of the US Department of Justice through its Office of Legal Counsel (OLC). The lengthy memorandum issued by OLC attorney John Choon Yoo dated January 9, 2002 invented a new category of human – "illegal enemy combatant" – to provide lawyerly cover for the now-transparent system of random detention, physical punishment of internees, psychological abuse, and long-term imprisonment.[16] A thick volume produced by attorneys with the American Civil Liberties Union contains autopsy reports, interview transcripts, government memoranda, sworn statements, depositions, and hand-written notes that in total present a disturbing documentary account of a rationalized and fully institutionalized system of creative brutality.[17] The documentary film *Outside the Law* (2009) provides vivid first-person testimony to imprisonment and ritual torture as told by those that somehow endured the process and lived to tell of it.[18]

One of the more enterprising MK-ULTRA projects was to bring together one hundred Chinese subjects that had been studying in the US when the communists came to power in 1949. The objective of the CIA was to mold them into agents that then could be placed behind the bamboo curtain to provide intelligence on the East Asian communist menace. Wolff "promised to tell them about the inner reaches of the Chinese character" and to help select the "most useful possible agents."[19]

In 1954, a town house was rented on the Upper East Side of Manhattan to serve as the headquarters of the research team whose charge was to observe the Chinese students and plumb the depths of their minds. The legendary Dr. Sidney Gottlieb himself had a hand in this particular line of behavioral science inquiry. Recent accounts of this dark history contend that the system of mind control research, development, and application remains in place to the present day albeit in a far more sophisticated guise.[20]

The pervasiveness of pharmacological mind control is evident to those that work in a classroom environment with the current generation of students who have been labeled as "depressed" or plagued by "attention deficit hyperactivity disorder" (ADHD) and then promiscuously prescribed selective serotonin reuptake inhibitors (SSRIs).[21] Young people who would otherwise be in prime physical and intellectual condition have been transformed into zombie-like creatures whose flat affect and deadened eyes betray their forced chemical romance with the military-pharmacological complex.[22]

In the guise of dispassionate intellectual inquiry and innovation in the sciences, the contemporary university is a corporate-owned national network of laboratories populated with a concentrated and contained control group of students on psychoactive drugs. Academic institutions such as Virginia Tech, where twenty-three year old student Seung-Hui Cho went on a killing spree (April 2007) that resulted in the death of thirty-two people, remain as sites for current government-sponsored mind control programs that supposedly were halted after being publicly exposed in hearings and officially acknowledged in a Congressional report issued (1977) by the Select Committee on Intelligence.[23] Independent researcher Webster G. Tarpley observes that the Fort Hood, Texas shooter Maj. Nidal Hasan was a graduate of the same institution as Cho. Located in Blacksburg, Virginia Tech maintains a close institutional relationship with the government intelligence community that includes housing of DARPA (Defense Research Advanced Programs Agency) operations devoted to "human robotic mind control programming."[24]

Paranoia Strikes Deep

According to Hotchner, Hemingway complained that the feds had his telephones tapped; automobile and rooms bugged. He claimed that his mail was being intercepted and sifted through. Well known to the general public and widely admired, the author was tailed wherever he went. Then in November 1960 Hemingway was admitted to St. Mary's Hospital in Rochester, Minnesota for psychiatric treatment. He underwent electro-shock therapy administered over the course of eleven separate sessions. Hemingway became even more depressed and attempted suicide on more than one occasion. Hotchner asked his friend why he would want to kill himself. Hemingway said that everything he valued in life – friends, sex, health, and creative work – had been stolen from him. He ended his life on July 2, 1961. Documents obtained through the Freedom of Information Act (FOIA) indicate that Hemingway indeed had been under FBI surveillance since the 1940s.

Prior to her suicide, Chang had told close friends that "powerful" forces linked to the government were closing in on her. She left written statements that unambiguously outlined the contours of the plot laid against her while attempting to complete a historical account of what is known popularly as the "Bataan Death March." Most attributed her mounting "paranoia" to stress, overwork, and exposure to stories told to her by war survivors. Chang was also a new mother, so some felt that this only compounded matters. Kamen discovered, however, that Chang had hidden the fact that her son had been adopted. This ruled out the "post-partum depression" theory.

In one of the notes addressed to her parents, Chang wrote:

> *There are aspects of my experience in Louisville [in a mental hospital in August 2004] that I will never understand. Deep down I suspect that you may have more answers about this than I do. I can never shake my belief that I was being recruited, and later persecuted, by forces more powerful than I could have imagined. Whether it was the CIA or some other organization, I will never know. As long as I'm alive, these forces will never stop hounding me....*
>
> *Days before I left for Louisville, I had a deep foreboding about my safety. I sensed suddenly threats to my own life: an eerie feeling that I was being followed in the streets, the white van parked outside my house, damaged mail arriving at my P.O. Box. I believe my detention at Norton Hospital was the government's attempt to discredit me.*
>
> *I had considered running away, but I will never be able to escape from myself and my thoughts. I am doing this because I am too weak to withstand the years of pain and agony ahead.*[25]

Read in proper context, these words make perfect sense. They are far from being the ravings of a "paranoiac." Ying-Ying Chang, who suspects that Japanese rightists might have been behind the harassment of her daughter, accepts the claims that she had been approached personally and threatened. Nor does she dismiss the possibility that images of "horrible atrocities and ugly images of children torn apart by wars" had been streamed purposely to the television set of the Louisville hotel where Chang had been staying while on a research trip. Indeed, "non-lethal" devices with psychotronic capability do exist in the arsenal of advanced weapons systems developed by the US Department of Defense (DoD) in coordination with the Department of Justice (DoJ), National Science Foundation (NSF), and (of particular relevance in the case of Chang) the National Institutes of Health (NIH).[26]

Chang stood as the unofficial spokesperson for the post-1965 Taiwanese American cohort composed of scientists and engineers who were militating for a stronger political voice commensurate with their significantly large representation within the academic/military/corporate complex.[27] Moreover, she had the temerity to accuse the US government and President George W. Bush himself of stonewalling the demands for reparations being made by Taiwanese Americans to the government of Japan. Because Japan is the key American military ally in East Asia, this long-term strategic alliance would ensure that reparations paid to the victims of the Pacific War would not be forthcoming. Because of her prominent stature internationally, however, Chang presented a threat to the postwar political economic accommodation forged between the US and Japan.

Predictably, assertions that ultranationalist Japanese elements were implicated in the death of Chang appeared online and in print almost immediately after the news of her suicide appeared. She became a martyr for the truth among many in the People's Republic of China, but especially among overseas Chinese in the US. In the former case, reminders of the "Asian Holocaust" perpetrated by Imperial Japan has been useful to the communist oligarchs in deflecting attention from the tens of millions of fellow Chinese that were sacrificed to consolidate power during the reign of Mao.[28] Today, orchestrated anti-Japan agitation via the Internet helps maintain one-party dictatorial control in a nation roiling with internal conflict and rebellion in its far-flung regions.

For Taiwanese Americans – a large number (including both parents of Chang who earned Ph.D.s at Harvard) of whom have been recruited since the 1950s specifically to staff highly specialized positions within the death-dealing US military-industrial complex – the "Asian Holocaust" has been an effective rallying point around which to gain the degree of political clout that matches their professional status and economic standing in the larger American society. Moreover, a shared historical memory of the widespread destruction and atrocities committed by the Imperial Japanese military during World War II eases political tensions between the PRC and Taiwan through a shared sense of victimhood directed against a common target: Japan. The factions engaged in intense current ideological battles within the immigrant Taiwanese American community have deployed anti-Japan sentiment as a politically effective organizing tool.[29]

Gold Standard

In the battle over historical memory and the role that Iris Chang played in activating it, however, there is one possible scenario that has been overlooked: That she might have been silenced for having ventured too close to truths that if exposed would have put the United States of America – not Japan – in a most unflattering light. More significantly, the investigative trail she was following with her most recent book project involving The Philippines could have led to greater exposure of the not widely known historical circumstances that undergird the very basis of the postwar economic and political order as commanded by the US. Veteran self-described "anti-fascist researcher" Dave Emory, who hosts a radio program on KFJC-FM (Los Altos, California) that features his incisive and thoroughly sourced investigative reports, states that "There is evidence to suggest that Ms. Chang's death may have resulted from mind control, administered to neutralize her as a threat to the clandestine economic and national security relationships that have governed US/Japanese affairs in the postwar period."[30]

Chang had endorsed an astounding book published by the independent Verso imprint titled *Gold Warriors: America's Secret Recovery of Yamashita's Gold* (2003) authored by Sterling and Peggy Seagrave.[31] Well-researched and heavily documented (including a CD containing facsimiles of original papers), the book reveals the systematic looting by Japan of the countries it had conquered and occupied during the war. It details the mind-boggling maneuvers whereby hundreds of tons of precious metals, gems, and countless art treasures that had been looted by the Japanese Imperial Army throughout Asia fell into the hands of Ferdinand Marcos and his cronies in the waning days of World War II.

America's special friend Marcos had succeeded in locating much of "Yamashita's gold" through the torture of key informants that were induced to locate vast stores of purloined wealth that had been skillfully hidden under the supervision of the retreating Japanese invaders. In an earlier book, *The Marcos Dynasty* (1988), Seagrave was perhaps the first author to subject this US-supported dictatorship to critical scrutiny and it is among the better works that illuminate the dark side of American imperium.[32] Importantly, a vast quantity of gold bullion produced from the wartime booty came into direct possession of the United States. The late Chalmers Johnson, an esteemed international authority on both modern China and postwar Japan, avers that this ill-gotten fortune was instrumental in helping fund the postwar economic recovery of Japan while forcing its political system into a one-party "democracy" under the sway of its American partner.[33]

Iris Chang began her career as a hard charging and ambitious crusader for truth. Beginning with her first book *Thread of the Silkworm* (1996), she had only touched upon the duplicity of government shot-callers and the utter cynicism by which their political-economic interests are pursued.[34] The subject of the work, research scientist Tsien Hsue-Shen, helped found the Jet Propulsion Laboratory (JPL) at Caltech. He was sacrificed to anti-Red hysteria that took hold when the Communist Party came to power with the Chinese Revolution.

With *The Rape of Nanking*, Chang discovered that historical truth is not necessarily welcomed. This is the point at which she came face-to-face with *real politik* grounded in cynicism, opportunism, and exploitation. While her previous work received accolades and brought early success to Chang, political-economic oligarchs will tolerate truth-seeking only up to a point: Should anyone come too close to exposing the source of their totalistic power, like the Venetian families of yore they will not hesitate to have such persons eliminated. Poisons have been their proven specialty, with Zoloft now replacing deadly nightshade or hemlock.

So long as the work of Iris Chang satisfied the agendas of the different interest groups, governmental entities, and political factions that benefitted from the good will and public sympathy garnered by *The Rape of Nanking*, she functioned as a useful asset. But with her final book project, thorough and meticulous researcher that she was, Chang independently of the Seagraves might have uncovered truths that would undermine the very foundation of the US monetary system, which had been taken off the gold standard by President Richard Nixon in 1971.

Not coincidentally, early in his political career Nixon reportedly received large cash payments from Ferdinand Marcos, who as dictator of The Philippines had enjoyed generous political and financial support from the US.[35] Ed Rollins, former campaign director for Ronald Reagan, wrote in his memoirs of ten million US dollars allegedly handed over by top political operators from The Philippines.[36] Indeed, political-economic structural corruption has defined the relationship between the US and The Philippines from colonial times to present.[37] During the course of her research, fueled as it was by a personal and political commitment to those who experienced profound losses during wartime, there is a strong possibility that Chang finally concluded that her own American government was complicit if not at the center of the multiple holocausts of the twentieth century. Her familiarity with the Seagrave book certainly had provided Chang with ample historical research that pointed to corruption among a highly select circle within the government, corporate, and military power elite.

Breakdown

In August 2004, while conducting interviews with survivors of Bataan in Louisville, Kentucky, Chang exhibited signs of mental instability. With the assistance of a certain "Colonel Kelly" whose presence she stated had frightened her severely, Chang was committed to the Norton Psychiatric Hospital. There she was diagnosed as having experienced a "brief reactive psychosis." For at least three days Chang was subjected to "antipsychotic" drugs until her parents arrived to take their daughter back to California.

Once returned home, she was placed on a regimen of anti-depressant drugs that did little to improve her condition. Brett Douglas, the IT engineer to whom she was married, appeared to offer scant emotional support to his wife other than insisting that she hew to the treatment prescribed her by medical professionals. His seeming callousness toward her was remarked upon by Kamen in *Finding Iris Chang* when upon visiting with Douglas at his home for an interview, she was introduced to a Chinese woman also named "Iris." He had met her online only months after the suicide death of his wife.

The horrifying treatment Chang was subjected to at Norton Psychiatric Hospital has a historical precedent in the rapid but controlled decline of James V. Forrestal after he was asked to resign from the Truman Administration as the first US Secretary of Defense in March of 1949 and then treated for depression. Once a partner and president of the Wall Street investment bank Dillon, Read and Company, Forrestal expressed disagreement with what he perceived to be the alarming embrace by many US government officials of the Communist State model. White House operatives had the chief of neuropsychiatry at the Bethesda Naval Hospital evaluate the once formidable Roosevelt appointee who had served the nation through wartime and then into the early years of the Cold War. His mental state deteriorated rapidly when subjected to a psychiatric treatment.

Like Hemingway, Forrestal told of being followed and having his telephone tapped. His personal physician was denied visits at least six times. When his brother finally arranged to pick him up from Bethesda for a visit to the countryside in May of 1949, Forrestal was conveniently discovered dead. An investigation claimed that he committed suicide, but no note was found that might have suggested motives for taking his own life.[38] Although not principally a writer like Hemingway or Chang, the approximately 3,000 pages in total comprised by his diaries were combed through by the White House and Pentagon before being published in censored and truncated form by Viking Press in 1951.

Nor was Forrestal the only high-level government apparatchik to have run afoul of those whom he believed to be his compatriots only to be brought low by mental breakdown, dementia, or suicide. Storied former CIA director William E. Colby (d. 1996) was the victim of a curious drowning accident while canoeing on the Wicomico River in Maryland. Among those who attended the public tribute held at the National Cathedral in Washington were Gen. William C. Westmoreland, Secretary of State Henry A. Kissinger, and "secret army chief General Vang

Pao," the latter figure having been cultivated by the CIA as a key military leader among Hmong tribesmen in Laos during the Vietnam War.[39]

The death list includes such illustrious intelligence figures as OSS chief Maj. Gen. William J. Donovan, CIA chief of counter-intelligence Jesus Angleton (who also exhibited signs of grave mental instability), *Washington Post* publisher and CIA asset Philip L. Graham who, like Hemingway, killed himself with a shotgun and CIA Office of Policy Coordination head Frank G. Wisner. After almost fifty years of government denial and corporate media dismissal of their crusade for truth, the family of US Army biochemist Frank Olson (d. 1953) finally prevailed by amassing enough evidence that his "suicide" that followed his being dosed with a hallucinogenic substance while on CIA business was in fact a case of murder. Olson had been researching pathogens for their prospective use as offensive weapons but was experiencing doubts over his involvement with such work.[40]

Given the documented history that has befallen select insiders by means of mind manipulation or direct psycho-pharmaceutical intervention, it seems reasonable to raise the question whether Chang falls within this consistent pattern.

Last Will

Although the "suicides" of Ernest Hemingway and Iris Chang are separated in time by close to five decades, they are connected in a closed loop formed by the dark history of authoritarian regimes that actively suppress the truths that would threaten their rule. The oligarchs will not hesitate to order that the life force be snuffed out of those who dare bring light to the world. Instead of murdering directly two admired literary figures of worldwide stature and thereby run the risk of official inquiries, Hemingway and Chang were most likely harassed, gang-stalked, and psychiatrically maimed to the point where they found it too painful to live. The myth of the high-strung, sensitive, self-destructive artist makes it all the more convenient to not look beyond the respective victims for the causes of their death and turn a blind eye to the darker forces at work.

The twin orthodoxy of psychiatry and pharmacology provided respectable cover to preclude a closer look into the deaths of

Hemingway and Chang. As in the case of Hemingway, however, the death of Iris Chang is not a closed book. Further investigation into the circumstances of her mental breakdown, coerced psychiatric treatment, and the identification of persons such as the mysterious "Colonel Kelly" who had her committed in Louisville, will shatter the easy and conveniently premature conclusion that the death of Chang was due to so-called "mental illness" alone.

In time, it might be seen that in her death the final gift to humankind bequeathed by Iris Chang will be the exposure of the system announced publicly in 1969 by José M. R. Delgado of Yale University in *Physical Control of the Mind*.[41] For Chang was far from being "mad" or "paranoid." Rather, Chang to the very end was engaged in a quite sane but desperate struggle for the recovery of the humanity that had been stripped from her. Instead of allowing herself to be forced into a permanent state of narcotized semi-awareness and zombie-like passivity, Chang mustered the courage to end her life by a method so disturbing and sensational that questions concerning the circumstances leading to this final act of resistance will be asked far into the future. This is made clear in the intimate account given by Ying-Ying Chang, who was closely involved with her daughter in seeking therapeutic approaches that in the end failed to restore the élan vital that had been sapped and replaced by fear and loathing.

In this, Chang left the door open for future researchers and writers to enter the dark house of pain to poke about just as she had done. Once inside, she had gained deeper knowledge of the slithering political realities that go largely unremarked by corporate journalism and unexamined in foundation-funded academic research.[42] Chang had stumbled into a nest of vipers and was bitten hard. Though slowly poisoned, her core strength caused her to remain lucid against the externally imposed madness. By force of will and sheer fortitude Chang left behind a wealth of written clues, personal leads, and questions that cry out for follow-up.

The political importance of her legacy risks being minimized as Chang continues to be memorialized in books, statuary (Hoover Institution, Stanford University), and films by those no doubt motivated by the utmost sincerity.[43] Let the example of Hemingway and his state-facilitated suicide serve as a reminder that repressive governments over the course of human history are the leading cause of violent death and represent an ever-present threat to individual freedom and dignity. If Iris Chang claimed that government forces were "hounding" her, then it would be wise to heed this last testament and treat it with the grave seriousness it warrants. It would honor her memory were the public to critically examine the history of human experimentation and mind control programs in the US and question the premises that underlie the contemporary psycho-pharmaceutical control grid.

Endnotes

1) A. E. Hotchner, "Hemingway, Hounded by the Feds." *New York Times* 01 Jul. 2011. Http://www.nytimes.com/2011/07/02/opinion/02hotchner.html?pagewanted=all.

2) Anthony Summers, *Official and Confidential: The Secret Life of J. Edgar Hoover* (New York: Pocket Star Books, 1994).

3) M. Wesley Swearingen, *FBI Secrets: An Agent's Exposé* (Boston, Massachusetts: South End Press, 1995).

4) Lydia Saad, "Americans: Kennedy Assassination a Conspiracy." *Gallup* 21 Nov. 2003. Http://www.gallup.com/poll/9751/americans-kennedy-assassination-conspiracy.aspx.

5) Mark Lane, *Last Word: My Indictment of the CIA in the Murder of JFK* (New York: Skyhorse Publishing, 20011).

6) Iris Chang, *The Rape of Nanking: The Forgotten Holocaust of World War II* (New York: Basic Books, 1997).

7) Stephanie Losee, "The Demons You Know." *Salon.com* 13 Dec. 2007. Http://www.salon.com/mwt/feature/2007/12/13/paula_kamen.

8) Paula Kamen, *Finding Iris Chang: Friendship, Ambition, and the Loss of an Extraordinary Mind* (New York: Da Capo Press, 2007).

9) Ying-Ying Chang, *The Woman Who Could Not Forget: Iris Chang Before and Beyond the Rape of Nanking – A Memoir* (New York: Pegasus Books, 2011).

10) Ray Moynihan and Alan Cassels, *Selling Sickness: How the World's Biggest Pharmaceutical Companies Are Turning US All Into Patients* (New York: Nation Books, 2005), 22.

11) John Marks, *The Search For the "Manchurian Candidate: The CIA and Mind Control* (New York: W. W. Norton, 1991).

12) Andrew Goliszek, *In the Name of Science: A History of Secret Programs, Medical Research, and Human Experimentation* (New York: St. Martin's Press, 2003), 155.

13) Don Gillmor, *I Swear By Apollo: Dr. Ewen Cameron and the CIA-Brainwashing Experiments* (Montréal, Canada: Eden Press, 1987).

14) Naomi Klein, *The Shock Doctrine: The Rise of Disaster Capitalism* (New York: Metropolitan Books, 2007), 39-41; Michael Otterman, *American Torture: From the Cold War to Abu Ghraib and Beyond* (London: Pluto Press, 2007).

15) Alfred W. McCoy, *A Question of Torture: CIA Interrogation, From the Cold War to the War on Terror* (New York: Owl Books, 2006), 21-59.

16) McCoy, 113.

17) Jameel Jaffer and Amrit Singh, *Administration of Torture: A Documentary Record From Washington to Abu Ghraib and Beyond* (New York: Columbia University Press, 2007).

18) *Outside the Law: Tales From Guantánamo* (2009). Produced and directed by Polly Nash and Andrew Worthington. DVD 75 min. London: Spectacle.

19) Marks, 160.

20) Dominic Streatfeild, *Brainwash: The Secret History of Mind Control* (New York: St. Martin's Press, 2007).

21) Peter R. Breggin, M.D., *Medication Madness: A Psychiatrist Exposes the Dangers of Mood-Altering Medications* (New York: St. Martin's Press, 2008).

22) David Healy, *Let Them Eat Prozac: The Unhealthy Relationship Between the Pharmaceutical Industry and Depression* (New York and London: New York University Press, 2004).

23) "Project MKULTRA, The CIA's Program of Research In Behavioral Modification." Joint Hearing Before the Select Committee on Intelligence and the Subcommittee on Health and Scientific Research of the Committee On Human Resources United States Senate. Ninety-Fifth Congress First Session 03 Aug. 1977.

24) Webster G. Tarpley, "Nidal Malik Hasan of Virginia Tech, Bethesda, and Fort Hood: A Major Patsy in a Drill Gone Live? *Tarpley.net* 14 Nov. 2009. Http://tarpley. net/2009/11/16/nidal-malik-hasan-of-virginia-tech-bethesda-ond-fort-hood-a-major-patsy-in-a-drill-gone-live/.

25) Kamen, 58.

26) Marshall G. Thomas, *Monarch: The New Phoenix Program* (Lincoln, Nebraska: iUniverse, Inc., 2007).

27) An overview of this historically specific immigration cohort is found in Bernard P. Wong, *The Chinese in Silicon Valley: Globalization, Social Networks, and Ethnic Identity* (Lanham, Maryland: Rowman & Littlefield Publishers, Inc., 2006).

28) Frank Dikötter, *Mao's Great Famine: The History of China's Most Devastating Catastrophe, 1958-1962* (New York: Walker & Company, 2010).

29) David Pierson, "Split Over Taiwan's Future." *Los Angeles Times* 03 Apr. 2005. Http://www.latimes.com/news/local/la-me-nutaiwan3apr03,0,7633279.story?coll=-la-home-local.

30) Dave Emory, "The Death of Iris Chang." *For The Record* #509 (radio program) 01 May 2005. Http://spitfirelist.com/for-the-record/ftr-509-the-death-of-iris-chang/.

31) Sterling Seagrave & Peggy Seagrave, *Gold Warriors: America's Secret Recovery of Yamashita's Gold* (London & New York: Verso, 2003).

32) Sterling Seagrave, *The Marcos Dynasty* (New York: Harper & Row, 1988).

33) Chalmers Johnson, "The 1955 System and the American Connection: A Bibliographic Introduction." *Japan Policy Research Institute* (July 1995). Http://www.jpri. org/publications/workingpapers/wp11.html.

34) Iris Chang, *Thread of the Silkworm* (New York: Basic Books, 1995).

35) Anthony Summers, *The Arrogance of Power: The Secret World of Richard Nixon* (2001), 164.

36) Ed Rollins with Tom DeFrank, *Bare Knuckles and Back Rooms: My Life in American Politics* (New York: Broadway Books, 1996), 214.

37) James S. Henry, *The Blood Bankers: Tales From the Global Underground Economy* (New York and London: Four Walls Eight Windows, 2003). Chapter Two, "Philippine Money Files" is particularly relevant, 43-94.

38) See "The Willcutts Report: On the Death of James Forrestal." Http://jamesforrestal. ariwatch.com/WillcuttsReport.htm#Introduction1.

39) John Prados, *Lost Crusader: The Secret Wars of CIA Director William Colby* (New York: Oxford University Press, 2003), 6.

40) H. P. Albarelli, Jr., *A Terrible Mistake: The Murder of Frank Olson and the CIA's Cold War Experiments* (Walterville, Oregon: Trine Day, 2011).

41) José Manuel Rodríguez Delgado, *Physical Control of the Mind: Toward a Psychocivilized Society* (New York: Harper & Row, 1969).

42) Horace Freeland Judson, *The Great Betrayal: Fraud in Science* (Orlando, Florida: Harcourt, Inc., 2004).

43) Iris Chang played by actress Olivia Cheng becomes the focal point in the Canadian docudrama adaptation, *Iris Chang: The Rape of Nanking* (2007). Directed by Anne Pick and William Spahic. Reel To Reel Productions (Canada).

President George W. Bush and
Secretary of Labor, Elaine Chao.

CHAPTER FIVE

USEFUL IDIOTS:
ASIAN AMERICANS AND THE
CAMPAIGN FINANCE SCANDAL

Tennessee Gore and the Temple of Doom

On April 29, 1996 Vice-President Albert A. Gore, Jr. made a fund-raising visit to the Hsi Lai (西來寺) Buddhist Temple in Hacienda Heights, California. The event had been arranged by a Democratic National Committee operative known as John Huang (Jian-Nan Huang) – a Taiwanese American who gained US citizenship in 1976 – in tandem with a Los Angeles-based co-ethnic named Maria Lynn Hsia (Hsia Ling). A US citizen like Huang, Hsia worked locally as an "immigration consultant." The origins of $140,000 in "soft money" contributions collected were called into question and Gore's appearance at the temple raised the possibility of his having engaged in illegal campaign finance practices.

The circumstances surrounding the suspect donations in turn became a referendum on the influence of foreign elements upon the US electoral system. More specifically, it was claimed that the Chinese American principals involved were dealing directly with individuals of influence among the ruling oligarchy within the People's Republic of China. This relationship was viewed by critics of the Clinton administration as posing a serious threat to US national security.

Against the backdrop of a seemingly alien religion and exotically-garbed adherents of the $25 million Buddhist temple located in Hacienda Heights – a Los Angeles County suburb where large numbers of middle-class Taiwanese and other Chinese American immigrants have settled in recent years – news media wags predictably dubbed the brewing controversy "Chinagate." Emerging from the dust kicked up by the barrage of news reports, investigative journalism, television accounts, blog rants, and formal government inquiries that ensued was a striking cast of Asian and Asian American characters. Their sudden and dramatic appearance in the national media revived long-held suspicion of Asian Americans as a disloyal force standing ready to do the bidding of their recent or ancestral homeland. The political function of the Hsi Lai Temple, however, is beyond dispute: Founder of the Fo Guang Shang (佛光山) Buddhist order, with temples established the world over, Hsing Yun (星雲) has enjoyed close ties with the *Kuomintang* in Taiwan; a key political-economic and military partner with the US for the past six decades.

One academic observer of Buddhist religion as practiced in the US has noted that Master Hsing Yun and his devotees have been suspected as being "clandestine agents" for the government of Taiwan and its business elite, particularly since he "served for nearly a decade on the Central Advisory Committee of the ruling Kuomintang (KMT) party."[1] The author notes, however, that temple leadership claimed it was more interested in advancing the position of the Chinese American community than peddling influence for the government of Taiwan.

But in practice there is no firewall between the Taiwanese government and Taiwanese Americans: US citizenship or permanent resident status does not magically preclude involvement with a foreign government or its representatives , whether innocent (religious worship) or devious (influence peddling). Indeed, the issue of citizenship is rendered moot by the direct involvement of foreign nationals in "American" concerns such as the Carlyle Group, which has placed on company payroll both domestic and foreign government officials including Fidel V. Ramos (former president, The Philippines); Anand Panyarachun (former prime minister, Thailand); Thaksin Shinawatra (former prime minister, Thailand); Park Tae Joon (former prime minister, South Korea) and well-connected individuals recruited from US client states in Asia.[2]

For nasty right-wing screed writer Ann Coulter, Democratic National Committee operative John Huang personified the evil specter of Asian American participation in presidential political fund-raising activity. During the run-up to the 1996 election, Huang directed approximately $3.4 million (most of it subsequently returned to donors) in soft money to the DNC. But it was not only such an enormous sum of cash shunted to the DNC that upset Coulter. After all, her favored conservative candidates and office-holders were likewise beneficiaries of a plutocratic electoral system fueled by politically combustible soft-money sources.[3] Rather, Coulter accused Clinton of no less than "treason" for accepting funds from foreign sources in exchange for favorable trade agreements benefiting China and, more dangerously, for compromising US national security by allegedly allowing Huang access to Top Secret intelligence information. "Selling national security for campaign donations is treasonous," asserted Coulter.[4]

More to the point, the task assigned to Huang as intermediary to such "red capitalist" industrial kingpins as Wang Jun is consistent with the courting of Chinese investment and sales by mainline Yankee capitalist transnational corporations such as Lehman Brothers, Inc. As head of the $23 billion China International Trust and Investment Corporation (CITIC), which the *Washington Post* characterized as the "most influential financial and industrial conglomerate" in the PRC, the meeting of Wang with President Clinton and other luminaries "had more to do with American companies trying to cozy up to China than with the Chinese trying to gain influence in the United States."[5] As such, staged partisan debates between Sen. Arlen Specter (R-Pennsylvania) and Sen. John Glenn (D-Ohio), refereed by Jim Lehrer on *NewsHour* one day prior to the US Senate investigation in to campaign finance abuse, diverted attention from the collective money-grab taking place across the political spectrum as corporations jockeyed for position in the new China Trade.[6]

Lippo Suction

Rich Lowry, editor of the conservative journal of opinion *The National Review* and a frequent guest on "The O'Reilly Factor" and "Hannity & Colmes" on Fox News Channel, weighed in with a detailed indictment of President Clinton titled *Legacy: Paying the Price for the Clinton Years.* Although far superior to Coulter's intellectually malnourished volume on the right's favorite whipping boy, both titles were issued by right-wing ideology mill Regnery Publishing, Inc.[7] As with most other authors under this imprint, Lowry shares a Sinophobia reminiscent of 1950s-vintage Cold War rhetoric but updated to grapple with the contemporary US-China relationship. The once abject nation now props up the faltering American economy by holding most of its foreign debt to the tune of over one trillion severely devalued US dollars as of 2008. At the same time, among the American corporate planners and political elite, China has been set up as an instrument for the hollowing-out of US manufacturing while crushing the remnants of the working class (especially organized labor) and squeezing further the already hard-pressed middle class.

Intended or not, contemporary anti-China themes abounding in the popular news media and related think-tank reports has had the effect of casting blanket suspicion upon Chinese Americans specifically and Asian Americans more generally. Lou Dobbs on his eponymous CNN hour-long daily program, for example, resurrected the deep Cold War appellation "Communist China" in routine reporting on the People's Republic of China. He sometimes teamed up with fellow reporter Kitty Pilgrim on stories concerning "Communist China" designed to raise the ire of the dwindling numbers of an older audience demographic that hewed to corporate-monopoly TV as it primary news source.

As an example, a story reported by Pilgrim titled "Who's Killing You?" concerned the lack of follow-up by the 2008 presidential candidates who had vowed to eliminate the importation of lead-contaminated toys from "Communist China."[8] Meanwhile, the US national manufacturing base eroded and planned de-industrialization proceeded apace while "Communist China" stories ran on *Lou Dobbs Tonight*. The effect was to divert anger from US corporations and globalist economic planners responsible for transferring American manufacturing overseas thereby creating massive unemployment and amplifying the social ills that attend poverty.

Beyond what these TV news programs revealed about the alarmist corporate news media vitriol concerning contemporary US-China trade relations, the xeno-paranoiac climate of opinion shaped by publishers such as Regnery, websites, and journals of opinion representing the full political spectrum (including left-liberal organs) did much to cast suspicion on Chinese Americans (both native-born and immigrant) while having minimal influence on international trade policy or consumer protection. Chinese Americans, the majority of whom are immigrants, remain suspected of harboring primary loyalty to the country of their birth while being willing to betray the national interests of their adopted US homeland. Such manufactured distrust fed into the ongoing, systematic criminalization of Chinese Americans that has dogged them as a group from the time of their first large-scale entry into the US beginning in the mid-to-late nineteenth century. It is worth noting that they were the first civilians subjected to the "first campaign of mass identification and registration" by the federal government.[9]

In *Legacy*, for example, Lowry reviewed the well-documented involvement of the Indonesia-based multi-national $5 billion conglomerate Lippo Group – headed by an ethnic-Chinese businessman named Mochtar Riady (Lee Mo Tie) – in US political culture through its illegal campaign contributions to favored American leaders such as Bill Clinton. In 1992, Lippo heir apparent James Tjahaja Riady was said to have donated $750,000 to the DNC.[10] John Huang had first met Mochtar and James Riady at a 1980 financial seminar held in Little Rock, Arkansas. Huang subsequently went to work for the Riady family as head of LippoBank USA in Los Angeles. The featured speaker at the event was none other than Bill Clinton, then governor of Arkansas.[11]

From this confluence of events Lowry outlined an elaborate influence-peddling scheme involving the Lippo Group and the government of China itself. High-level military officers attached to the People's Liberation Army were reported to have gained access to the White House through the efforts of Huang and other influential campaign rainmakers who had proven their ability to raise massive sums of money with the prospect of even more loot in the offing.

Lowry drew from the proceedings of the Committee on Government Affairs convened by the US Senate on July 8, 1997. The hearings were chaired by Sen. Fred Thompson (R-Tennessee) and were meant to uncover abuses of campaign finance practices as regulated by the Federal Election Campaign Act (FECA) of 1971. An amendment to the act passed in 1974 created the Federal Election Commission (FEC). The Commission was given authority to administer the public funding program while enforcing the provisions of FECA. Although Lowry focused almost exclusively on the laxity of the Democratic National Committee, its Republican counterpart likewise was found to be less than vigilant in vetting the individuals and organizations behind the enormous sum of money required to fill the coffers of preferred political challengers and those standing for re-election. In practice, shady Americans of diverse ethnic backgrounds are identified in the final Committee report published in March 1998. Yet Lowry takes selective interest in what the Committee describes as "circumstantial evidence" that China had contributed funds to US campaigns in violation of federal law that bans foreign money. The Thompson committee also averred that state secrets had been breached by Chinese "intelligence" units thanks to Huang, Hsia, and others of their suspect ethnicity.

Also singled out for special mention by Lowry was Yah Lin "Charlie" Trie. An immigrant from Taiwan who came to the US in 1974, he arrived in Little Rock, Arkansas to join his older sister Dailin Outlaw, who ran a chain of Chinese restaurants. She later bequeathed the restaurant called "Fu Lin" to her brother before she left the area. There in the state capital, Trie became friendly with power brokers and local politicians. Many a political fundraiser was held at Fu Lin, a local haunt of Gov. Bill Clinton. Tiring of the restaurant business, Trie was encouraged by Clinton to get in on the booming US-China trade.

By 1991, Trie moved into the realm of global entrepreneurial capitalism by establishing the Daihatsu International Trading Co., appropriated from the Japanese automobile manufacturer Daihatsu. The ambitious immigrant proceeded to demonstrate his ineptitude for business by losing a good deal of money while incurring expenses more usual to that of an upper-level executive with a large corporation.

His fortunes changed dramatically for the better after his former customer at Fu Lin became President of the United States. It did not take Trie long to realize that merchandise such as Made-in-China wrenches that he tried brokering to Wal-Mart was not his most marketable product. Rather, his most precious commodity was the direct line he had to chief executive Bill Clinton. Not long after his special friend became president, Trie became a fixture in Washington and began making large contributions to the DNC.[12]

Along with Huang, Trie is thought to have generated about eighty percent of the $2.8 million later returned by the DNC. Their aggressive fund-raising tactics gave both gentlemen easy access to the White House, which they visited along with other Asian and Asian American supplicants dozens of times during the mid-1990s. One of the key sources of money that passed through the hands of Trie was supplied by prominent businessman Ng Lap Seng of Macao, who gained ready access to the Clinton White House while donating generously to the Democratic National Committee.[13] He owned real estate in the US, restaurants in Hong Kong, and the Fortuna hotel and casino in Macao. Seng also was a partner of Wang Jung, "chairman of one of China's largest financial conglomerates, who also heads one of the country's leading arms firms."[14]

These visits, however, were not the only cause for alarm. Again drawing from insinuations made by Sen. Thompson about a PRC connection between Mochtar and James Riady, Huang, Hsia, and another would-be player named Sam Wong "Ted" Sioeng (also present at the Hsi Lai Temple event held for Gore), Lowry concluded that the "president's fund-raising operation was infiltrated by Chinese agents, many of whom were openly courted as contributors and given intimate audiences with the president and other senior administration officials."[15] The politically embarrassing improprieties committed by the DNC in exercising its mandate of attracting and distributing donor money was thereby linked to a far more sinister plan to undermine US national security and economic welfare with the full complicity of President Clinton. Lowry, unlike Coulter, did not invoke the "T" word – treason – in condemning the cozy relationship between Clinton, his Asian American money bundlers, and Asian foreign nationals seeking advantage. But Lowry shared with her the conviction that the president was responsible for selling sophisticated US military technology to the People's Republic of China.

High-level cooperative efforts between the US and the PRC were not simply a partisan affair of Republicans versus Democrats. That is, the transfer of specialized military technology to China cannot be attributed to the Clinton administration alone. Investigative reporter Robert Parry, whose incisive work extends back to the Iran-Contra affair that surfaced in 1986, wrote extensively beginning in the late 1990s about the Unification Church of Rev. Sun Myung Moon. He has documented that it was during the Reagan and Bush regimes that issues relating to "Chinese espionage" were first raised. In violation of US law, the Regan White House wanted to get SA-7 missiles from China into the hands of the Contras in Nicaragua through a false front provided by the government of Guatemala. But since the PRC did not want to assist the Guatemalan military, the Chinese government through its embassy in Washington was let in on the surreptitious maneuvers. In exchange, the Reagan administration "decided to share sensitive national security secrets with the Chinese by 1984."[16]

Rodent Droppings

Predating the complementary books of Lowry and Coulter by a few years was an explosive volume that hit the *New York Times* best-seller list even before the brouhaha over the DNC campaign money-machine controversy completely blew over. *Year of the Rat* (1998) by Edward Timperlake and William C. Triplett II contained just enough truth-shadings and dubious inferences to make the story line of direct Chinese government and military influence on the White House quite compelling reading by those predisposed to the idea of alien forces controlling the US from within. "In exchange for Communist Chinese money flowing into Clinton-Gore coffers," the authors breathlessly relate, "the administration turned a blind eye to – or, worse, lent support to – dangerous Chinese activities."[17]

In truth, elements within the US government have often enough supported regimes and leaders only to later turn them into contrived enemies out of political expediency born of raw cynicism. In the Asian world alone, the figures Mao Zedong and Ho Chi Minh are but two examples of this process; both enjoyed the support of the US through the Office of Strategic Services (OSS). Indeed, the relationship between Wall Street and Japan did not cease during World War II nor was the connection severed with the Third Reich.

If indeed Charlie Trie was a member of the Four Seas triad *Si Hai Bang* (四海幫) as claimed by Timperlake and Triplett, then his affiliation would be comparable to that of three generations of the Bush dynasty tapped into The Order of Skull and Bones at Yale University along with a distinguished roster of leaders in the US business and political sphere. The Order of Death traces its American origins to 1832 when it was co-founded by William Huntington Russell, whose family wealth and power stemmed from the huge profits they reaped through dealing opium and other commodities.[18] Such illicit proceeds in turn were laundered through the colleges, universities, fraternal lodges, and churches they founded to accumulate cultural capital and perpetuate political advantage while using these same institutions to construct elaborate philosophical, scientific, and theological rationalizations for their group supremacy over the non-White and the heathen.

Although the knee-jerk defenders of Asian American sleaze and convicted criminals would be loath to admit it, there have been a good number of Asian Americans beyond the more obvious scapegoat Wen Ho Lee who have been implicated in espionage and related illegal activity. The editors of *AsianWeek*, "community" activists, professional organizations like the Committee of 100, academic types whose credibility rests upon rallying student support-on-demand, and even Asian American Studies programs in the university turn a blind eye to the misprisions and evil deeds of co-ethnics gone bad to manage the perception of collective victimization and a shared defensive identity predicated upon historically conditioned racial oppression.

Even overlooking the fact that growing numbers of Asian American individuals work at morally reprehensible anti-human pursuits as war-machine developers, bio-technicians, engineers, medical researchers, behavioral scientists, and social planners within the massive military-corporate system funded by an unwitting captive public, there is no ignoring such figures as Peter Hong-Yee Lee, Bin Wu, Larry Wu-Tai Chin, Eugene You-Tsai Hsu, Chi Mak and wife Rebecca Lai-wah Chiu, Douglas Tsou, Denise K. Woo, David Wei Dong, John Joungwoong Yai, and Robert C.

Kim. Tsien Hsue-shen, unfairly singled out as he was during the 1950s anti-communist purges even as the US government protected and rewarded former Nazi scientists such as Wernher von Braun, contributed to the refinement of nuclear weapons – first for the US and then for the PRC – whose one and only purpose is to destroy human life on a mass scale at one extreme while producing debilitating chronic illness among friend and foe alike.[19]

These names, however, must be placed in the larger context of routine espionage and intelligence work that is embedded in the ordinary functions of the national security state. Cases include that of civilian US Naval intelligence analyst Jonathan Jay Pollard who was convicted of spying for Israel, CIA counterintelligence officer Aldrich H. Ames who specialized in the Soviet Union and Russia, and FBI agent Robert P. Hanssen who passed state secrets to the Soviet Union.[20]

Israel, the chief recipient of US military weapons systems and state-of-the-art aircraft funded at great cost to the American taxpayer, maintains sophisticated domestic and foreign spy operations against the US. An article by John J. Mearsheimer and Stephen M. Walt issues a bold and detailed challenge to the Israel Lobby and its supporters in the US government. The authors question whether Israel has been a "loyal ally" because of its unauthorized transfer of sensitive military technology to China. Moreover, they cite a US General Accounting Office report that states Israel "conducts the most aggressive espionage operations against the US of any ally."[21]

To sustain the economic dynamism of Asian capitalist "Tigers" a great deal of money is circulated to help cultivate and maintain amicable relations among those who are best positioned to benefit from the enormous wealth being generated among the elites of the nations involved. Whether or not Bill Clinton and members of his administration were in the pocket of the PRC, as Timperlake and Triplett argue, it deflects attention from the political reality that the distinction between friend and foe is never clear; that ambiguities inhere in constantly shifting alliances, alignments, and liaisons. Moreover, foreign governments routinely invest in the US political system and control those who occupy influential positions within it. Mock surprise such as that expressed by Timperlake and Triplett greet every new startling revelation. Perhaps their journalistic function is simply to raise a chorus of ritual indignation to distract from ongoing structural corruption that – at the highest level – is truly color-blind and beyond nationality.

The focus on supposed Chinese government influence on the national leadership also has the benefit of deflecting attention from the American Israel Public Affairs Committee (AIPAC) and agents of influence linked to the ruling family of Saudi Arabia, in addition to secondary and tertiary states, who advance a geopolitical agenda that benefits only the elite stratum and the underlings who do their bidding in that part of the world.

Read another way – in a manner probably not intended by its authors – *Year of the Rat* points to the emergence of important new realities within the Asian American community that have emerged over the past four decades since 1965. Chief among these novel social facts is the arrival of a different breed of well situated, wealthy, cosmopolitan, and often desperately ambitious immigrant operators who want nothing less than full and complete access to the highest levels of economic and political power in US society. Their *petit bourgeois* class origins, multi-lingual ability, transnational orientation, elite education, exposure to American supranational media culture, and congruence with a core capitalist predatory social psychology place them a world apart from the earlier waves of pre-1965 Asian immigrants who were primarily of the rural peasantry or urban working class and emigrated to the US under much harsher regime of overt anti-Asian racism.

That this new contemporary class of Asian and Asian American transnational capitalists would want to protect and extend the scope of their family wealth is entirely consistent with the US political process, which is under plutocratic control for the benefit of dynastic rulers. Even though unsuccessful in their immediate goal of leveraging big money into political advantage, this first highly visible foray of wealthy and privileged Asian Americans into the upper reaches of the White oligarchic leadership might foreshadow their eventual entry into ultra-elite circles.

Already, select Asian Americans are being granted selective admission into the Euro-American-dominated administrative elite. Examples include Sen. Mitch McConnell (R-Kentucky) and US Secretary of Labor Elaine Chao, former Sen. Phil Gramm

(R-Texas) and economist/regulatory head Wendy Lee Gramm, and CBS president Leslie Moonves and network personality Julie Chen representing mass media. Moreover, as in the cases above, an intimate cross-racial political alliance between Asian Americans and Whites is coming into being. Related examples are former Secretary of Transportation Norman Yoshio Mineta, "torture memos" author John Choon Yoo, political philosopher Yoshihiro Francis Fukuyama, and conservative pop-pundit Dinesh D'Souza, each of whom have Euro-American spouses.

As the ultimate White-Yellow Power Couple, Global media overlord Rupert Murdoch and wife Wendi Deng (邓文革) are a more recent manifestation of this gendered and racialized marriage of mutual benefit. Already, the strategic incorporation of Deng into the Anglo-American global mass media network has resulted in the penetration of the ripe and ready China communications and entertainment market on a scale inconceivable by even the most visionary and grasping nineteenth-century Christian missionary.

It did not take long after her marriage to Murdoch in June 1999 before Deng began to assert herself as strategic business partner in addition to her function as wife and mother of two heirs to the imperial media mogul throne. By July 2007 the thirty-nine-year old Deng was formally brought into the News Corp. leadership after being named Chief of Strategy for MySpace operations in China. After News Corp. acquired MySpace.com by purchasing Intermix Media for $580 million in July 2005, Deng began making trips to the land of her birth to "lay the political and business groundwork to launch MySpace China" whose majority owners are Chinese nationals.[22]

Only the intense backlash caused by 2011 revelations of routine phone hacking, spying, and payoffs engaged in by Murdoch properties did their political influence begin to be questioned by establishment figures and government agencies hoping to contain the scandal.[23] After rumors of an affair between Deng and former Prime Minister of the United Kingdom Tony Blair were confirmed by her husband, their marriage of fourteen years came to an end in 2013. By early the following year, the American and British press was awash with the sordid details of the relationship between Deng and Blair. The women Murdoch once described as "a nice Chinese lady" had emerged over time as a powerful force unto herself.[24] By this public act of sexual humiliation, Murdoch was seen as a doddering cuckold unable to maintain the loyalty of his wife let alone control a coveted media empire.

While critics have pointed out that such an ownership arrangement could bolster the already tight censorship grip that the government of China keeps on internet and other media, Fox News Channel in the US already serves a similar function for the state by stocking its newsroom with government hacks, retired generals, and corporate lobbyists masquerading as "expert" analysts and commentators. Along with other major corporate TV networks such as NBC, CNN, CBS, and ABC, Fox TV and radio newscasts are nothing more than propaganda, given that the "symbiotic relationship where the usual dividing lines between government and journalism have been obliterated."[25] Along the same lines, perhaps Wendi Murdoch will succeed in convincing the Chinese politburo that MySpace would be useful in their monitoring of its restive population along similar lines as the US where so-called "social networking" sites are being sifted through for potential intelligence nuggets.[26]

Campaign Love Child

One of the more shrill sources of official condemnation came courtesy of Rep. Dan Burton (R-Indiana), whose visceral dislike of Clinton was expressed by his calling the president a "scumbag" in an April 1998 interview with the editorial board of the *Indianapolis Star.* As chair of the House Government Reform and Oversight Committee, Burton let fly with all manner of accusations, innuendoes, half-truths, and falsehoods against the President and his Taiwanese American supporters as the campaign finance scandal played out through the late 1990s. The self-described "political pit bull" characterized DNC campaign fund-raising functions as the haunt of criminals, drug dealers, and Chinese arms dealers. The partisan nature of his attack comes as no surprise. State level structural corruption, however, is not limited to either political party within the duopoly enjoyed by both Democrats and Republicans. Both parties are but limbs on the same deformed institutional beast bred and fed by the corporatist establishment.

Criminality and illicit activity is central to the ongoing functions of the state at all levels. Even Rep. Burton is not immune: It was revealed during the height of the Burton-led government investigation that he may have engaged in unethical if not illegal campaign practices by having staff members from his offices in the Capitol solicit money from potential donors. They reportedly used "heavy-handed" pressure tactics in getting lobbyists and attorneys to pony up. Although Burton enjoyed a one hundred percent approval rating from the Christian Coalition for his affirmation of "family values," an investigative journalist found that the would-be moral paragon had a penchant for extramarital affairs and a reputation for sexual harassment. Outdoing Clinton, Burton admitted to having fathered a "love child" in 1982 during his first campaign for Congress.[27] While the showboating congressman denounced Vice-President Gore for attending the Hsi Lai Temple event, Burton benefited from the monetary contributions of American Sikhs who donated through their *Gurdwara* or place of worship to gain support for the separatist political movement of their co-religionists in India.

Burton and the claque of right-wing journalists endeavored to portray the ingrained corruption of pay-to-play government as the exclusive province of Democrats. But in a minority report issued (1998) by a conclave of Democratic senators who sat on the same investigative committee chaired by Burton, it was pointed out that the practice of well-heeled opportunists buying access to the president, legislators, cabinet officers, senior White House officials, and other VIPs is a bi-partisan affair. Senators John Glenn (D-Ohio), Carl Levin (D-Michigan), Joseph I. Lieberman (D-Connecticut), Daniel K. Akaka (D-Hawaii), Richard J. Durbin (D-Illinois), Robert G. Torricelli (D-New Jersey), and Max Cleland (D-Georgia) recounted the tale of Michael Kojima, a Japan-born naturalized US citizen who contributed nearly $600,000 to the Republican Party for the privilege of sitting at the head table with President George H.W. Bush at a 1992 fund-raising dinner.[28]

Not only was the $600,0000 sum perhaps the largest ever contributed by an individual according to Federal Election Commission records, but there was compelling evidence that the ten Japanese nationals who attended the dinner as guests of Kojima paid dearly in foreign funds for the privilege of occupying ringside seats to the American political process. Unfortunately for Kojima, heavy media coverage of the unseemly revelations brought him to the attention of angry creditors who had believed him to be insolvent. Press reports also attracted the notice of the Los Angeles County District Attorney's office, which described him as "America's most wanted deadbeat dad." A warrant was issued for his arrest on the charge of failing to make child-support payments to former wives. Kojima disappeared from public view shortly after the payola hit the fan, but almost half of the $600,000 was kept by the Republican National Committee after privately settling a lawsuit involving his creditors and two ex-wives of the Japanese American mystery man.

Flexible Transnational Dupes

Within the social science departments and ethnic studies programs of the American academy a set of grand sounding but dubious set of related terms has gained currency. These terms are complementary to the even more grandiose concept of "globalization," which by now has grown into a cliché much in the way that "narrative," "deconstruction," and "postmodern" can be heard issuing from the mouths of current news readers, discussants, and presumably qualified specialists seen on cable television. Terms such as "flexible citizenship" or its close variant, "transnational citizenship," and "cultural citizenship" have been put forth to describe and explain the rapid, complex, wide-ranging, and often contradictory impact on myriad and diverse but identifiable populations that have been set into dizzying motion by politico-economic forces intended by the central banks and families that control them to propel humanity into the next phase of wealth generation via the process of "creative destruction," as early on observed by Marx and his adherents, but today embraced by a wide range of thinkers across the political spectrum.

There is a deeper and far more sinister possibility, however, that might account for the intense media and government interest in this ragtag assembly of Asian American hustlers that were brought forward for public scrutiny and justifiably punished for their misdeeds at this specific moment in time. According to E. P. Heidner in a well-researched and heavily documented article, Clinton was brought to political prominence and groomed for the presidency by a network of influential persons rotated through sensitive positions in banking, intelligence, government, and the law profession that wield unimaginable power derived from laundered CIA drug money, investment fraud, inside trading, and most significantly the confiscation by the US of the "Black Eagle Gold Fund" established on behalf of former President Ferdinand Marcos of the Philippines.

Heidner goes even further by connecting this national security dictatorship to engineering of the subprime mortgage crisis, the looting of pension funds, extorting financial bailouts from the US Congress, and bankrupting "key American industries" whose assets could be purchased for pennies on the dollar. Most dramatically, the author points to the complicity of this "partnership that condoned the murder of 3,000 people on September 11, 2001 to keep their secret and past crimes hidden."[29] Building on the research by Heidner, who approached the attacks on the World Trade Center as a criminal investigation, Mark H. Gaffney in *Black 9/11* meticulously draws linkages between private and government intelligence corporate entities such as American International Group (AIG) and the insurance brokerage Marsh & McLennon whose two floors of offices in the North Tower of the WTC happened to be the point of impact for American Airlines Flight 11.[30]

In the grand scheme of the international "black money" enterprise that has financed the corporatist shadow government since the end of World War II, the cast of Asian American characters were but bit players in a far more extensive new world order scenario. Even as such agents of influence assisted in the further degeneration of the American body politic by corrupting the political process, these sorry individuals were little more than flexible transnational dupes for the far more sophisticated gamesmen of the Anglo-American intelligence banking combine. Gaffney concludes his study by fingering those "diabolically evil forces that have betrayed and subverted our democratic values." He writes:

> They and their allies presently dominate Wall Street, both political parties, and the courts. Congress (which they have bought), not to mention the White House (also bought) and the major

US corporate media outlets (which they own); and by which means they have put many of our countrymen to sleep.[31]

He neglects to mention, however, the one institution philosophically and in practice charged with the responsibility to pursue truth: The university. For even with its positive contributions to the advance of the sciences, arts, and the humanities it too has become little more than the research and development arm of the corporatist state that owns it lock, stock, and barrel.

Endnotes

1) Stuart Chandler, "Placing Palms Together: Religious and Cultural Dimensions of the His Lai Temple Political Donations Controversy" in Duncan Ryūken Williams and Christopher S. Queen, eds. *American Buddhism: Methods and Findings in Recent Scholarship* (Surrey, Great Britain: Curzon Press, 1999), 42.

2) Dan Briody, *The Iron Triangle: Inside the Secret World of the Carlyle Group* (Hoboken, New Jersey: John Wiley & Sons, Inc., 2003).

3) The use of "soft money" originated in a 1979 law that allowed for donations to be used for "party building activities," but it evolved into the loophole that allows unrestricted money to fill Republican and Democratic coffers. Rebecca Carr, "As Soft Money Grows, So Does Controversy." *Congressional Quarterly* (1996). http://www.cnn.com/ALLPOLITICS/1996/news/9611/21/campaign.finance/soft.money.html.

4) Ann Coulter, *High Crimes and Misdemeanors: The Case Against Bill Clinton* (Washington, DC: Regnery Publishing, 2002), 255. In keeping with the obsessions shared by others of her political stripe, Coulter devotes Part One of the foregoing title to Clinton's sexual indiscretions and in Part Three attacks him on Whitewater and "Fostergate." Alluding to Clinton's ties with Asian and Asian American campaign donors, Coulter refers to him as the "Manchurian Candidate."

5) Steven Mufson, "To Chinese Firm, Access Becomes A Key Commodity." *Washingtonpost.com* 26 Mar. 1997. Http://www.washingtonpost.com/wp-srv/politics/special/campfin/stories/cf032697.htm.

6) *Online NewsHour with Jim Lehrer*. PBS 08 Jul. 1997. Http://www.pbs.org/newshour/bb/congress/july97/hearing_7-8.html.

7) In addition to Coulter and Lowry, the Regnery stable of authors reads like a "Who's Who" of contemporary right-wing punditry, including Michelle Malkin, Kenneth R. Timmerman, David Horowitz, Barbara Olson, Dinesh D'Souza, and Bill Gertz. For a brief history of Regnery Publishers, see Nicholas Confessore, "Hillary Was Right." *The American Prospect* Volume 11, Issue 5. January 17, 2000. http://www.prospect.org/print/V11/5/confessore-n.html.

It its early days, the Regnery publishing house (founded in 1947) reportedly was subsidized by the CIA.

8) *Lou Dobbs Tonight*. CNN 02 Jun. 2008.

9) Christian Parenti, *The Soft Cage: Surveillance in America From Slavery to the War On Terror* (New York: Basic Books, 2003), 76.

10) Rich Lowry, *Legacy: Paying the Price for the Clinton Years* (Washington, DC: Regnery Publishing, Inc., 2003), 140.

11) "Campaign Finance Key Player: John Huang." *Washington Post*, 24 Jul. 1997. Http://www.washingtonpost.com/wp-srv/politics/special/campfin/players/huang.htm.

12) Robert Suro, "Clinton Fund-Raiser to Plead Guilty." *Washington Post*, 22 May 1999, A2.

13) Charles R. Smith, Clinton White House and Warships Sold to China." *Newsmax.com* 03 Apr. 2007. Http://archive.newsmax.com/archives/articles/2007/4/3/113339.shtml.

14) "Campaign Finance Key Player: Ng Lap Seng." *Washingtonpost.com* 24 Jul. 1997. Http://www.washingtonpost.com/wp-srv/politics/special/campfin/players/seng.htm.

15) Lowry, 141.

16) Robert Parry, "Chinese Espionage Was a Reagan-Bush Scandal." *Consortium News* 16 Feb. 2001. Http://www.consortiumnews.com/2001/021601a.html.

17) Edward Timperlake and William C. Triplett II, *Year of the Rat: How Bill Clinton and Al Gore Compromised U.S. Security for Chinese Cash* (Washington, DC: Regnery Publishing, 1998), 263.

18) Hunt Janin, *The India-China Opium Trade in the Nineteenth Century* (Jefferson, North Carolina: McFarland & Company, 1999) 24. It was his first cousin Samuel Wadsworth Russell whose skill as a Yankee trader that built Russell and Company into a dominant force in the international drug trade.

19) The Tsien case is discussed in David Caute, *The Great Fear: The Anti-Communist Purge Under Truman and Eisenhower* (New York: Touchstone, 1979).

20) See Adrian Havill, *The Spy Who Stayed Out in the Cold: The Secret Life of FBI Double Agent Robert Hanssen* (New York: St. Martin's Paperbacks, 2002). Hanssen led a live of moral rectitude as a member of the ultra-conservative Roman Catholic Opus Dei yet had a penchant for videotaping his wife having sex with other men. Also, Pete Earley, *Confessions of a Spy: The Real Story of Aldrich Ames* (New York: G. P. Putnam's Sons, 1997). This volume is based on interviews and correspondence from Ames censored by the CIA.

21) John J. Mearsheimer and Stephen M. Walt, *The Israel Lobby and U.S. Foreign Policy* (New York: Farrar, Straus and Giroux, 2008), 76.

22) "Wendi Murdoch to work with MySpace." *China Economic Review*, 04 Jul. 2007. Http://www.chinaeconomicreview.com/it/category/wendi-deng/.

23) Greg Farrell, "News Corp. Said to Get U.S. Letter Seeking Information For Bribery Probe. *Bloomberg* 20 Sep. 2011. Http://www.bloomberg.com/news/2011-09-20/news-corp-said-to-get-u-s-letter-seeking-information-for-bribery-probe.html.

24) Mark Seal, "Seduced and Abandoned." *Vanity Fair* (March 2014), p. 3. Http://www.vanityfair.com/society/2014/03/wendi-deng-note-tony-blair.

25) David Barstow, "Behind TV Analysts, Pentagon's Hidden Hand." *New York Times* 20 Apr. 2008. Http://www.nytimes.com/2008/04/20/washington/20generals.html?_...=&adxnnl=1&adxnnlx=1214565951-nyWu6OzL2roFrYIO5iGD3Q.

26) Nick Juliano, "In Search for Foreign Intelligence, Spies turn to YouTube, MySpace, Blogs." *The Raw Story* 07 Feb. 2008. Http://rawstory.com/news/2008/In_search_for_foreign_intelligence_s...

27) Russ Baker, "Portrait of a Political "Pit Bull." *Salon* 22 Dec. 1998. Http://www.salon.com/news/1998/12/cov_22newsa.html.

28) Committee on Governmental Affairs, "Investigation of Illegal or Improper Activities in Connection With 1996 Federal Election Campaigns." Senate Report 105-167, Vol. 4, 105th Congress 2d Session, 10 Mar. 1998, 5413-31.

29) E. P. Heidner, "Collateral Damage (Part 2): The Subprime Crisis and the Terrorist Attacks on September 11, 2001. *WikiSpooks* 25 Dec. 2008. Http://wikispooks.com/wiki/File:Collateral_Damage_-_part_1.pdf.

30) Mark G. Gaffney, *Black 9/11: Money, Motive and Technology* (Walterville, Oregon: Trine Day, 2012).

31) Gaffney, 216.

Johnny Chung with First Lady
Hillary and President Bill Clinton.

CHAPTER SIX

FALSE FLAG:
TRANSNATIONAL ASIAN AMERICA
AND POLITICAL OPPORTUNISM

Sleaze Factor

On a scale perhaps unlike that of any other preceding administration, the Presidency of William Jefferson Clinton was plagued by seemingly endless controversies both personal and political. Not long after Clinton took office, trusted family friend and Deputy White House Counsel Vincent Walker Foster, Jr. was found dead on July 20, 1993 at Fort Marcy Park located in a Virginia suburb outside Washington, D.C. He was considering quitting his position according to those close to him and had gone so far as to draft an outline for a letter of resignation. Foster was a childhood friend of Bill Clinton and later enjoyed a professional relationship with Hillary Clinton as partners with the Rose Law Firm in Little Rock, Arkansas. It has been claimed that the partnership went far outside the bounds of standard professional practice. As was subsequently revealed over the course of the two-term presidency, the provincial *arrivistes* had brought with them heavy political baggage to the White House. And once installed in their new base of operations at 1600 Pennsylvania Avenue, together they engaged in a pattern of boldly opportunistic, legally dubious, money-generating ventures of even greater magnitude.

Following the death of Foster, both the president and Hillary Rodham Clinton became targets of a full-scale investigation concerning the "Whitewater" real estate investment scheme that was transacted in Arkansas prior to their ascension to the national political stage. Kenneth W. Starr as independent counsel led an official inquiry into an array of allegations that in the end left both the Clintons free to rule the nation while erstwhile friends and associates James B. (Jim) McDougal, his wife Susan C. McDougal, and Governor Jim Guy Tucker were convicted of fraud and sentenced to prison. By her account, Susan McDougal says that the collapse of Madison Guaranty with her husband as CEO had more to do with "stupidity and incompetence" rather than financial fraud and conspiracy.[1] The day before he was due to testify against the Clintons, the former professor of political science at Ouachita Baptist University died of a heart attack while being held in solitary confinement. McDougal was one of many Clinton associates who died at convenient moments, Secretary of Commerce Ronald H. Brown being another.

The Whitewater scandal was fed by allegations of a long-standing raunchy affair between the decedent Foster and Clinton that supposedly commenced in 1977. Right-wing media mercenary David Brock in an *American Spectator* article featured the revelations of Larry Patterson and Roger Perry, Arkansas State Police troopers assigned to ensure the personal safety of Governor Bill Clinton. In this capacity they had many occasion to witness the unseemly private behavior of both him and his wife.[2] Brock later had a crisis of faith as a Republican hatchet man and laid bare the inner life of a low-level political operative and others like him in a self-pitying confessional.[3] He founded the left-liberal organization Media Matters for America in 2004. MMA has been funded in part through foundations and non-profit organizations backed by globalist financier George Soros whose own criminal history makes the Clintons seem angelic by comparison.[4]

Rumors of foul play in the death of Foster began almost immediately. The public affairs documentary series *Frontline,* aired in October 1997, attempted to untangle the skein of financial transactions and complex real estate transfers while outlining the involvement of Hillary Clinton, who at the time was a partner with the Rose Law Firm.[5] In an interview with Viet D. Dinh, who served as counsel to the Senate Whitewater Committee, he states "Mrs. Clinton was the one who ordered the destruction of records" and that at minimum she had knowledge of their whereabouts. While careful not to accuse her of wrongdoing, Dinh observes that billing records accidentally discovered in the White House in the summer of 1995 point to her involvement in "very, very important questionable transactions."[6] Dinh was to resurface later as the principal architect of the USA Patriot Act that was rolled out only forty-five days after the 9/11 false flag attacks on select US landmarks.

What began in November 1995 as a series of erotically charged encounters between the President and a starry-eyed White House intern named Monica S. Lewinsky snowballed into an interminable and costly inquisition led once again by Clinton nemesis Kenneth Starr, this time cast in the role of Special Counsel. The "Starr Report" issued in 1998 poked into even the most intimate aspects of the chief executive's sexuality. The report provided dates, times, locations, and even semen-soiled physical evidence (navy blue Gap dress; FBI specimen Q3243) of "sexual encounters" between the president and his intern amour. The turgid account went into clinical detail concerning specific sex-acts between the two parties – oral sex, fondling, phone sex, kissing, mutual masturbation – and in so doing yielded a salacious investigative story line that verged on the pornographic.

Lewinsky had been fired from the White House staff for being, according to deputy chief of staff Evelyn Lieberman, a "clutch"; one who aggressively sought out the attention of the president. After being sent to the Pentagon to work in public affairs, Lewinsky met a career federal government employee named Linda Tripp. The two bonded through the exchange of workplace gossip and talk about clothes, hairstyles, and dieting. Lewinsky had hinted to Tripp that she was having an affair with a high-level government official. After some prodding she told Tripp that the recipient of her ministrations was none other than the President of the United States.

Seizing a golden opportunity, Tripp secretly recorded telephone conversations she had with Lewinsky hoping to get useful smut on Clinton. The former White House staffer described paying the president a private visit before beginning her new duties at the Pentagon. In their chat, Clinton expressed disappointment upon learning that Lewinsky would be leaving the White House and promised her a job should he win reelection in November 1996. "You can do anything you want," said the chief executive.

"Well, can I be the assistant to the president for blow jobs?" she joked.

According to Jeffrey Toobin, who wrote a bestselling book on the affair, "Before this conversation with the president ended, Lewinsky again auditioned for that position (this time while the president was on the telephone with his adviser Dick Morris)."[7] Not long afterward in August 1996, Morris was forced to resign his position after being exposed for engaging in weekly trysts with prostitutes at his suite in the Jefferson Hotel located just four blocks from the White House.[8] It was Morris who had revived Clinton's career after being defeated in his second run for governor of Arkansas, but he was cut loose anyway. Perhaps his fate was sealed by sharing unflattering observations about the Clintons with one of the call girls, Sherry Rowlands, who apparently leaked the story to the *Star* tabloid.[9]

Despite protestations of innocence, Clinton was not able to wriggle free of the accusations that had ensnared him. The Starr Report concluded: "There is substantial and credible information supporting ... eleven possible grounds for impeachment." As a consequence, the House Judiciary Committee on December 19, 1998 approved four articles of impeachment with which to try Clinton. On January 7 the following year, Chief Justice William Rehnquist opened the impeachment trial in the Senate. On February 12, votes were taken on Article I, perjury, and Article II, obstruction of justice. The president was acquitted on both counts and Clinton was left to complete his second term in office, much to the chagrin of well-funded conservative groups that had done all they could to hamper the president's ability to govern by placing him on the defensive in the face of unrelenting political attacks.[10] Having adroitly maneuvered himself out of the traps set by his political enemies, Clinton enjoyed exceptionally high personal popularity among the general public for the remainder of his presidential tenure.

Although Hillary Clinton continued to be intensely disliked in certain quarters, she too rode out the turbulence and went on to be elected US senator representing the state of New York while her husband's second term in office came to an end. As for Kenneth Starr, in 2004 he was named dean of the law school at Pepperdine University in Los Angeles.

The private institution located on prime real estate overlooking the Pacific Ocean in Malibu is known for its conservative politics and benefitting from the large contributions of right-wing billionaire godfather Richard Mellon Scaife. It was he who also helped fund various anti-Clinton schemes. An admitted philanderer, despite his financing of "family values" campaigns, Scaife later confessed to being thoroughly charmed by Clinton after a "very pleasant" two-hour fifteen-minute private lunch with the former president. He laughingly said that womanizing "is something that Bill Clinton and I have in common." [11] Any lingering animosity between the two was set aside after Scaife wrote a check for $100,000 in support of the Clinton Global Initiative. In 2006, Starr became "counsel of record" for private mercenary army Blackwater (renamed "Xe" in 2009) USA whose role in the Iraq War has been condemned by critics but nonetheless functioned with impunity.[12]

Bulletproof Bill

Accusations once leveled, even if subsequently proven untrue, often grievously wound the intended target. Clinton, however, escaped seemingly unscathed from one scandal after another before resettling into private life after completion of his second term in office. While still first lady, Hilary Clinton wasted no time in taking advantage of her personal popularity in New York City by running for the US senatorial seat vacated by the venerable Daniel P. Moynihan whose career in government service dated back to the Kennedy administration. After first taking care to establish New York residency through the joint purchase of title to a house in Chappaqua, about forty miles from Manhattan, Rodham Clinton won the 2000 senatorial race by receiving fifty-three percent of the vote to forty-three percent garnered by her much weaker opponent Rick Lazio.

In an effort to polish the image of Democratic congressional members tarnished by their association with the scandal-plagued power couple, Rep. Henry A. Waxman (D-California) released a lengthy report in 2001 that debunked a long list of select allegations against the Clinton administration.[13] In the report, Rep. Dan Burton and other Republican leaders were criticized for wasting well over $23 million during 1997-2000 in various and sundry investigations initiated by the House Committee on Government Reform and Oversight. Counter-theories surrounding the death of Vince Foster and accusations of an "enemies list" maintained by the White House, the selling of burial plots in Arlington National Cemetery, the alleged cover-up by Atty. Gen. Janet Reno concerning the 1993 government siege of the Branch-Davidian homestead in Waco, Texas, the transfer of sensitive military technology to the PRC, and the Chinese infiltration of the US political system through campaign contributions were among the many headline-grabbing allegations made by Burton and Co. that soon faded from public consciousness.

Both husband and wife got the last word on the troubles caused by what Ms. Clinton famously proclaimed in 1998 as the "vast right-wing conspiracy" that had dragged them through the mud for several years running: They published hers-and-his best-selling autobiographies within a few years of vacating the White House. As might be expected, *Living History* (2003) by Hillary Rodham Clinton is a self-serving portrait of her upper-middle class beginnings in Illinois and methodical rise to political prominence.[14] The embarrassingly public tribulations – and there were many – the Clintons faced during their turbulent life together are taken up one-by-one and adroitly explained away by the former first lady. Pilloried are enemies of Hillary while die-hard supporters are thanked by name. Personal scores having been settled in print, Clintonian good intentions are restated and family honor presumably restored. Most importantly, *Living History* cleared the way for what her detractors had feared most: A presidential campaign and possible Clinton re-occupation of the White House.

To prevent a Clinton II White House from being put into place, the US senator came under sustained attack from mostly conservative quarters. To maintain the illusion of undying enmity between the two political parties joined at the hip, predictably loud denunciations spewed from the usual mega-corporate radio and cable personalities. In addition the alternative media in particular were effective in mounting an anti-Hillary campaign. A flurry of books (most self-published to circumvent print monopoly suppression), internet postings, Podcasts, and DVDs were issued to publicize the private transgressions and despicable dealings of the pair.[15]

The first eight chapters of *My Life* (2004), the Bill Clinton autobiography that reached almost 1,000 pages in length, are calculated to evoke sympathy for the low born but bright, personable, and ambitious Southern boy with dreams of greatness. Named William Jefferson Blythe III after a father who died in an automobile accident before he was born, he knew early on – by age sixteen – that politics was his destiny. Included in the photographs section is Boys Nation delegate Clinton meeting President John F. Kennedy only four months prior to his assassination in November of 1963. The face of the future US president shines in the radiant glory of the Kennedy promise that had enraptured the postwar generation.

The combined heft of these autobiographies notwithstanding, they do not outweigh the volumes of books and independent documentaries that render an altogether different portrait of the Clintons. One of the recurrent allegations leveled at both Clintons was too politically sensitive and physically dangerous for most mainstream media outlets to pursue: That they were involved with ongoing government drug distribution operations, money laundering, sweetheart Pentagon contracts, and illegal international arms deals centered around the town of Mena, Arkansas. "The Clintons' lines of direct or indirect knowledge and association had laced unmistakably through and around the crimes of Mena," writes respected investigative journalist and historian Roger Morris.[16]

Daniel Hopsicker produced a series of DVD documentaries and published a companion book that follows the trail that connects CIA opium operations in Southeast Asia during the Vietnam War, government joint-ventures with the Mafia, the Bay of Pigs fiasco, the Kennedy assassination, Watergate, and the current "War on Drugs" being waged as part of an overall new world order pacification program. In his probe, Kenneth Starr briefly touched upon the possible connection between drug money and Clinton campaign finances "before slinking back into the safer precincts of Oval Office blow jobs," writes Hopsicker.[17]

Clinton devotes a good deal of space in explaining his role in the Whitewater investigation, the Paula Jones lawsuit, claims made by Gennifer Flowers of a twelve-year affair, his admitted dalliance with Monica Lewinsky, and the impeachment trial that followed. Clinton tells how he, amidst the scandals and controversies, also went about the job of meeting world leaders, overseeing the national and global economy, formulating social policy, and protecting the US against enemies foreign and domestic as commander-in-chief. The sustained personal attacks, however, took their toll on his health. To unblock severely clogged arteries, Clinton underwent quadruple heart bypass surgery in September 2004 and press coverage indicated a difficult recovery. Six months later he had to undergo a thoracotomy to remove scar tissue in his lungs. But by late 2007, the Man from Hope was back campaigning for his wife in her bid for the Democratic presidential nomination against Sen. Barack Hussein Obama (D-Illinois) who was to prevail over Sen. John McCain (R-Arizona) in the national election.

FOB Power

Despite the centrality of mega-campaign donors to their dual careers as professional politicians, neither *Living History* nor *My Life* gave adequate credit to the legions of high-income individuals and large corporations who donated so generously to the wellsprings of American democracy. Certainly the Asian American donors who made their ill-fated attempt at similarly gaming the US political system were given far less respect than they had paid for. Indeed, these wannabe movers and shakers who believed they had earned the trust, confidence, and gratitude of their good old boy Bill Clinton are portrayed in *My Life* as more of an annoyance than anything else.

At the tail end of his 1996 re-election campaign, Clinton recalls that his "momentum had been slowed in the last two weeks by allegations that the DNC had received several hundred thousand dollars in illegal campaign contributions from Asians, including people I had known as governor." [18] His good buddy Little Rock restaurateur Charlie Trie is not even mentioned by name in the Clinton autobiography, which reportedly earned him a $10 million advance from the publisher.

These "Asians," who had considered themselves part of the president's inner circle or FOBs ("Friends of Bill"). But in the end they were used and discarded like the "FOBs" of an earlier Asian American immigrant generation, when this disparaging acronym stood for "Fresh Off the Boat." For all the effort expended and money they lavished upon the DNC and President Clinton, Charlie Trie, Maria Hsia, Pauline Kanchanalak, John Huang, Johnny Chung, and James Riady did not even warrant passing mention in the Clinton autobiography. And this after Huang and Riady each had donated $100,000 to help stage the 1993 presidential inaugural gala.[19] Contributions to the celebration, it should be noted, are not considered campaign contributions although they certainly do bear the odor of a political pay-off.

Johnny Chien Chuen Chung immigrated to the US only as recently as 1983. He reportedly began his new life in America as a mere busboy at the Holiday Inn, yet within little more than a decade found himself on such good terms with the Clintons that he visited the executive mansion about fifty times, "bringing his well-connected Chinese friends to various functions, including a couple of White House Christmas parties."[20] On May 11, 1999, Chung gave testimony before the House Committee on Government Reform and Oversight where he summed up his thoughts on the Clintons. "Today I have mixed feelings about the President and the First Lady but I can't help but think that they used me as much as I used them," said Chung. "I also think, however, that it was grossly unfair for the DNC to attack me when they were fully aware that I was doing a lot of business and cultivating friendships with people from the People's Republic of China."[21]

In a 1997 *Los Angeles Times* interview, Chung perceptively observed, "I see the White House like a subway: You have to put in coins to open gates."[22] Between 1994 and 1996, Chung dropped a total of $366,000 worth of "tokens" into DNC turnstiles, although the money later was returned due to suspicions that it came from foreign nationals; specifically Chinese businessmen. As a relatively recent Asian immigrant, Chung did not understand that his non-White racial identity precluded him from gaining entry into the inner sanctum of the American political system simply by delivering bundles of cash to the gatekeepers. Not yet. This will come later, now that willingness to ante up on a big-time level has been established by Chung and his cohorts. For better or worse, "Chinagate" represents a break-through in the political evolution of Asian Americans because for the first time it marks them as players eager to contribute serious money that will get them into the big game.

Barbara Olson – attorney, conservative television commentator, *National Review* contributor, wife of US Solicitor General Theodore B. Olson, and implacable foe of Hillary Clinton – mocked the pretensions of Charlie Trie by citing verbatim a passage from a personal note he wrote to Bill Clinton. This pathetic message from a rank political amateur expressed concern over US-China tensions: "Why U.S. has to sent the aircraft carriers and cruisers to give China a possible excuse of foreign intervention and hence launce a real war?" Highlighting his ungrammatical "broken English," Olson writes "This is the first time an American president has ever received a threat of war from a fund-raising bag man who ran a Chinese restaurant in Little Rock."[23]

Sadly, Olson perished on American Airlines Flight 77 when it supposedly hurtled into the Pentagon on 9/11 as Vice-President Dick Cheney awaited the attack with an incredulous Secretary of Transportation Norman Y. Mineta at his side in the Presidential Emergency Operations Center. In the end, Olson was sacrificed as collateral damage in the war on terror conducted by the government she so faithfully served as one of its propagandists.

As Chinese immigrants, Chung, Trie, and their compatriots doubtless experienced individual acts of discrimination in daily life but were oblivious to its deep structural foundations. Had these Yellow greenhorns been equipped with rudimentary knowledge of the larger 150-year legacy of anti-Asian racism in their adopted homeland, they would have understood that they were attempting to surmount legal, legislative, and social barriers that had been erected by the ruling White racial oligarchy long before their historical predecessors from southern China began arriving in large numbers during the nineteenth century.

The very act of purchasing a piece of the actually-existing democratic process could not be countenanced by the White ruling class even at the end of the twentieth century. These post-1965 aspiring political power-players proved woefully ignorant of the intensely hostile and in some instances violent reaction to early Chinese laborers by the White ethnic working class and hate-mongers in elective office who succeeded in halting immigration from the Celestial Kingdom with the passage by the US Congress of the Chinese Exclusion Act of 1882.

Chung, Trie, Huang, Hsia, and others incorrectly assumed that money alone – even large sums of it – was sufficient to grant them access and acceptance by the White ruling class. In the end, they were proven to be not much more than deluded free-spending immigrants who received negligible political return on their substantial monetary investment in White power. The Congressional investigation by the Committee on Government Affairs led by Sen. Thompson was little more than a ritual public humiliation of the Asian American community; even for those who do not share the money-grubbing mentality and retrograde politics of the principal characters involved in "Chinagate."

Chicken Run

As stated above, the Waxman Report was intended more as an image makeover for the Democratic Party rather than an honest effort to clear the good names of those caught in the swirl of self-serving government-sponsored inquiries. For all its revelations concerning the abuse of investigative power, sheer vindictiveness, and hypocrisy that marked the Burton committee, the Report captured only part of the story: Although the Waxman Report attempted to put to rest the notion that the PRC was directly involved in compromising the inner workings of the US government or its agencies, absent from its pages was an acknowledgement of very real attempts by the likes of John Huang, Johnny Chung, Charlie Y. T. Trie, Maria Hsia, Pornipol "Pauline" Kanchanalak, Yogesh K. Gandhi and a host of other privileged and well-connected Asian Americans to weasel their way into the company of top-level decision makers among the US political and corporate leadership.

On June 21, 2000, Pauline Kanchanalak pleaded guilty to the charge of making false statements to the Federal Election Commission and for facilitating illegal campaign contributions by a foreign corporation. A total of $253,000 in donations to the DNC was returned after it was revealed that the money passed through the hands of her wealthy mother-in-law Praitun Kanchanalak.

Like her daughter-in-law Pauline, Praitun Kanchanalak was a permanent legal resident of the US and therefore permitted to make individual contributions to campaigns within certain limits. But the use of "straw donors" and laundering of foreign money are both forbidden by law. Nonetheless, the donations handled by Pauline Kanchanalak won her colleagues "regular access" to the White House and earned her a recommendation for a post with a US trade policy committee. Kanchanalak was unable to assume duties with the committee, however, because she lacked US citizenship; a basic job requirement that somehow went unmentioned as she shoveled more cash into the DNC furnace.[24]

The politically savvy Pauline Kanchanalak had married into a prominent Thai family. With her husband Chupong or "Jeb," they resided in McLean, Virginia and operated a "consulting" firm.[25] In the manner of many contemporary Asian elite immigrant transnationals, they shuttled between the US, Thailand, and other countries in the region in tending to their far-flung business interests. In 1992, with the backing of the Thai government, a consortium of Thai corporations formed the US-Thailand Business Council. Chupong Kanchanalak was named executive director of its Bankok office. In its US branch, a "Republican foreign policy expert" named Karl D. Jackson headed the council beginning in 1994.[26]

Through the lobbying outfit she and her husband founded in the early 1990s, Ban Chang International, Kanchanalak most notably represented the Thailand-based agro-industrial conglomerate, Charoen Pokaphand Group.[27] CP (as it is commonly known) is headed by one of the richest men in Asia, Dhanin Chearavanont, who reportedly is worth $1.3 billion.

Despite his adopted Thai name, the chairman and CEO of CP is in truth ethnic Chinese (Chia Ek Chow); a group resented for its achievements in business and the larger economy. His father and uncle emigrated from Guangdong Province in 1921, settled in Bankok, and together they opened a seed shop that grew to include feed and fertilizer products. Upon taking over the business in 1964, Chearavanont expanded into poultry production and emulated US agribusiness practices of vertical integration that led to CP becoming the top chicken processor in Asia.[28]

CP played a central role in the initial take-off of the H5N1 virus or "avian flu" throughout Southeast and East Asia beginning in the fall of 2003. Because of close personal and political ties between the Chearavanot family and Thai government leaders, CP executives were able to cover up the outbreak long enough to minimize financial losses and delay the inevitable drop in value of its stock market shares before the local population and foreign importers of the diseased poultry products were officially notified of the spreading pestilence. Only after two farm boys became ill from avian flu did Prime Minister Thaksin Shinawatra finally admit publicly that the H5N1 plague had been visited upon chicken livestock across the country and throughout the region. In response, the European Union, Japan, and South Korea halted the importation of poultry from Thailand. The Bush Administration, "grateful for Thaksin's support of US interventions in Afghanistan and Iraq," according to avian influenza chronicler Mike Davis, "avoided public criticism of the cover-up."[29]

CP poultry operations, however, currently account for only ten percent of total revenues for the multinational corporation that has 100,000 employees working for 250 affiliated companies in twenty countries. More important to the long-term growth of CP is the abundance of business opportunities represented by China after the "one country, two systems" (*yì guó lǐng zhì* 一國兩制) economic reforms initiated by Deng Xioping (鄧小平) in 1979. By 2004, China generated $4 billion in sales for the CP Group or about thirty percent of its total income.[30]

Chronic economic instability and the propensity for financial crisis in countries such as Thailand, that perforce function under the constraints of US-imposed neoliberal economic policies enforced by the World Trade Organization (WTO), compelled businessmen like Chearavanont to use substantial sums of money to lather select American politicians whose committee decisions would have a direct effect on the maintenance and enlargement of his already enormous family wealth. This created the opportunity for contemporary transnationals such as the Kanchanalak couple to act as power brokers between Asian business concerns and the US political establishment.

Non-Passive Persistence

In the American popular imagination, the surname "Gandhi" typically resonates with only the most positive of associations. During an especially turbulent period of intensifying political militancy and even violent civil rebellion, psychologist Erik Erikson published the acclaimed *Gandhi's Truth* in 1969, which won both the Pulitzer Prize and National Book Award. The feature film

Gandhi (1982) received Academy Awards for Best Picture, Best Director (Richard Attenborough) Best Actor (Ben Kingsley), and five others totaling eight altogether.

By the time the citizen of India known legally as Yogesh Kathari immigrated to the US in 1988, the popular culture milieu had been sufficiently conditioned for him to adopt "Gandhi" as his own family name as part of his American makeover. Claiming to be the great grand-nephew of Mohandas Karamchand Gandhi, he established a foundation in the name of his putative relative. Based in Northern California, the ostensible mission of Gandhi International Memorial Foundation was to recognize the humanitarian contributions of such stellar individuals as Mother Teresa, Nelson Mandela, and Mikhail Gorbachev. Only the most hardheaded skeptic would dare gainsay the illustrious international roster assembled by the ever-resourceful and persistent Yogesh Gandhi.[31]

In a bid to further elevate the status of the foundation he headed, Gandhi attempted to secure an audience with President Clinton, informing him by letter in February 1996 that he had been named recipient of the "Gandhi World Peace Award." It was requested that he receive the award in a public presentation ceremony. Gandhi was rebuffed, however, after Doris O. Matsui and her staff at the White House Office of Public Liaison ran a background check on his foundation and concluded that it lacked legitimacy. A letter dated April 17, 1996 issued by the White House expressed regrets that the president would be unable to accept the award. Gandhi, despite his best entrepreneurial efforts, had failed to pass the sniff test at this vetting. This would not, however, be the end of the affair.

Not to be deterred, Gandhi arranged with John Huang (who was still pushing forcefully for a formal title with the DNC) to attend a power dinner in Washington, DC on May 13, 1996. Once at the Sheraton-Carlton Hotel, he presented the Gandhi World Peace Award to President Clinton during a brief, hurriedly arranged private reception in a room separate from the main dining area.

Despite precautions taken at the semi-secretive hand-off, multimillionaire "rightwing Japanese cult figure" Fukunaga Hogen was caught in a photograph presenting President Clinton with the Gandhi World Peace Award. [32] On that same evening, a $325,000 check made out to the DNC was given by Gandhi to either Huang or Charlie Trie. Gandhi, however, requested that the check not be cashed until sufficient additional funds had been deposited into the specific account from which the large sum of money was to be drawn.

By the time the check cleared on June 3, 1996 a total of $500,000 had found its way into the bank account courtesy of a Japanese national named Tanaka Yoshio, who had attended the banquet. Tanaka was a wealthy businessman who promoted health products and concocted an entity known as the Earth Aid International Foundation. Tanaka had been working with Gandhi in promoting Fukunaga, who had founded one of the many new religions, cults, and millenarian movements, or *Shinshūkyō* (新宗教), that have arisen during the postwar period in Japan as a response to social dislocation, economic restructuring, cultural disorientation, and alienation from the mainstream political system.

An article published by the *Yomiuri Shimbun* (1999) stated that publicizing encounters with world figures such as Clinton, Mikhail Gorbachev, Mother Teresa, and Pope John Paul II was an effective means for Fukunaga to recruit new members to the cult. So slick was Fukunaga that he purchased a set of rings in Rome and asked the pontiff to wear one of them while the *Hō No Hana Sanpōgyō* (法の華三法行) leader wore the other. The exchange later was played up by the cult as "an expression of solidarity in efforts to achieve world peace." [33] The Pope himself had been scammed.

In July 2005, Fukunaga was convicted in Tokyo District Court for having defrauded followers of *Hō No Hana Sanpōgyō*, popularly described as a "foot-reading cult" of ¥150 million. The sixty-year-old cult leader, whose real name is Fukunaga Teruyoshi, was sentenced to twelve years in prison.[34] By the time Fukunaga began attempting to raise his profile in the US by meeting with the likes of President Clinton, he was already feeling the heat of accusations lodged by former followers who demanded the return of money they had surrendered to him out of religious devotion.

On March 4, 1998, Yogesh K. Gandhi was arrested by the FBI on suspicion of federal mail fraud. Also participating in the arrest were agents of the US Justice Department. In addition to the accusation of mail fraud, Gandhi later was charged with violating election laws and tax evasion. Although he stood to spend several years in jail and possibly would have been required to pay hundreds of thousands of dollars in fines, Gandhi got off much more lightly than that. He pleaded guilty in June 1999 to all charges and was sentenced to a year in prison the following December. In addition, he was ordered by the US District Court in San Francisco to remit $237,000 in unpaid taxes.[35]

James Riady, a foreign national, paid the largest penalty among the campaign finance transgressors. He was assessed a record-breaking $8.6 in criminal fines for violating federal election laws.[36] By mid-1999, the Justice Department's $30 million investigation had begun to lose steam as public interest in the story waned. John Huang negotiated a plea agreement that had him confess to two minor offenses committed in 1993 and 1994 but without an admission of wrongdoing in the 1996 campaign drama.

Having failed to pin anything substantive on Huang, the Department of Justice gave plea deals to the lesser of former Democratic Party fund-raisers, Johnny Chung and Charlie Trie.[37] Chung pleaded guilty in 1998 to charges of tax evasion and violating campaign laws. In exchange for his role as a cooperating witness in the investigation, he was placed on probation for five years as punishment. Trie cut a similar deal and received a sentence of three years maximum on probation after pleading guilty to one felony count and one misdemeanor count of breaking federal election laws.

As for Hsia, right-wing Asian American journalist and Michelle Malkin indignantly reported that after being convicted by a federal jury in the spring of 2000 on five felony counts relating to political donation-laundering, her legal representation managed on appeal to whittle it down to one felony count. Hsia was sentenced to ninety days of home detention, assessed a fine of $5,300, and placed on probation for three years.[38]

As a minority mouthpiece (Malkin is the daughter of Filipino immigrants, Dr. Apolo and Rafaela Maglalang) she sits comfortably among the mostly White men and women of contemporary arch-conservative pop pundits. Malkin is remarkably consistent when it comes to pointing out the misprisions and peccadilloes of her ideological arch-enemies within the Democratic Party as if they differed fundamentally from Republicans. Malkin, however, missed the larger dubious contribution that Hsia and her co-ethnic collaborators were making to US political culture: That Asian Americans could be just as cynical, conniving and opportunistic as White people if given even a sliver of an equal opportunity to work the system for their own benefit. But then this lesson might have hit too close to home for Malkin.

Yellow Power Couple

If Bill Clinton and Hillary Rodham were the ultimate late twentieth century Washington power couple, then Maria Hsia and her domestic partner Howard Hom, were their down-market counterpart operating at the other end of the country in Los Angeles, California. In 1988, Hsia, Hom, James Riady, John Huang, and other like-minded individuals determined to organize themselves as a distinctively "Asian American" interest group whose ostensible purpose was to raise their profile among the national political leadership.

Toward that end, the couple formed the Pacific Leadership Council (PLC) with the Lippo Group's moneyman Riady serving as one of its three founding co-chairs. The public relations face of their collective endeavor was to encourage the active participation of the rapidly growing post-1965 Asian American community in mainstream politics. The shadow purpose of activity cynically promoted as so-called "Asian American" political empowerment was the base pursuit of financial gain for each respective member of the clique. Donation laundering would be a means to exert influence upon local and national political leadership under the "Asian American" ethnic banner.

Maria Lynn Hsia, a native of Taiwan, was born in 1951 and came to the US on a student visa in 1973. She returned to her home country in 1974 for a short while, but returned to the US and was granted permanent resident status in 1975. Hsia soon found a professional niche working for a succession of law firms specializing in US immigration cases. After four decades of highly restrictive race-based legislation that had made it all but impossible for Asians to settle lawfully in the US, the Immigration Act of 1965 raised the numerical ceiling high enough to precipitate a historically significant influx of peoples from allied satellite countries within the US Cold War orbit.

In particular Taiwan, South Korea, and the Philippines were direct beneficiaries of this fundamental reworking of immigration law and legislation. The upper tier of the new Asian immigrants – that is, those able to meet the not negligible expense of specialized legal services – were the client base of firms for which Maria Hsia worked as an "immigration consultant." Nor were Hsia and Hom the only operators providing this service for contemporary Asians hoping to gain permanent entry to the US. As yet there is scant empirical scholarly literature on this topic since most research on immigration in Asian American Studies seems to be mired in fuzzy concepts carried over from the 1980s such as "diaspora," "transnationalism," and "post-colonialism."

Academic myopia notwithstanding, the immigration services racket remains robust: In 2004, a disbarred former attorney named Walter Wenko (age 59) and his non-attorney wife Miao Huang (age 48), who operated Asian Pacific Legal Services, were fined $1.85 million by the California Office of the Attorney General for having bilked at least 350 clients out of fees ranging from $1,000 to $8,000 to obtain work permits, green cards, and expedite the immigration process.[39]

Beginning as an attorney for the Immigration and Naturalization Service, Howard Hom learned the nuances, subtleties, and real-world application of the complex legal apparatus regulating the admission of foreign-born Americans-in-the-making. In 1986, he put his training and experience gained as a privileged insider with the INS to use by forming a fateful business partnership with Hsia. Together, they worked side by side as tireless advocates for the new Chinese immigrant huddled masses. In a scenario that somehow does not quite match the romantic cachet of Bill Clinton's heady first encounter with Hillary Rodham at the Yale Law Library, Hom and Hsia met in the summer of 1979 while enrolled in a Cantonese language class at the University of California, Los Angeles.

By 1980, Hom and Hsia were living together. But alas, their love was not to last. Their personal and business relationship faltered and in 1990 they went their separate ways. Not missing a beat, in 1991 "Hsia and Associates" was born. Apparently, immigration consulting services provided to Taiwanese nationals seeking residence in the US paid quite well. In 1982, Hsia reported an income of $637,000.00. Like any self-employed professional her income varied from year to year, but she earned enough on average to own a home in the ultra-exclusive City of Beverly Hills. Completing the picture of immigrant success, Hsia drove a Rolls Royce around town.

Formal diplomatic recognition of Taiwan by the US ended on January 1, 1979 in favor of a potentially far more advantageous economic relationship with the People's Republic of China. This marked a pivotal moment in the reconstitution of the larger Asian American population. The PRC did not recognize the sovereignty of the contested island across the Strait, which had become the refuge of the US-supported Kuomintang (國民黨), or Nationalist Party, as the Chinese Civil War (國共內戰) took its course and the Communist Party emerged victorious in 1950.

With the formal end of the Cold War commitment by the US large numbers of Taiwanese looked to America as a safe harbor in a turbulent sea of political and economic uncertainty.[40] By the 1990s, the larger Asian American community had built a substantial economic infrastructure and professional presence in the science and high-technology sectors that more recent immigrants could build upon. Having stopped the equality revolution of the 1960s-70s in its tracks through a process of attrition that ranged from co-optation to assassination, social engineers within academia positioned the "new" Asian Americans as the ideal postindustrial producers for an economy driven by science and technology as opposed to high-wage/benefit unionized manufacturing.

Simultaneously the military "defense" sector was expanded to satisfy the well-positioned corporate constituency that received government contracts while returning a hefty portion of public tax money to elected officials in the form of campaign "contributions." The intensification of the military-corporate economy created the demand for highly educated intellectual coolie labor drawn from East Asian client states of the US.

Recognizing and acting upon the epochal opportunity this diplomatic about-face represented, it fell to entrepreneurs such as Hsia to facilitate the movement of well-educated, high-income individuals from Taiwan to the US. In 1989, for example, Hsia and an associate identified as Tina Bow each contributed $1,000 to the Republican primary campaign of Sen. Mitch McConnell (R-Kentucky). Hsia was quoted in the *National Journal* (1990) as crediting McConnell for playing a "key role" in arranging meetings between Pacific Leadership Council members with Bush administration officials while crucial provisions of what was to become the Immigration Act of 1990 were being considered.[41]

Through the PLC, Hsia lobbied hard for measures that would limit INS deportations and pushed for a new provision that gave preferential consideration to "investor immigrants." These wealthy investors, so the argument went, supposedly would create new jobs while infusing the US economy with another source of overseas capital. Viewed from another angle, the transfer of wealth would benefit the US, while costing little beyond administrative expenses associated with the processing of applications, since investor immigrants were not likely to become indigent and enter the welfare rolls.

Tina Bow relates her "rags to riches" story on the website she maintains with an El Salvadoran immigrant and former drug dealer named Mario Rivera. In 2000, the duo co-founded a non-profit foundation known as Simply Help. Based in Rosemead, a largely working-class city in the San Gabriel Valley area of Los Angeles County that over the past three decades has become a favorite place of settlement for recent Asian and Latino immigrants, their organization provides direct assistance to "3rd-world and developing countries" such as China, Cambodia, Nicaragua, Guatemala, El Salvador, and other Latin American countries in the form of training schools and supplies.[42]

Born in Taiwan to a military family, Bow claims to have risen from humble origins. After working as a flight attendant for China Airlines for four years, Bow had the good fortune of marrying into a wealthy family that operates a major manufacturing concern in Taiwan. After immigrating to the US, for ten years Bow worked in the high-end real estate business in Beverly Hills. She became involved in local politics only to see her friends brought low by what she describes as the "Chinese Donation Scandal."

Chastened by her foray into the American political system, Bow turned her energies away from the pursuit of "material success" to "spiritual cultivation." After meeting Rivera at one of her properties where he had been hired to perform maintenance work, despite his lack of demonstrable skills, Bow determined that he would be better suited to render humanitarian aid and assistance unto the poor. Thus began their partnership.

During the course of daily business conducted at such operations as Hsia and Associates, the cultural, political, and economic composition of the Asian American population was being refigured radically as the larger society and its basic institutions were being altered by their large-scale entry into the universities, the professions, and the lower managerial rungs of the corporate world. In forming the Pacific Leadership Council in Los Angeles, Huang, Hsia, and other recent immigrants appropriated the concept of "'Asian America" to advance the corporate agenda of its foreign benefactor, the Lippo Group, while at the same time making inroads into the primary institutions in the US.

Her hobnobbing with high-profile politicos helped create the perception among clients and prospective customers that Hsia was a power-player and a force to be reckoned with locally, nationally, and globally. For a brief moment, Hsia and her cronies enjoyed paid access to the highest reaches of government under the guise of "Asian American political empowerment." They learned the hard way that mere proximity to the White power establishment is not the same as being *of* it. For the courtesy shown the supplicant can be withdrawn in a trice by the reigning monarch and his courtiers.

Corruption Asian American Style

Resident PBS moralist Bill Moyers served as correspondent for a *Frontline* episode aired in 1998, titled "Washington's Other Scandal."[43] The piece tells of the politically "corrupting" influence of $2.2 billion in soft money donations generated during the 1996 election cycle. He explains how the search for funds to pay for premium-priced television "issue ads" and related campaign expenses led both major political parties down a ruinous path away from democratic governance. Moyers restates the obvious by piously noting that paid sleepovers in the Lincoln Bedroom, pricey coffee klatches with well-heeled contributors, face-time sold by candidates to wealthy petitioners, and private closed-door sessions between corporate contributors and Congressional leaders at five-star resort hotels are emblematic of thoroughgoing rot within the system.

In a supplemental interview with Sen. Joseph I. Lieberman (D-Connecticut), carried on the *Frontline* website, Moyers observes that campaign finance practices that benefit only corporations and wealthy donors have resulted in a "kind of coup d'état of the democratic process."[44] The senator finds the analogy interestingly apt and does not refute it, perhaps because Lieberman also has received his share of corporate campaign blandishments.[45]

The name "John Huang" comes up more than once in the *Frontline* report. According to notes kept by Harold Ickes, Deputy Chief of Staff (1994-97), he and Huang met at the White House on October 2, 1995 to follow up on the President's insistence that their top earner be given a job with the DNC and granted a title commensurate with the cash clout he wielded. The following month, on November 13, two of Clinton's lieutenants interviewed Huang for a job in fundraising. Donald L. Fowler, DNC Chair (1995-97), approved the title specially created for his new hire: "Vice Chairman for Finance." So began, with official sanction from the DNC, the concatenation of events that later came to be known through the press as "Chinagate." Shifting the focus to an assemblage of disreputable Asian Americans on the make had the effect of perpetuating the false notion that "outside" forces are the corruptors of government and the legislative process rather than structural corruption itself being the prime mover within the universe of criminality.

Ordinary Asian Americans who believe as a matter of naïve faith in electoral politics were tainted by the campaign finance scandal fall-out. Aaron Brown, sitting in for Ted Koppel on the June 28, 1999 edition of *Nightline,* introduced a feature by John Donvan who reported on the ill effects suffered by Chinese Americans who once more were placed under collective suspicion by government spy agencies. One of the casualties, former US Marine Hoyt Zia, left his job of five years in Washington, DC over the cloud of suspicion that descended upon him. "Do you think that if you were white you would still have a job in Washington, you'd be staying and none of this would have happened to you?" Donvan asks. "Oh, absolutely," Zia replies. "If I were white or maybe just non-Asian there wouldn't have been the connections that these conspiracy theorists drew connecting me with China."[46]

As Zia is shown packing his household belongings for a new job in Hawaii images are evoked of Japanese Americans awaiting their removal to civilian concentration camps along with their worldly possessions. While this heart-rending tale won the gratitude of certain Asian American interest groups, Donvan did not capture the full scope of intrigue behind the forlorn departure of Zia and family into Hawaiian exile.

Huang and his crew represent a new breed of Asian Americans who have little in common with earlier generations of immigrants to the US other than a very loosely shared ethnic identity forged over 150 years of colonialism, racial oppression, labor exploitation, exclusionism, deportation, and even mass incarceration. Historically, each Asian immigrant group brought with them to the US native criminal traditions and adapted them to American conditions. Although they were continually being policed and harassed by the larger dominant society and its law enforcement and legal institutions, the traditional Asian American criminal organizations functioned for the most part within the province of their respective ethnic communities.

By co-opting the "Asian American" designation as its operational umbrella, this particular post-1965 cohort has given a perverse twist to the radically new concept of "pan-ethnicity," which was conceived originally as a collective socio-cultural identity, meant to stand as a political bloc *against* hegemonic White power rather than *supporting* it as is the case today.[47] At its inception, the concept of "Asian America" meant opposition to the institutions that maintained White racial supremacy and a challenge to the dominant culture and repertoire of social behavior meant to sustain it. As a demographic category it currently lacks the oppositional force it once held for significant numbers of Asian Americans and their political allies.

Soy Milk of Politics

In contrast to the established Chinese American community, the post-1965 immigrant cohort represented by Huang, Chung, Trie, and many others might be harbingers of a time when Asian Americans will be in a position to corrupt the political process just as the White bourgeoisie have done in the pursuit of greater wealth and expansion of social privilege, to be shared with similarly placed individuals and transferred among family members, to widen the network of power for each subsequent generation.

Perhaps more realistically, White elite power will continue to court international capital delivered by the local Asian American comprador class, cream exceptional intellectual talent from its educated ranks, forge family power-links via the adoption of Asian babies and intermarriage, and perhaps share token resources with an elite segment of the collaborating group. This will serve to strengthen White oligarchic power while conjuring the illusion of equality, access, and ethnic diversity in US liberal pluralist society.

If it were only a matter of dealing with the ingrained problem of multi-ethnic influence peddling within a widely acknowledged and cynically accepted plutocratic system of governance, the arrival on the national scene of Asian American political hustlers would be of only slightly more consequence than the recent Asianization of Major League Baseball team rosters and the break-through of Wang Zhizhi followed by Yao Ming into the National Basketball Association. But as can be seen in the case of the attempt by the Thai conglomerate CP to create a favorable investment climate for itself in China by injecting large sums of money into the US political system via Asian American operatives such as John Huang and his ilk, the consequences could quite literally spell death for millions whose health and welfare have been compromised by fabulously lucrative deals consummated in private.

This is an unacceptable and dangerous perversion of governance in a constitutional republic. As such, political insiders of this devious sort must be taken to task rather than reflexively defended by the Asian American ethnic press as simply targets of racist accusations or scapegoating. The conservative *AsianWeek* based in San Francisco has been one of the better examples of this self-protective mechanism in action while online, *Goldsea* beats the drum of triumphal Asian Americanism. Moreover, spokespersons from the academic world, elected officials, and self-appointed "community" advocates are quick to defend or rationalize white collar criminal practices committed by Asian American individuals. Thankfully, no longer does a defensive consensual silence necessarily greet specific instances of wrongdoing by Asian Americans as in times past. But neither is much attention paid to structural corruption and the expanded role that Asian Americans are now playing in its perpetuation.

While the press and certain journals of opinion such as the *National Review* (which ran a March 24, 1997 issue with caricatures of the Clintons and Gore as "Chinamen") made much of the oddly dressed exotics who worship at the altar of strange gods, those implicated in the Clinton-era campaign finance transactions were Americans like any other save for their ethnicity, relative wealth, and tangible advantages of their social class. And like any other Americans with the wherewithal, "these people" want to draw upon their considerable financial power and make it work for them in the political arena. This new expectant bourgeois stratum within the larger Asian American population seeks to influence key policies and participate in decisions that have an immediate and long-term impact upon their goal of expanding private wealth on a level that only can be achieved by standing at the levers of the political economic machinery. The major difference is that, unlike others of wealth, power, and influence in the US, these would-be players happen to be Asian American, not White. There is nothing novel about their brand of political clientelism save for their Asian racial identity in a society that remains implacably under the control of White oligarchic rule despite the growing presence of select Asian Americans in positions of high visibility.

The coming years will see increasing numbers of Asians relocating to the US as a refuge from political instability caused by worsening economic crises orchestrated by globalist institutions such as the World Bank and the International Monetary Fund. The Thompson Committee, for example, in investigating the involvement of the Riady family with high-level American politicians and officials, suggested that as ethnic Chinese they were vulnerable to native Indonesian resentment against a minority group that controlled most of the national economy.

While numbering only six million within a total population of 200 million in Indonesia, eighty percent of all businesses are owned by Chinese Indonesians. A month-long series of attacks against ethnic Chinese commencing in 1965 as Sukarno was swept from power was particularly vicious, resulting in thousands of deaths and injuries. Faced with discriminatory laws imposed by the government and threatened by periodic riots targeting the Chinese minority such as those that broke out in May of 1998, there is strong incentive for those of means to seek safe harbor in the US.

As the US economy continues its downward slide in these early years of the new century, more Asian Americans such as Elaine Chao will be tapped by the supranational power-plutocracy to front for its globalist designs. Now that the much-touted shift to the political economic bloc represented by East and South Asia has been realized, nineteenth century characterizations of Asian Americans as a deracinated alien presence within the republic will be tempered by the strategic planting of hand-picked professionals in positions of authority whose primary function is that of managing pacification at home or perhaps negotiating deals overseas within their countries of origin. This will be achieved through the clever appropriation of "race," "ethnicity," and "gender" by the very establishment that resisted (and in certain instances attempted to subvert) the civil rights agenda of the past half-century.

In response to the reality of the token transracial adoption of Asian Americans into the power nexus, a renewed analytical emphasis on the advantages of social class will be needed to peel away the mask of presumed disadvantage claimed by the new comprador stratum and expose the raw power-politics of the system they so loyally serve.

Endnotes

1) Susan McDougal with Pat Harris, *The Woman Who Wouldn't Talk: Why I Refused to Testify Against the Clintons & What I Learned in Jail* (New York: Basic Books, 2004), 95.

2) David Brock, "His Cheatin' Heart." *American Spectator* Jan. 1994. Http://spectator.org/archives/2004/06/23/his-cheatin-heart.

3) David Brock, *Blinded By the Right: The Conscience of an Ex-Conservative* (New York: Three Rivers Press, 2003).

4) Jacob Laksin, "David Brock: Media Liar." *FrontPageMagazine.com* 21 Sep. 2005. Http://www.frontpagemag.com/readArticle.aspx?ARTID=7186. *FrontPageMagazine. com* is edited by former leftist now conservative commentator David Horowitz.

5) *Frontline: Once Upon A Time in Arkansas* Oct. 7, 1997. Written by Michael Kirk and Peter J. Boyer. Http://www.pbs.org/wgbh/pages/frontline/shows/arkansas/etc/tapes.html.

6) "Interview: Viet Dinh," *Frontline: Once Upon A Time in Arkansas* 07 Oct. 1997. Http://www.pbs.org/wgbh/pages/frontline/shows/arkansas/interviews/vietdinh.html.

7) Jeffrey Toobin, *A Vast Conspiracy: The Real Story of the Sex Scandal That Nearly Brought Down a President* (New York: Touchstone, 2000), 109.

8) Richard L. Berke, "Call-Girl Story Costs President A Key Strategist." *New York Times* 30 Aug. 1996. http://query.nytimes.com/gst/fullpage.html?res=9A02EED-91638F933A0575BC0A960958260.

9) Howard Kurtz, "The Hooker, Line and Sinker." *The Washington Post* 04 Sep. 1996. Http://www.washingtonpost.com/wp-srv/local/longterm/tours/scandal/morris.htm.

10) An entire chapter is devoted to "The Scandal Industry's Secret Sugar Daddies" such as multi-millionaire Richard Mellon Scaife in Joe Conason and Gene Lyons, *The Hunting of the President: The Ten-Year Campaign to Destroy Bill and Hillary Clinton* (New York: St. Martin's Griffin, 2000).

11) Michael Joseph Gross, "A Vast Right-Wing Hypocrisy." *Vanity Fair* (February 2008), 107.

12) Jeremy Scahill & Garrett Ordower, "From Whitewater to Blackwater." *The Nation* 26 Oct. 2006. Http://www.thenation.com/doc/20061113/whitewater_to_blackwater.

13) Committee on Government Reform, US House of Representatives, "Unsubstantiated Allegations of Wrongdoing Involving the Clinton Administration." Minority Staff Report, March 2001.

14) Hillary Rodham Clinton, *Living History* (New York: Simon & Schuster, 2003).

15) Since major publishers and media entities are adjuncts of the larger system of domination and control, self-produced and independent sources are indispensible in researching the underside of individuals and institutions that are protected by silence, spin, and intimidation. Examples include the trilogy by renegade investigative journalist Victor Thorn, *Hillary (and Bill): The Sex Volume* (Washington, DC: American Free Press, 2008); *Hillary (and Bill): The Drugs Volume* (Washington, DC: American Free Press, 2008); *Hillary (and Bill): The Murder Volume* (Washington, DC: American Free Press, 2008). See also Patrick Matrisciana, ed. *The Clinton Chronicles Book* (Hemet, California: Jeremiah Books, 1994). There is a companion VHS tape (*The Clinton Chronicles*) based on the book.

16) Roger Morris, *Partners in Power: The Clintons and Their America* (New York: Henry Holt and Company, 1996), 416.

17) Daniel Hopsicker, *Barry & 'The Boys': The CIA, The Mob and America's Secret History* (Eugene, Oregon: Mad Cow Press, 2001), 272.

18) Bill Clinton, *My Life* (New York: Vintage Books, 2005), 731.

19) *AllPolitics*, "Huang, Riady Gave to '93 Clinton Inauguration." CNN.com, 11 Nov. 1996. Http//www.cnn.com/ALLPOLITICS/1997/9611/26/huang.donor/index.html. It should be noted that donations to the inaugural festivities are not subject to the same legal restrictions as campaign contributions.

20) Christopher Andersen, *American Evita: Hillary Clinton's Path to Power* (New York: Avon Books, 2005), 160.

21) Roberto Suro, "Not Chinese Agent, Chung Says." *Washington Post*, 12 May 1999, A2. Http://www.washingtonpost.com/wp-srv/politics/special/campfin/stories/chung051299.htm.

22) Roberto Suro, "Chung Makes Deal With Prosecutors. *Washington Post* 06 Mar. 1998, A01. Http://www.washingtonpost.com/wp-srv/politics/special/campfin/stories/cf030698.htm.

23) Barbara Olson. *Hell To Pay: The Unfolding Story of Hillary Rodham Clinton* (Washington, DC: Regnery, 2001), 290.

24) "Campaign Finance Key Player: Pauline Kanchanalak." *Washington Post* 20 Jul. 1998. Http://www.washingtonpost.com/wp-rv/politics/special/campfin/players/kanchanalak.htm.

25) Lena H. Sun and John Pomfret, "The Curious Cast of Asian Donors." *Washington-post.com* 27 Jan. 1997, p. A01. Http://www.washingtonpost.com/wp-srv/politics/special/campfin/stories/donors.htm.

26) Committee on Governmental Affairs, "Investigation of Illegal or Improper Activities in Connection With 1996 Federal Election Campaigns." Senate Report 105-167, Vol. 5, 105th Congress 2nd Session, 10 Mar. 1998, 7248.

27) Keith Hammond and Laurel Druley, "Returned to Spender." *Mother Jones*, 17 Apr. 1997. Http://www.motherjones.com/news/special_reports/coinop_congress/97mojo_400/returned.html.

28) Robert Horn, "Charoen Pokphand Group." *Time*, 19 Apr. 2004. Http://www.seas.upenn.edu/ ~aneeshk/miniWeb/time/globalbusiness/article/0,9171,1101040419-610053,00.html.

29) Mike Davis, *The Monster At Our Door: The Global Threat of Avian Flu* (New York: The New Press, 2005), 106.

30) "Asia's 25 Most Powerful." *Fortune*, 17 Oct. 2005. Http://www.fortune.com/fortune/asiapower/snapshot/0,25171,16,00.html.

31) Chief among skeptics is Christopher Hitchens as found in his exposé *The Missionary Position: Mother Teresa in Theory and Practice* (New York: Verso, 1997). Ironically, he was later called upon by the Vatican as a witness in the beatification of Mother Teresa, who is being fast-tracked for eventual sainthood.

32) Rupa Kurian, "Sentencing Date for Yogesh Gandhi Set" *Rediff On The Net*, 01 Jul. 1999. Http://www.rediff.com/news/1999/jul/01us3.htm.

33) "Guru Lured Members By Chasing Celebrities." *Yomiuri Shimbun*, 03 Dec. 1999. Http://www.rickross.com/reference/ho_no_hana/ho_no_hana6.html.

34) "Honohana foot-cult guru gets 12 years for fraud." *The Japan Times*, 16 Jul. 2005. Http://search.japantimes.co.jp/print/news/nn07-2005/nn20050716a3.htm.

35) R. S. Shankar, "Yogesh Gandhi to Serve 1 Year in Prison." *Rediff On The Net*, 28 Dec. 1999. Http://www.rediff.com/news/1999/dec/28us.htm.

36) "James Riady Pleads Guilty; Will Pay Largest Fine in Campaign Finance History for Violating Federal Election Law." US Department of Justice, 11 Jan. 01. Http://www.usdoj.gov/opa/pr/2001/January/017crm.htm.

37) Roberto Suro, "Campaign Fund Probe Winds Down." *The Washington Post*, 30 May 99, A5. Http://www.washingtonpost.com/wp-srv/politics/special/campfin/stories/finance053099.htm.

38) Michelle Malkin, "Maria Hsia's revenge." *townhall.com*, 13 Feb. 02. Http://www.townhall.com/columnists/michellemalkin/pritnmn20020213.shtml.

39) David Pierson, "Couple Fined $1.85 Million for Legal Fraud," *Los Angeles Times* 01 Mar. 04, B3.

40) The US maintains informal diplomatic relations and extends military aid via the Taiwan Relations Act passed by the US Congress in 1979. The American Institute in Taiwan although supposedly private is the institutional conduit for the US Department of State. Similarly, the Taiwan Economic and Cultural Representative Office (TECRO) is headquartered in Washington, DC and maintains a presence in other US cities.

41) Bill Straub, "Woman in fund scandal aided McConnell campaign." *Cincinnati Post*, 14 Mar. 1998. Http://www.cincypost.com/news/1998/mccon031498.html.

42) The organization maintains a website both in English and Mandarin. Http://www.simplyhelp.org/en/index.html.

43) *Frontline*, "Washington's Other Scandal" 06 Oct. 1998. Produced by Sherry Jones. Written by Bill Moyers, Sherry Jones, and Elizabeth Sams. Directed by Foster Wiley. Frontline coproduction with Washington Media Associates.

44) *Frontline*, "Washington's Other Scandal" 06 Oct. 1998. Interviews: Sen. Joseph Lieberman. Http://www.pbs.org/wgbh/pages/frontline/shows/scandal/interviews/lieberman.html.

45) Sen. Lieberman is also tied to Big Pharma not only though his position in Congress but by benefit of his wife who was hired in 2005 by the lobbyist firm of Hill & Knowlton as a "senior counselor" in its "health care and pharmaceuticals practice."

Joe Conason, "In Bed With Big Pharma." *Salon.com* 01 Sep. 2006. Http://www.salon.com/opinion/conason/2006/09/01/hadassah_lieberman/.

46) "The Asian American Issue," *Nightline* 28 Jun. 1999. ABC News. Transcript available at Http://www.geocities.com/jetdogy5/AaronBrownCNN011.html.

47) See Yen Le Espirtu, *Asian American Pan-Ethnicity: Bridging Institutions and Identities* (Philadelphia: Temple University Press, 1992).

Judge Paul Linebarger his son Paul Myron Anthony Linebarger, (better known known as Science Fiction. writer Cordwainer Smith), who tapped Joe Kiyonaga for CIA.

CHAPTER SEVEN

ENEMIES FOREIGN AND DOMESTIC: THE GOOD SHEPHERD AND RENEGOTIATION OF RACIAL IDENTITY IN THE NATIONAL SECURITY STATE

Ethno-Political Narrative

On the PBS interview program *Charlie Rose*, (18 Dec. 2006) a full hour was dedicated to a discussion that included actors Robert De Niro, Matt Damon, and Angelina Jolie. The occasion was the debut of *The Good Shepherd* (2006), a film that went beyond previous examples of intrigue, derring-do, secrecy, and heroism characteristic of the "spy" genre. De Niro explained that he had envisioned making a film about the genesis of the CIA and its role in the shaping of the postwar international political landscape.[1] Written by Eric Roth (*Forrest Gump* [1994]; *The Curious Case of Benjamin Button* [2008]), *The Good Shepherd* is devoid of the conventional heroism and existential angst typically ascribed to the Cold Warrior of the Anglo-American alliance as seen in such classics as *The Spy Who Came In From the Cold* (1965) or the more recent cinema adaptation and remake of the Graham Greene novel, *The Quiet American* (2002).[2]

The film has elements that expose the lineaments of the national security state in its formative moment during the World War II period and into the Cold War. In subsequent decades, the CIA came to stand as the sign-symbol for scores institutions, Military (e.g. Defense Intelligence Agency; Office of Naval Intelligence), corporate (e.g. Lockheed-Martin), government (e.g. National Security Agency; Department of Homeland Security), private mercenary (e.g. Xe [formerly Blackwater]), and civilian spy organizations (e.g. CACI International). This combination of entities has been busily transforming the American republic into a corporatist totalitarian state operating on behalf of private banking families.[3] It is no accident that more than a few founding leaders of the CIA were attorneys with Wall Street firms such as Sullivan & Cromwell.[4]

The scholarly, anecdotal, fictionalized, and crackpot literature concerning Central Intelligence Agency and allied institutions would fill a respectably large private library. Countless documentaries produced for the *History Channel*, cable television programs (*Conspiracy Theory with Jesse Ventura*), and podcasts (*Alex Jones Show*; *For The Record*) devote a good deal of programming to the dark arts as practiced by the CIA within the larger national security state. Even videogames – which generate enormous profits and compete for the film entertainment dollar – such as Tom Clancy's *Splinter Cell* draw from this history. Finally, innumerable websites, such as Alex Constantine's *Anti-Fascist Encyclopedia* and *Global Research*, devoted to political intrigue both historical and contemporary have proliferated along with the growth of the internet.

Constitutive of the narrative line of *The Good Shepherd* is an underlying racial and ethnic tension and conflict that has its historical basis in the renegotiation of White social identity between the dominant Anglo-Protestant elite and groups on the ascent – Jews, Irish Catholics, and Italian Americans (commonly referred to as "White ethnics") – that began with the mass mobilization of the civilian population required to wage war against the Axis nations during World War II. The principal argument of the present chapter is that the growth of the US national security state born in the midst of wartime mobilization and concentration and convergence of power among civilian government, the military, and corporate entities provided a point of entry for those groups once denied full access to social privileges and political-economic access controlled by the "White" Protestant elite.

Due to the geographic expansiveness, racial variety, and cultural heterogeneity of the postwar international order led by the US, White ethnics were admitted selectively to key institutions within the larger political economic system to help administer the workings of the "American Century" and thereby generate more wealth and power for the hereditary Anglo-American elite families. *The Good Shepherd* dramatizes that historical moment when Jewish Americans, Irish Americans, and Italian Americans were on the threshold of being incorporated into the dominant White society with the benefits and advantages that accrue to such negotiated status.

By analyzing *The Good Shepherd* as an "ethno-political narrative" the historical process by which a demonstrably more advantageous social identity is constructed in the popular culture can be better understood. On a practical level, by laying bare the historical reworking of "White" racial/ethnic identity we are better prepared for the manipulative and cynical uses of "race" in the exercise of political-economic power. The case in point (discussed below) is the rise, recruitment, and installation of suspected Anglo-American intelligence asset Barry Soetoro or "Barack Hussein Obama."

Equally important, this move to the inclusion and incorporation of the newly constituted White social group was achieved by their being counterpoised against a common non-White enemy. The Japanese served this purpose during World War II as later did the "Red" Chinese for the Cold War. By subjecting *The Good Shepherd* to historical or "extrinsic" analysis that foregrounds racial formation and ethnicity in postwar American society, the contemporary function of this film as both a mobilizing and unifying propaganda tool (albeit subtle) in the "asymmetrical" undeclared wars of the present can be more easily understood.

The Good Shepherd has been critiqued by the CIA itself and, apart from predictable quibbles, given the thumbs up.[5] Moreover, De Niro expressed interest in doing two sequels to the original despite unremarkable box office returns for a $90 million movie. Its primary relevance today, however, lies in CIA-guided films like *The Good Shepherd* that help massage the ambient ideological climate via "public media" to help maintain and advance the Anglo-American globalist agenda that requires an increasingly "diverse" cast of characters as "Great Game" players on far-flung playing fields riven by ethnic, religious, and national antagonisms.

Ethnic Types

Early on, the OSS availed itself of a most unusual spy in Moe Berg – professional baseball player and graduate of Princeton – who was convinced that his "dark, saturnine complexion" allowed him to "fit in" almost anywhere overseas he was sent. It is nonetheless clear that his master controllers were exclusively of the Anglo-Protestant elite social class.[6] Later, during the early phase of the Cold War, a Japanese American veteran of World War II named Joe Yoshio Kiyonaga was recruited by the CIA out of the School of Advanced International Studies (SAIS) at Johns Hopkins by legendary "guru of psychological warfare" Paul Linebarger and posted to Japan and later Latin America.[7]

Born and raised in Hawaii, Kiyonaga had been a volunteer with the storied 442nd Regimental Combat Team composed of Japanese American volunteers and fought in the Italian Campaign during World War II. Kiyonaga would become among the first in a cohort of CIA field personnel whose race and ethnicity could be exploited as an asset to assist in the maintenance of a majority non-Anglo-American population in an array of nations that viewed the end of World War II as an opportunity to realize political economic independence from the imperial world system. The Anglo-Saxon elite drawn from banking families and educated at the Illuminist colleges they founded and controlled exploited non-White status-anxious personnel like Kiyonaga that could provide protective coloration for the high-level shot callers that represented Wall Street and The City of London.

In the 1960s White "ethnic" types such as Greek American Gust Avrakotos (focal point of *Charlie Wilson's War*; book version) would be brought in for Mediterranean and Central Asian operations, but his resentment of the "blue blood" Ivy League types like Archie Roosevelt runs consistently as a theme throughout his career. As he put it crudely, the "only reason half of them got anywhere is because they jerked off Henry Cabot Lodge's grandson at some prep school."[8] But like his non-Anglo predecessors the career of Avrakotos was delimited by his Greek ethnicity and working class origins. Both Avrakotos and Kiyonaga struggled in vain to break the blue-blood barrier that was not breached until George Tenet of Albanian Greek parentage served as Director of Central Intelligence (DCI) from 1997 to 2004. It appears, however, that even Tenet was used and burned by high-level strategists to help lend official cover for the attacks of 9/11 and subsequent invasion of Iraq in the Anglo-American "war on terror."

Kiyonaga had enjoyed life in postwar Japan living in the exclusive Meguro district of Tokyo, where he lived in the former residence of Gen. Charles Willoughby. He entertained any number of individuals within the Japanese political establishment and enjoyed rounds of golf with many of them. As a "political action" and propaganda specialist, he succeeded in collecting a number of "agents" for the CIA including high-ranking members of the Communist Party. At age forty, however, he was passed over for promotion and his career had stalled by the late 1950s once he returned to CIA headquarters as a desk jockey. When he made it known to superiors that he was married to a White woman and not a "meek little Japanese wife" his career began to take off again with a posting to Brazil.[9] It helped that Brazil had a large and economically formidable Japanese-Brazilian population. Kiyonaga, however, never made it to retirement. He was dead of stomach cancer at age fifty-nine.

Praetorians of Color

Finally, the present analytical exercise is meant to lay the groundwork for deeper, less abstract, historically-grounded approaches to the study of cinema and its close relationship to geo-strategic wars of American imperium that attended the birth of the moving picture itself beginning with the filming of the US conquest of The Philippines.[10] The chapter concludes with vexing questions (typically dismissed by hirelings of corporatist media as "conspiracy theory") concerning the recent incorporation of select non-White political actors into the national security system itself. This is seen in the strange case of alleged intelligence asset Barry Soetoro/Barack Hussein Obama and his ascension to the office of the US presidency.[11]

One of the more immediate implications of admitting select women and racial minorities to the higher reaches of the national security state is that scholarly inquiry will be forced to radically rethink the seemingly progressive catechism of thought concerning "race," "ethnicity," and "gender" that predominates in film studies. Early in 2011, for example, the three major "cheerleaders" for balls-out military attack on Libya were of the female gender: Secretary of State Hillary R. Clinton, National Security Advisor Samantha Power, and US ambassador to the United Nations Susan E. Rice (who also identifies racially as "Black").

In ways that have not yet been recognized in film scholarship, the liberal socio-dramas of Stanley Kramer in the 1960s to the mainstreaming of certain aspects of African American life by Spike Lee during the 1990s has helped set the stage for a Barry Soetoro/Barack Hussein Obama. Not only was his candidacy marketed as a corrective to the widely reviled Bush administration, in a larger historical sense an "Obama" victory would serve as a final collective expiation of liberal guilt over African American slavery and all related expressions of such abjection. Despite his being hailed as the first "Black" US president, he in truth is one-half "White," with an Asian (Indonesian) step-father who adopted him, and was socialized primarily among Asian Pacific – not African American – peoples.[12]

If film is indeed an effective means of mass predictive programming, then the series of national security-themed films that have positioned African Americans in lead roles – including a remake of *The Manchurian Candidate* [2004] substituting Denzel Washington for Frank Sinatra as Bennett Marco – ranging from Will Smith (*Men in Black* [1997]) to Morgan Freeman as CIA director in *The Sum of All Fears* (2002) are early warning signs of what might be called "multi-cultural corporatism." A preview – although admittedly a cheesy one – of the pending globalist political-economic agenda is seen in *The Art of War* (2000) with Wesley Snipes as an agent with a United Nations covert-action unit aligned against intrigue by the twenty-first century threat posed by China.

Power of Ethnicity

In 1940, as America appears headed for war, an outdoor social gathering on the forty-acre Deer Island private retreat maintained for the secret society known popularly as Skull & Bones is depicted in *The Good Shepherd*. Directed by Robert De Niro, the film ambitiously dramatizes the formation of the Office of Strategic Services (OSS) and the doings of its postwar incarnation as the Central Intelligence Agency (CIA). All manner of covert operations including political assassination, murder, sabotage, guerilla warfare, money laundering, and the more routine aspects of espionage provide the historical backdrop for the lives of its principal characters. As the narrative gets underway, De Niro himself does a cameo turn as "Gen. Bill Sullivan." The character is modeled after legendary OSS founder Maj. Gen. William J. Donovan, who earned the nickname "Wild Bill" from the men under his command.[13]

Decorated veteran of The Great War, successful attorney but failed gubernatorial candidate (1932) against Herbert H. Lehman, Donovan had been a law school classmate of Franklin D. Roosevelt at Columbia University, a bastion of hereditary privilege enjoyed by the Anglo-American Protestant elite since the colonial period when it was chartered by the British crown as King's College. Donovan graduated in 1907 and established himself at a prominent Buffalo, New York law firm before volunteering for military service during World War I and distinguishing himself on the battlefields of France. He then entered a life of public service and international intrigue on a scale that helped to lay the foundation for what CIA alumnus George H.W. Bush (Yale Skull & Bones 1948) proclaimed on September 11, 1990 before a joint session of the US Congress as the "New World Order."

Among his exploits prior to the formation of the OSS was providing financial support to a Catholic intelligence agency known as Pro Deo headed by Father Felix Morlion. Donovan helped relocate the priest in New York after the cleric and his spy organization were placed in jeopardy by German military victories in Western Europe during World War II. This provided Donovan excellent access to the "secret affairs of the Vatican" which maintained its sovereign neutrality for the duration of the war.[14] One of the practical benefits of cooperation between the Vatican and US intelligence operations was the acquisition of "strategic" bombing targets in Japan provided by Church contacts that led to massive civilian casualties.

Thus was completed the centuries-long mission of the Jesuits – held in distrust upon their initial incursions into Japan during the sixteenth century – of transubstantiating body, mind, and spirit into earthly profits. In recognition for his service to the Vatican, Donovan was awarded the most prestigious of Papal knighthoods: the Grand Cross of the Order of Saint Sylvester. It was bestowed by Pope Pius XII whose support of the Third Reich social and political agenda has been documented by mainstream contemporary scholarship.[15]

Earnest acolyte Edward Wilson (Matt Damon) is invited to a private audience with Gen. Sullivan (De Niro) in his cabin during the Deer Island festivities.[16] Echoing the transformative scene when Wilson was "tapped" as one of only fifteen students admitted each year into The Brotherhood of Death (Skull and Bones) at Yale University, the Battle-Hardened Veteran offers the Callow Young Man a rare opportunity to serve his nation by joining other similarly illumined individuals in a no-holds-barred contest against the hostile world-historical forces that threaten American corporate interests. In conveying the seriousness of his undertaking, Sullivan emphasizes that the grand mission "isn't about a bunch of frat boys playing with each other's pricks" but rather "is for real ... for America."

Outlining his vision for the intelligence organization that he had proposed to President Franklin D. Roosevelt, Sullivan expresses his concern regarding the potential for the abuse of power when held in so few hands. "I see this as America's eyes and ears," he says. "I don't want it to become its heart and soul." Sullivan tells Wilson that he asked the president to institute "civilian oversight" of the new organization lest it violate the spirit and substance of its mandate. "I always seem to err on the side of democracy," says Sullivan without apparent irony. For at its inception, the OSS and what was to be institutionalized as the CIA was intended by its founders to get results without regard to civil liberties, human rights, democracy, and related procedural niceties that stood in the way. It is not coincidental that the name "Edward Wilson" bears similarity to that of Edwin P. Wilson, a onetime CIA operative whose storied career-path cut a clean swath through conventional morality.[17]

Concluding his recruiting pitch to Wilson, Sullivan informs the young prospect that in anticipation of the US formally entering the war, President Roosevelt was seeking to assemble a "foreign intelligence service" composed of men "from the right backgrounds." By this criterion it was meant that fine young men drawn from Northeastern establishment families that dominated American political-economic life would be groomed to manage *sub rosa* the larger society through a network of seemingly legitimate institutions (investment banks, academia, the military, arts and culture organizations, private foundations, research centers, newspapers, publishing houses) in which ordinary citizens unquestioningly place their faith.[18] So prevalent were graduates of Ivy League institutions such as Yale within the OSS that wags would joke that the acronym stood for "Oh So Social." Donovan, described as a "dedicated Anglophile," recruited fully forty-two members from the Yale class of 1943 alone.[19] In its incarnation as the CIA, "the Company" in its early years retained the clubby feel of its socially exclusive membership.[20] Although one of the few Roman Catholics of influence among the almost exclusively Protestant establishment of the period, Sullivan specifies that the "right backgrounds" would include White Christians only. "In other words," says Sullivan, "no Jews or Negroes and very few Catholics and that's only because *I'm* Catholic."

A massive body of critical literature concerning the OSS, CIA, and the all-embracing national security state that has evolved over the past six decades gives the lie to the disclaimer uttered by Sullivan/De Niro: The CIA and the non-representative elite stratum of men who ruled it were never interested in preserving "democracy" either in theory or in practice. Rather, its mission has been to render material support to authoritarian client regimes directly put into power or at least countenanced by the US while destabilizing governments that dared resist American political-economic domination or in any fashion demonstrated independence from the global corporate-imperial system.[21] Countless declassified US government documents, findings of Congressional investigations such as the Church Committee (1975), independent reportage, eyewitness accounts, scholarly tomes, memoirs, and mainstream news coverage have made public the horrifying scope of CIA activity and its boundless creativity in devising strategies of neutralizing its perceived enemies and sacrificing "allies" when necessary.

Torture, paramilitary attacks, blackmail, mind-control experimentation (MK-ULTRA), doping, assassination, bribery, sabotage, drug distribution, forgery, gun-running, industrial espionage, counterfeiting, breaking and entering, poisoning, false-flag terrorism, kidnapping, illegal surveillance, chemical and biological weapons attacks, data mining, business fraud, prostitution, political imprisonment, election rigging, money laundering, bombings, and related criminal acts are an incomplete list of the standard CIA repertoire.[22] Organized crime syndicates, terrorist groups, or even rival spy organization – excepting that of Great Britain – would be hard pressed to match the scope and intensity of CIA machinations since its formation through the National Security Act of 1947.

Ethnicity of Power

The private conversation between spymaster Sullivan/De Niro and his young prospect Wilson/Damon reveals the centrality of racial and ethnic identity in the formation and strategic cultivation of elites in American society. But while the warning voiced by Sullivan accurately portrays the still-tenuous position of Roman Catholics within the dominant Anglo-Protestant society during the immediate prewar years in the US, neither were they as a group utterly vulnerable to the caprice or ill will of their presumed social betters.

Long before the founding of the American republic, however, the Roman Catholic Church had been engaged in centuries of aggressive empire building. It employed strategies ranging from brutal main force to pacification via mass conversion, with a well-schooled clerical hierarchy managing this sophisticated global management system for the benefit of the Vatican and its trusted cardinals.[23] Its carefully calculated shifting political alliances from the Holy Roman Empire under the Habsburg dynasty to contemporary hyper-powers such as the US give testament to the genius of its highly adaptable organizational structure and the guile of the men who run it.

Militarily, the Church has not been without its defenses: At the end of the 11th century during the First Crusade, an armed auxiliary known formally as the Sovereign Military Order of Malta (SMOM) was designated by the Church to advance its religio-economic interests.[24] In addition to Donovan, others within the US intelligence community who were members of this exclusive Catholic military order included Allen W. Dulles, William J. Casey, John A. McCone, George H.W. Bush, James Jesus Angleton, and Vernon A. Walters.

Each of these individuals (including non-Catholics like Dulles and Bush) played significant roles in shaping the dark history of the US. Casey, for example, headed the successful presidential campaign (1980) of Ronald W. Reagan (honorary SMOM) and subsequently was appointed CIA director. From there, Casey was in position to oversee a range of subversive projects while shielding the president from the damning extra-legal specifics of the Iran-Contra scandal that broke in 1986.[25] The Knights of Malta also claimed high-ranking US military officers amongst its membership, including Gen. William C. Westmoreland, Gen. Alexander M. Haig, Jr., and the German-born Maj. Gen. Charles A. Willoughby (Adolf Tscheppe-Weidenbach).[26]

Sullivan's caution regarding his Roman Catholic religious affiliation is reminiscent of the social anxiety expressed by Henry A. Kissinger when as National Security Advisor to President Richard M. Nixon he once worried, according to his biographer, about there being "too many Jews" at a certain closed meeting. His boss, after all, delighted in acts of reflexive humiliation toward subordinates and openly referred to the former professor of government at Harvard as his "Jew boy."[27] Yet for advice and political protection Nixon relied upon any number of Jewish appointees and advisors, such as attorney Leonard Garment, speechwriter and *New York Times* political columnist (since 1973) William Safire (born Safir), and economist Arthur F. Burns (born Burnseig). Even so, he saw himself as the target of liberal Jews in the media establishment, especially those critical of his administration such as the politically influential owner and publisher of the *Washington Post* Katherine Graham, (*née* Meyer).[28]

Although Nixon has often been characterized by observers as "paranoid" and obsessed with the belief that certain forces were out to "get him," the *Washington Post* itself is considered by students of the national security establishment to be one of many media entities under CIA control. Philip L. Graham, husband and predecessor of Katherine Graham as publisher before the onset of mental illness followed by suicide at age forty-eight, had been named as the linchpin of OPERATION MOCKINGBIRD, devised to shape public opinion through strategic media outlets.[29]

Executive editor Ben Bradlee, descendent of the prominent colonial Crowninshield family line and Nixon nemesis, was also known to have worked in propaganda and intelligence during his career. His star reporter Bob Woodward, who along with Carl Bernstein reported on the "Watergate" burglary that eventually brought down President Nixon, served in the Office of Naval Intelligence (ONI) prior to joining the *Washington Post*.

Bedfellas

For Wilson/Damon, his role as a mid-level functionary within the racial and class hierarchy of mid-century American society is decidedly unproblematic as he sails almost dream-like through a world that he feels destined to inherit. "They were the pure line, a natural extension of schoolboy societies, secret oaths and initiations, the body of assumptions common to young men of a certain discernable dash," Don DeLillo writes in *Libra*. His eerily perceptive novel of the John F. Kennedy assassination imaginatively retraces the blazingly mundane conspiratorial vectors that came together at one precise moment in Dealey Plaza.[30]

The lives of those such as Wilson/Damon appear to outsiders like Italian American mobsters to be devoid of passion; bland, opaque, and lacking in outwardly identifiable human qualities. In the heart of the film, with his career as a CIA operative in full swing during the early 1960s, Wilson/Damon has a telling encounter with a rough-edged Mafioso named Joseph Palmi (Joe Pesci). This tough-talking figure is a composite of Santo Trafficante, Jr., Carlos Marcello (born Calogero Minacore), Frank Sturgis (born Frank Angelo Fiorini), Sam Giancana (born Momo Salvatore Giancana), John Roselli (born Filipo Sacco), and other Italian Americans known to have collaborated in different capacities with US intelligence organizations for their mutual benefit. As the two discuss a piece of work that the CIA needs the Mafia to carry out, a sincerely befuddled Palmi/Pesci wonders aloud to Wilson about what he sees as a lack of passion and life-force shared by the Anglo-Saxon people:

"We Italians," says Palmi, "we got our families and we got the church. The Irish have the homeland. The Jews, their tradition. Even the Niggers, they got their music. What about you people, Mr. Wilson? What do you have?"

"The United States of America," Wilson responds evenly, with all the aplomb that attends his privileged social class and ethnicity. "The rest of you are just visiting," he adds flatly, driving home his point.

This calmly delivered rejoinder concludes the furtive meeting between the two shadow warriors. Wilson makes it clear that although they are co-conspirators in black-ops intrigue, it is only expedience that brings their respective worlds together for the joint task of subverting the Castro regime that had come to power in 1959.

The US corporate-banking establishment had a bone to pick with the defiant Cuban leader, who charted an independent course for his nation that had been held in servitude to American corporations and criminal syndicates under the Batista regime. In parallel, the Cuban revolution meant a major loss of revenue for the Mafia, led by the Russian Jewish American mobster Meyer Lansky (born Majer Suchowliński) widely respected for his financial genius.[31] He and his Sicilian American business partners had a score to settle with Castro for being deprived of gambling, prostitution, and offshore banking operations. It made practical sense for the Mafia to combine its specialized skills with those of the CIA even as it was headed by that paragon of the Presbyterian elite, Allen W. Dulles.[32]

But even in a clandestine operation so large as this, Palmi and his *goombata* are regarded as mere instruments – not equals – of the then-dominant Anglo-Protestant majority. Again, DeLillo (son of Italian immigrants) in *Libra* has the CIA operative Larry Parmenter express his disdain for "those roly-poly wops" he has to deal with strictly out of the need to protect overlapping business interests in Cuba.[33]

Larger than life OSS/CIA spook and convicted Watergate burglar E. Howard Hunt held similar social attitudes as DeLillo's Parmenter and his movie-version counterpart Wilson/Damon. "He was a complete self-centered WASP who saw himself as this blue blood from upstate New York," observed his son St. John Hunt. "'I'm better than anybody because I'm white, Protestant and went to Brown, and since I'm in the CIA, I can do anything I want.' Jew nigger, Polack, wop – he used all those racial epithets. He was an elitist. He hated everybody."[34]

Hunt, a consummate professional almost to the end, claimed in his final confession to have been a direct participant in the assassination of President John F. Kennedy. Significantly, he was Chief of Political Action for the CIA and its failed Bay of Pigs invasion and "personally recommended an assassination" of Castro.[35]

The conversation between Palmi and Wilson articulates the inter-group relations of the early 1960s, when White ethnics such as Italian Americans had not quite reached full accord with the dominant WASP majority but nonetheless were poised on the cusp of structural assimilation. Within less than two decades, Geraldine A. Ferraro (D-NY), the daughter of an Italian immigrant, would launch a career in the US House of Representatives and later be named as running mate of presidential candidate Walter F. Mondale (D-Minnesota) in the 1984 national election. Mario M. Cuomo (D-New York) would capture national attention by being elected governor of New York in 1983 and serving for the next decade before George E. Pataki (R-New York), grandson of János Pataki from Mátészalka, Hungary, turned him out of office. Although he reluctantly admitted family connections to organized crime, former New York mayor Rudy Giuliani was confident enough to run for the presidency based on his national visibility in the immediate aftermath of the 9/11 attacks on the World Trade Center.[36]

With Extreme Prejudice

Concluding the roundtable discussion of *The Good Shepherd* with guests De Niro, Matt Damon, and Angelina Jolie, host Charlie Rose asserts that the CIA of the present is "different" from its Ivy League origins. This is to suggest that, in keeping with the larger societal drive for equality since the time of the Great Society, the selective inclusion of individuals from more diverse social backgrounds has somehow transformed the institution itself. Agreeing with Rose, De Niro says that the CIA indeed has become more "open" in the years subsequent to the passing of its founders. Damon observes that as a student at Harvard during the late 1980s he would have been hard-pressed to find any one group of men bound by such narrow ethno-religious, racial or social class origins as those portrayed in *The Good Shepherd*. Implied is the notion that the realities represented in the film have been left in the past and has little relevance to "post-racial" American society.

What Rose and his guests miss, however, is that a more profound reworking of race-power in the US has taken place: In the same way that elite institutions of higher education have had to diversify their student body, faculty and administration by bringing ethnic and racial minorities into the fold, so too have other en-claves of traditional social privilege such as the officer ranks in the military, corporate boards, elective political bodies, and the CIA. This change in strategy by the Anglo-American elite is seen in the curiously rapid rise of the individual known today as Barack Hus-sein Obama.[37] His recruitment from families (Dunham, Obama, Soetoro) with likely connections to US and British intelligence and his elevation to the office of presidency is the culmination of a decades-long historical process set in motion during the postwar civil rights movement, but with the cruelly cynical twist of offer-ing up a "Black" leader under the full control of the corporatist banking establishment.[38]

In the climactic final sequence of *The Good Shepherd*, the fiancé/informant of Wilson's son Edward, Jr. is thrown out of a plane as she is en route to their wedding ceremony. On July 16, 1999 John F. Kennedy, Jr., along with his wife and sister-in-law, perished in waters off Martha's Vineyard. Both his father and un-cle also met early deaths after publicly threatening and thereby betraying the establishment to which they belonged. Decades of forensic evidence, confessions, and analysis undertaken by both government, academic, and independent researchers in countless books, articles, conference proceedings, and documentary films, indicate that the Kennedy brothers were dispatched by an identi-fiable cast of actors (many self-confessed participants) under the control of one or more intelligence agencies that serve as the en-forcement arm of the corporatist banking elite.[39]

Neither is the death of John F. Kennedy, Jr. settled: Indepen-dent filmmaker John Hankey has produced three related docu-mentaries that raise substantive questions concerning both his death and that of his martyred father.[40] The Kennedy scion was about to announce his candidacy for the US Senate from New York; the seat that was won by none other than Hillary Rodham Clinton. According to investigative journalist Wayne Madsen, had the FBI at first approached the plane crash as murder inves-tigation, there were a number of telltale clues, including evidence that a "massive electromagnetic event," crippled the Piper Sarato-ga Kennedy was piloting.[41]

On the morning of April 27, 2011 after spending two million dollars over two years thwarting legal challenges to the question of his eligibility to hold the office of the presidency, Barack Hussein Obama broke into the normal broadcasting schedule to present a document that purports to be definitive proof of his US citizenship.[42] After decades of overthrowing leaders of sovereign nations and replacing them with their own assets, it is not unlikely that Barry Soetoro/Barack Hussein Obama is but the latest in a succession of Wall Street/CIA corporatist surrogates put in office since the time of the short-lived Kennedy administration when the prince of Camelot was slain in full public view.[43]

If analyzed as an ethno-political narrative, as this chapter has articulated, *The Good Shepherd* provides a touchstone for gaining a deeper and more nuanced understanding of contemporary race-power as seen in the construction of Barry Soetoro/Barack Hussein Obama. Given the well-documented history of anti-democratic intrigue and illegal actions perpetrated by apparently respectable individuals working for seemingly legitimate institutions during the historical period under review, it is not far-fetched to entertain the notion that the president of the United States of America – whatever his true identity may be – is not The Good Shepherd the advertising propagandists have cynically fabricated, but is instead a Judas Goat that won the hearts and minds of a voting public desperate to expiate the original sin of American racial slavery.

Endnotes

1) *Charlie Rose* 18 Dec. 2006. Http://www.charlierose.com/view/interview/83.

2) Of course both John le Carré (David Cornwell) and Graham Greene worked in British intelligence as did Ian Fleming, creator of the more cartoonish parodies featuring "James Bond" who is noteworthy for his very lack of introspection and absence of psychological depth.

3) Tim Shorrock, *Spies For Hire: The Secret World of Intelligence Outsourcing* (New York: Simon & Schuster, 2008).

4) Burton Hersh, *The Old Boys: The American Elite and the Origins of the CIA* (St. Petersburg, Florida: Tree Farm Books, 2002).

5) David Robarge, Gary McCollim, Nicholas Dujmovic, Thomas G. Coffey, "The Good Shepherd: Intelligence in Recent Public Media." *Studies in Intelligence* Vol. 51, No. 1. Https://www.cia.gov/library/center-for-the-study-of-intelligence/csi-publications/csi-studies/studies/vol51no1/the-good-shepherd.html.

6) Nicholas Dawidoff, *The Catcher Was A Spy: The Mysterious Life of Moe Berg* (New York: Pantheon Book, 1994), 202.

7) Bina Cady Kiyonaga, *My Spy: Memoir of a CIA Wife* (New York: Perennial, 2001), 116.

8) George Crile, *Charlie Wilson's War* (New York: Grove Press, 2003), 41.

9) Kiyonaga, 151.

10) Library of Congress, *The Spanish American War in Motion Pictures*. Http://memory.loc.gov/ammem/sawhtml/sawsp1.html.

11) This is not unprecedented: President George H. W. Bush was director of the CIA (1976-77) and it is claimed that his involvement in covert operations extend much further back into his personal history. Webster Griffin Tarpley and Anton Chaitkin, *George Bush: The Unauthorized Biography* (Joshua Tree, California: Progressive Press, 2004). Richard M. Nixon similarly was connected to US intelligence networks both while in the Navy and in civilian life as an attorney with the law firm Sullivan & Cromwell (John Foster Dulles managing partner) prior to entering politics. Conrad Black, *Richard M. Nixon: A Life in Full* (New York: Public Affairs, 2008), 38.

12) The African *bona fides* of Barack Hussein Obama are presented in Peter Firstbrook, *The Obamas: The Untold Story of an African Family* (New York: Crown Publishers, 2011). Though limited analytically, his Indonesian and "White" political influences are discussed in Dinesh D'Souza, *The Roots of Obama's Rage* (Washington, DC: Regnery Publishing , 2010).

13) Richard Dunlop, *Donovan: America's Master Spy* (Chicago: Rand McNally & Company, 1982), 58-59. Allen W. Dulles, the first director of the CIA, is alluded to by De Niro/Sullivan when he complains of gout from which he was known to suffer.

14) Martin A. Lee, *Their Will Be Done. Mother Jones* Jul./Aug. 1993. Http://www.motherjones.com/news/feature/1983/07/willbedone.html.

15) John Cornwell, *Hitler's Pope: The Secret History of Pius XII* (New York: Penguin Books, 2000).

16) The retreat is located north of Alexandria Bay on the St. Lawrence River in New York. Its spelling is "Deer Iland" as specified by G. D. Miller, who donated the property to the organization in 1906. Antony C. Sutton, *America's Secret Establishment: An Introduction to the Order of the Skull & Bones* (Walterville, Oregon: Trine Day), 199.

17) Joseph C. Goulden with Alexander W. Raffio, *The Death Merchant: The Rise and Fall of Edwin P. Wilson* (New York: Simon and Schuster, 1984). Wilson was of humble social origins and later was burned by his government handlers.

18) Frances Stonor Saunders, *The Cultural Cold War: The CIA and the World of Arts and Letters* (New York: New Press, 2000); Robin Winks, *Cloak and Gown: Scholars in the Secret War, 1939-1961*, 2nd ed. (New Haven: Yale University Press, 1996).

19) Robert C. Christopher, *Crashing the Gates: The De-Wasping of America and the Rise of the New Power Elite in Politics, Business, Education, Entertainment and the Media* (New York: Simon and Schuster, 1989), 234.

20) For a richly detailed account of the Washington, DC social milieu at the time of the Kennedy presidency see Nina Burleigh, *A Very Private Woman: The Life and Unsolved Murder of Presidential Mistress Mary Meyer* (New York: Bantam Books, 1999). There were signs of foul play in the death of Mary Pinchot Meyer. She had been a mistress of John F. Kennedy.

21) L. Fletcher Prouty, *The Secret Team: The CIA and Its Allies In Control of the United States and the World* (New York: Skyhorse Publishing, 2008).

22) William Blum, *Rogue State: A Guide to the World's Only Superpower* (Monroe, Maine: Common Courage Press, 2000).

23) Desmond Seward, *The Monks of War: The Military Religious Orders* (New York: Penguin, 1996).

24) H. J. A. Sire, *The Knights of Malta* (New Haven and London: Yale University Press, 1994).

25) Barbara Honegger, *October Surprise* (New York and Los Angeles: Tudor Publishing Company, 1989).

26) Renowned investigative journalist Seymour Hersh identified contemporary

high-ranking individuals within the US military who are members of the Knights of Malta or Opus Dei. In a talk at Georgetown University, Hersh indentified Gen. Stanley McChrystal and Vice Admiral William McRaven in specific. Stephen C. Webster, "High-ranking Members of US Military Part of 'Knights of Malta,' 'Opus Dei,' Reporter Claims." *The Raw Story* 21 Jan. 2011. Http://www.rawstory.com/rs/2011/01/highranking-members-military-part-knights-malta-opus-dei-reporter-claims/.

27) Walter Issacson, *Kissinger: A Biography* (New York: Simon & Schuster, 2005), 561-2.

28) Katherine Graham, *Personal History* (New York: Knopf, 1997). Graham inherited the opinion-shaping newspaper from her father Eugene Isaac Meyer, well-connected Wall Street banker (e.g. War Finance Corporation) linked to the House of Rothschild and first (1946) head of the World Bank.

29) Deborah Davis, *Katherine the Great: Katherine Graham and Her Washington Post Empire* (New York: Sheridan Square Press, 1991).

30) Don DeLillo, *Libra* (New York: Penguin Books, 1991), 30. Dealey Plaza is also the site of the first established (since razed) Masonic Temple in Dallas.

31) Robert Lacy, *Little Man: Meyer Lansky & the Gangster Life* (New York: Random House, 1993).

32) Enrique Cirules, *The Mafia in Havana: A Caribbean Mob Story* (New York: Ocean Press, 2004). Based on research conducted in the Archivo Nacional de Cuba, the author verified the interlocking relationship between the CIA, Mafia, and US financial sector with Cuban banks serving as fronts. One such document was a letter signed by CIA director Allen Dulles to President Fulgencio Batista dated July 15, 1955 concerning the arrangement between the Cuban government and the US.

33) DeLillo, 129.

34) Erik Hedegaard, "The Last Confessions of E. Howard Hunt," *Rolling Stone* 21 Mar. 2007. Http://www.rollingstone.com/politics/story/13893143/the_last_confessions_of_e_howard_hunt.

35) Bernard Fensterwald, Jr., *Coincidence or Conspiracy?* (New York: Zebra Books, 1977), 160.

36) Wayne Barrett, *Rudy!: An Investigative Biography of Rudy Giuliani* (New York: Basic Books, 2001).

37) Webster Griffin Tarpley, *Barack H. Obama: The Unauthorized Biography* (Joshua Tree, California: Progressive Press, 2008).

38) Based in Washington, DC and boasting impeccable credentials as investigative journalist, intelligence community insider, and military veteran, Wayne Madsen has published on his subscription-only website a multi-part expose of Barry Soetoro, family background, and sketchy personal history that includes working after graduating from Columbia University for Business International Corporation (BIC); a known CIA front. In response to a series of articles published in his subscription-only online newsletter, Madsen was informed by high-level White House sources that he has been targeted for death. He has announced that his journalistic enterprise will leave the US for an undisclosed overseas location. Wayne Madsen, "White House Threats Must Be Taken Seriously." *Wayne Madsen Report* 04 Apr. 2011. Http://www.waynemadsenreport.com/articles/20110403. See also Janny Scott, "Obama's Account of New York Years Often Differs From What Others Say," *New York Times* 30 Oct. 2007. Http://www.nytimes.com/2007/10/30/us/politics/30obama.html?_r=2.

39) Lamar Waldron with Thom Hartmann, *Legacy of Secrecy: The Long Shadow of the JFK Assassination* (Berkeley: Counterpoint, 2009). This latest meticulously researched study benefitted by interviews with associates of assassination victims and other principals involved. Thousands of documents at the National Archives recently released yield more information for the historical record and contribute deeper insight into the dimly

perceived workings of power and supremacy in society.

40) *JFK II: The Bush Connection* (Alice In Arms, 2003); *The Assassination of JFK Jr: Murder By Manchurian Candidate* (2006); *Dark Legacy: George Bush and the Murder of John Kennedy* (Terra Entertainment, 2009). The latter title appears to line up with information that has been gathering over the years that implicate CIA operative George H. W. Bush in the events of November 1963.

41) Wayne Madsen, "UPDATE 1X. JFK Jr's Plane Crash Was Originally Treated As Murder Investigation." *Wayne Madsen Report* 12 Aug. 2009. Http://www.waynemadsenreport.com/articles/20090812_4.

42) Legal challenges to the Constitutional question of the identity and nationality of Barry Soetoro/Barack Hussein Obama has been led most notably by former Deputy Attorney General of Pennsylvania, registered Democrat and life member of the NAACP Philip J. Berg. *Obamacrimes.com.* Http://obamacrimes.com/?page_id=7.

43) Ron Nixon, "U.S. Groups Helped Nurture Arab Uprisings." *New York Times* 14 Apr. 2011. Http://www.nytimes.com/2011/04/15/world/15aid.html?_r=2&ref=todayspaper.

CHAPTER EIGHT

RACE IN YOUR FACE: CNN AND NEOLIBERAL MULTICULTURALISM

Prologue: Dobbs Jobbed

The dark and dismal November 2009 day when the venerable and querulous Lou Dobbs abruptly announced on air his resignation from the long-running program that bore his name, CNN lost its last remaining personality present at the 1980 inauguration of an institution responsible for revolutionizing the terms and conditions by which the English and Spanish language-literate world population is fed news and information.[1] He left behind a global news organization that through its twenty-four hour reportage and commentary upon the events of the historical moment did much – prior to its recent nosedive in viewership – to shape public opinion regarding both domestic and international affairs to the benefit of the Anglo-American axis.[2]

His frequent arch commentary ("Red Storm Rising") on the nation he consistently, in anachronistic Cold War parlance, referred to as "Red China" (usually in reference to the flood of cheaply-made products – including "poisonous" toys and tainted food products – exported to America) and sustained opposition to large-scale immigration from Mexico to the US ("Broken Borders") drove "socio-ethnic centric special interest groups" (his oft-invoked phrase) crazy with anger. Not one to shy away from confrontation, Dobbs once visited the New York "firehouse studio" of *Democracy Now!* for a live face-off with host Amy Goodman and co-anchor Juan Gonzalez to defend himself against accusations of inaccurate and biased coverage of Latino immigration.[3]

While earning the enmity of many Latino advocacy groups, Dobbs also managed to offend mainline Democrats of the sort that fit the Keith Olbermann MSNBC liberal audience demographic, Move On and Code Pink-style progressives, and much of the African American intelligentsia by daring to raise the simple and legitimate question concerning the birthplace of the individual known today as Barack Hussein Obama.[4] The Constitution requires the president of the republic as a condition of office to have been born in the USA. Those who dared press the issue of nativity in reference to Obama were dismissed as "birthers" suspected of being motivated by residual racial hatred against the half-White/partially Black chief executive.[5]

President of CNN-US Jonathan Klein had already been feeling the heat from Latino organizations that had mounted protests against Dobbs. But the turning point came during one specific show when CNN contributor (since March 2007) Roland S. Martin threw a conniption fit in response to Dobbs asking why Obama refused to present his US birth certificate to silence the doubters.[6] Shortly into the discussion that included US Representative Ted Poe (R-Texas) from a remote studio location, Martin began loud-talking ("C'mon!") both the congressman and Dobbs, arguing that since Obama already occupied the office as president number "forty-four" this was enough to preclude further discussion.

It was as if Obama were royalty. "You make it sound like he was anointed something beyond that," Dobbs remarked. Martin became more agitated even though Dobbs repeated that he himself believed Obama to be have been born in the US. The exchange became heated to the point that Dobbs asked Martin to cease shouting at the congressman. "Well, I think it is hilarious," said Martin, alluding to the controversy. "Then laugh," Dobbs retorted.

In a post-separation interview with co-anchor Terry Moran on *Nightline* (ABC News), after having the opportunity to reflect upon his career as a "populist" from the comfort of his three-hundred-acre estate in Sussex County, New Jersey horse country, Dobbs was markedly more conciliatory. With an eye on a possible run for political office, the former professional curmudgeon who rode the wave of popular resentment against government misprision, expresses his support of pathways to American citizenship for unauthorized immigrants. Moran, having dismissed the "ludicrous conspiracy theory" that questions whether Barack Hussein Obama indeed was born in the United States of America, allows

Dobbs to minimize the extent to which he fanned the flames of the so-called "birther" controversy.[7]

This well-crafted eight-minute public relations piece, meant to sell the new improved Lou Dobbs by playing up his softened political rhetoric, suggests that for the last few years of his tenure at CNN he simply exploited the themes of race, ethnicity, and immigration to provide daily relief to a viewing audience hurting from the engineered collapse of the US economy. Moran suggests to Dobbs that he might need the Latino vote should he decide to seek election to public office. The cagey news veteran does not deny the insinuation of political opportunism. Attired in a colorful argyle vest and shirtsleeves, a more avuncular Lou Dobbs affirms that, "Hell yes!" he indeed is "changing his tune" concerning immigration. By the end of the *Nightline* interview, Dobbs has been all but rehabilitated, reformed, and repackaged for future consumption as an elected servant of the people.

Ironically, the chief beneficiaries of the Dobbsian presence on CNN, radio (United Stations Radio Networks), and in print (*Money* magazine columns; top-selling books), were the very "socio-ethnic centric special interest groups" that agitated against him and then claimed credit for his demise. Without Dobbs to kick around any more, such groups lacked a highly visible media figure to rally their supporters against. Absent the media politics and accusations of anti-Latino racism on CNN, serious issues like NAFTA and the stealthy imposition of the North American Union by the governments of Canada, Mexico, and the USA would have to be confronted on their own merits.

Without the smokescreen of racially charged media politics, one of the key objectives of the globalist political-economic agenda – the merging of sovereign nations into a centrally controlled and governed North American bloc modeled after the European Union – was exposed for what it is: An attempt to bring the US under centralized global control by private offshore bankers. Dobbs was one of the few mainstream journalists to devote consistent coverage of this most alarming development being orchestrated by the ruling elite within the nations involved.[8] Moreover, few critics of any ideological stripe could gainsay his most important journalistic contribution: His impassioned focus on the accelerating economic death of all but the elite in US society in a series of reports titled "War On the Middle Class."

The deciding factor, however, in the demise of *Lou Dobbs Tonight* was that its Nielsen ratings had slid downward by fifteen percent prior to the plug being pulled.[9] For a brief moment in media history, in parallel with the implosion of the American economy and systematic dismantling of civil liberties in the aftermath of the 9/11 attacks, Lou Dobbs captured the hearts and minds of a large segment of the viewing public. His time, however, had passed; the internet and alternative media continued to eat into the news and information monopoly once held by cable TV, particularly among those under the age of thirty.[10] In the end, Lou "Mr. Independent" Dobbs became a liability at CNN not primarily for political reasons but because he no longer commanded the attention of the contemporary consumer audience as measured by the marked decline in program ratings.[11]

Neoliberal Multiculturalism

During the almost thirty-year tenure of Dobbs, CNN had refined and extended its function (along with Fox News and MSNBC) to set the acceptable range of ideological persuasion and political discussion allowed on corporate cable, as a conduit for the corporatist state, to produce political consensus and limit dissent to tolerable levels. One of the more effective strategies in expanding its domestic US audience demographic that has not yet fled network and cable news for internet sites, blogs, or comedic journalism such as *The Daily Show*, *The Colbert Report* or the moronic Fox News *Red Eye w/Greg Gutfeld*, has been the integration of non-White talent filling its on-air roster. This sends a strong message of multiracial liberal democracy to the substantial world audience that includes specialized channels such CNN International (since 1985), available in over 200 countries.

In the face of protests by groups that include the National Hispanic Media Coalition, Media Matters, National Council of La Raza, and the Institute for Latino Policy, Dobbs left behind a roster of colleagues that appeared to embody the post-civil rights era liberal multiculturalism that got underway during the late 1970s and through the 1980s as CNN rose to prominence.[12]

Veteran African American journalist Bernard Shaw, for example, worked for CNN from 1980 to his retirement in 2001. Along with Anglo New Zealander and 1966 Pulitzer Prize recipient Peter Arnett (father-in-law of John "Torture Memos" Choon Yoo), Shaw earned notoriety for his reportage in 1991 from Baghdad as the US military began its aerial decimation of the city.[13] In a simultaneous blow for female equality and racial synthesis, Christiane Amanpour gained international attention for her coverage of the Persian Gulf War beginning in 1990. Her hybrid Iranian-Anglo beauty seduced the eye while aurally the cadences and vocal inflections of a proper British education lent credibility to every impassioned battlefield utterance. For those years spent on dangerous assignment covering the wars and conflagrations of the US-led post-Soviet Union world order she was rewarded by being given her own international issues program titled *Amanpour* (2009-10) before leaving for ABC News in 2011.[14]

Following the trail blazed by the first AsianAmerican TV journalist of national stature, Connie Chung, Joie Chen began as CNN anchor in 1991 and lasted for ten years before moving on to CBS as a correspondent in 2002. After her contract was not renewed, the graduate of the Medill School of Journalism at Northwestern University left CBS in February 2008 and subsequently moved into a niche with an online media business.

Subsequent to Chen, Carole Lin held down anchor duties at CNN Center in Atlanta and worked as a correspondent from 1998 to late 2006. It was she who broke the news to an international audience of the sensational airliner attacks on the World Trade Center Towers on September 11, 2001. Connie Chung herself, the grand dame of Asian American female media figures, had a very brief run at CNN beginning in mid-2002. The hourlong *Connie Chung Tonight*, which reportedly paid her $2 million, was cancelled in March of the following year. The program was not received well by critics but garnered an appreciable base of Chung fans.

As the US invasion and occupation of Iraq proceeded apace and in the face of competition against *The O'Reilly Factor* on Fox, the new management at CNN decided it needed to get back to "serious" news reportage.[15] The daughter of a Kuomintang political officer who had relocated his family from the Republic of China to the US, Chung never was to regain the heights of TV journalism she had after winning the job in 1993 as co-anchor with the *CBS Evening News,* which at the time enjoyed the highest prestige among competing network programs. She left in May 1995 after losing a power struggle with co-anchor Dan Rather, heir to the throne vacated by *éminence grise* Walter Cronkite.[16]

With his ambition for high elective office having gone unfulfilled, including two successive campaigns for the US presidency, Jesse Jackson hosted a weekly public affairs program – *Both Sides With Jesse Jackson* – from 1992 to 2000. Other African Americans have served as anchors or correspondents for CNN including Fredricka Whitfield (since 2002); Suzanne Malveaux (White House correspondent since 2002); Tony Harris (2004-10); T. J. Holmes (2006-11); and Don Lemon (since 2006). Soledad O'Brien is of Australo-Afro-Cuban American heritage and began in 2003 as co-anchor of *American Morning* before being replaced by Euro-Nepalese American Kiran Chetry who began co-hosting the program in April 2007.

Two other Asian American women work as on-camera talent as well: Alina Cho (national correspondent since 2004) and Betty Nguyen (2004) was a weekend newsroom fixture as the first Vietnamese American anchor to appear on a national level before moving to CBS News in 2010. The sole male Asian American among the bevy of "hot" anchor babes of the sort celebrated in the men's magazine *Maxim* was Richard Lui. He hired on in 2005 and anchors for the less prestigious HLN franchise while also appearing on CNN International and CNN/US. Lui joined MSNBC in 2010.

Given their significant numbers in the general population, Latinos are underrepresented on the news set. The lone Latino male prior to his firing in October 2010 was Rick Sanchez. The son of Cuban American political exiles had been with the organization since 2004. He was seen as anchor on *CNN Newsroom* in addition to responsibilities with CNN International and CNN en Español.

Sanchez was let go after saying on a satellite radio show that Jon Stewart was a "bigot" for his "White, Liberal Establishment view" that does not allow him to "relate" to people like him. He refused to concede to host Pete Dominick on Sirius radio that

Stewart, being Jewish, was a member of an "oppressed minority" group like Sanchez and therefore would not be prejudiced against him.[17] On more than one occasion, Sanchez had been the butt of one-liners delivered by Stewart; whose demographically coveted viewership relies upon his program for "news" to a far greater extent than CNN.

Untied Nation

CNN founder Robert Edward "Ted" Turner III, despite his privileged upbringing as inheritor of a regional billboard empire built by a father who died by his own hand, was an early champion of what today is called "globalization." The "Mouth of the South" has opined freely on issues ranging from so-called climate change, argued for population reduction, and financially supported centralized supra-national global governance via the United Nations.

In 1998, Turner founded the United Nations Foundation with a $1 billion gift to help fund the globalist agenda in the guise of health care and environmentalism.[18] He has cunningly cast himself as a swashbuckling, gruffly pragmatic truth teller that cared not if his utterances offended the softhearted public. His carefully crafted public persona allowed the less sensational but far more dangerous professional eugenicists such as John P. Holdren (currently Obama's science and technology advisor) to seem humane by comparison.[19]

On April Fool's Day 2008, Turner famously appeared on *Charlie Rose* – itself a vehicle for globalists ranging from corporate leaders, research scientists, and political figures along with a sprinkling of artists, directors, actors, and intellectuals – to tout the dubious claims of the scientific dictatorship concerning "global warming" as a means of frightening the public into accepting mass population control and drastically reduced resource consumption.[20] Meanwhile, Turner promoted his breed of genetically pure bison meat while living on pristine private land holdings in Bozeman, Montana.[21] He is also father to five children; twice as many offspring as the average American family.

A consummate showman, "Captain Outrageous" anticipated the break-up of the Soviet Union by conceiving and staging the first "Goodwill Games" in Moscow (1986), ostensibly as a means of lessening international geo-strategic tensions. The CNN extravaganza was sold as an ideology-free athletic competition and alternative to the modern Olympics, which has been a showcase for nationalist pride and supremacy since the time of Hitler and his mass media propagandists of 1936 Berlin games. As a former billboard man and denizen of the "New South" undergoing transformation by the relocation to China of heavy manufacturing from highly unionized industrial cities of the North and investment of foreign corporations such as Japanese automobile makers in "right-to-work" states, Turner has profited enormously by dragging the American mass-mind into the age of neoliberal globalization through ownership and control of an extensive, inescapable, seamless, twenty-four hour a day news, information, entertainment and advertising media matrix that even Nazi propaganda mastermind Joseph Goebbels never came close to realizing.[22]

But while the Third Reich exploited racial nationalism as a binding force until its military defeat in 1945, the US during the latter years of twentieth century adopted the clever strategy of liberal multiculturalism – work-shopped at the university and then disseminated throughout the wider society via mass media – as a means of perpetuating class power and racial privilege within the global capitalist world system.

The break-up of the Soviet Union during the 1990s heralded a new age of triumphant capitalism according to observers such as Francis Fukuyama with his well-timed essay that appeared in the neoconservative house organ *The Public Interest*, later beefed up into a book.[23] Neoliberal economic theory was propagated at established centers of intellectual endeavor such as the University of Chicago with its historically close connection to the globalist Rockefeller family that founded the private institution. As an outgrowth of the national security state, the new cable and satellite technology exploited by Turner Broadcasting and CNN was ideally suited to market this crafted neoliberal *Weltanshauung* to America and internationally.

By the time Turner Broadcasting System, Inc. merged with Time Warner in 1996, the next phase in the evolution of centralized world government controlled by foreign central banks and administered domestically by the privately held Federal Reserve System was well underway. Moving into the twenty-first century, CNN programming would take the lead in advancing the neoliberal economic order while televising US military actions dictated by the neoconservative foreign policy establishment grouped around its neo-fascist Project for the New American Century .[24]

Passage to Chindia

Whereas the economic advance of Japan followed by the East Asian "Tigers" had been the object of much popular attention and scholarly research through the 1980s, China and India took center stage during the 1990s and into the first decade of the new century. A popular collection of essays, for example, aimed at the American corporate managerial class bears the whimsical title *Chindia: How China and India are Revolutionizing Global Business.* The title conflates the names of the two Asian countries whose immense populations currently inspire wonder among the *Business Week* types represented in this anthology.[25] Despite the largely uncritical cheerleading of the "Chindia" concept in this collection, select contributors cannot help but betray doubt concerning the possible disruption of the long march toward Chinese-style capitalist prosperity, based upon ongoing political protest and general social unrest arising from uneven economic development and the extreme concentration of wealth among the new oligarchs.

Though China manufactures the bulk of goods consumed at mega-retailers like Wal-Mart and is the number two (behind Japan) holder of US national debt in the form of Treasury bonds totaling $1 trillion, the Obama administration nonetheless adopted an antagonistic stance toward its creditor by selling $6.4 billion worth of weapons systems to Taiwan.[26] While CNN/Opinion Research Corporation polling results indicate that only half of Americans surveyed view the PRC as a military menace, over seventy percent perceived it as an economic threat.[27] India, on the other hand, has been elevated over China through clever diplomatic machinations as a trustworthy asset in that part of the Asian world while the Middle Kingdom is seen as the "most independent and uncontrollable element" within the international political order.[28]

Framing China as a moral pariah were recurrent news reports, documentaries, and publications that highlighted "human rights" issues concerning political autonomy for Tibet, freedom of religion, as in the case of Falun Gong and the growing Christian population, persecution of the non-Han minority in the Xinjiang Uighur Autonomous Region, use of slave and child labor, suspected cyber-attacks against US companies and government agencies, kidnapping and sale of females, forced abortions, harvesting of human organs for sale, and a "thirst" among the nouveau riche for tiger parts.[29] Images of the slaughter at Tiananmen Square (1989) are often recalled to reemphasize the reality of political repression in the world's largest communist state, while select dissidents such as Harry Wu and his anti-*laogai* campaign put a human face on the struggle against PRC authoritarianism.[30] *China Digital News* – a specialized Website maintained by the Graduate School of Journalism at the University of California, Berkeley – features an aggregation of articles not entirely flattering to the PRC, which of course blocks it.[31]

Mother India

In contrast to China, the India portrayed by its promoters is a thriving democracy that has moved beyond the political turmoil that set in after the termination of the British Raj in 1947 and subsequent decades of failed economic development along socialist lines. Its brand of dynamic entrepreneurialism and economic growth is presented as an exemplary case of a society freed through the move away from government bureaucratic strictures and excessive regulatory control. The adoption of neoliberal economics as theorized by US-trained policy makers and administered by the World Bank, International Monetary Fund, and World Trade Organization in support of information technology-driven capitalist development is responsible for an enviable rate of growth. Or so the self-validating narrative goes. Political activist Vandana Shiva and other opponents of mega-corporatism, however, tell a quite different story.[32]

South Asians in US academia lend scholarly assistance to what is put forth as the historically inevitable process of globalization as articulated by neoliberal theoretical legerdemain. As an example, Jagdish Bhagwati ("University Professor" at Columbia and "Senior Fellow in International Economics" with the privately-funded globalist Council on Foreign Relations) is but one visible NRI (Non-Resident Indian) placed in strategic institutional positions to promote India as key component in the restructuring of the capitalist world system according to the needs of the Anglo-American alliance and the elite families that accumulated great wealth during the earlier, classic phase of colonialism in imperial possessions such as India.[33]

On the applied level, two brothers – Atul Vashistha and Avinash Vashistha – have established themselves as corporate managerial experts in "business process outsourcing" (BPO) through their jointly operated firm neoIT.[34] In the same way that corporate planners shipped US manufacturing overseas to China, India has been set up by global capitalists to eviscerate the great American middle class through the exportation of jobs in the information and service sector of the economy. The documentary *American Jobs* (2005) devotes a segment to furloughed IT professionals displaced by foreign workers brought in by the Tata Group on H-1B visas lobbied for by the likes of Bill Gates.[35] The feature film starring George Clooney, *Up In The Air* (2009), captures the anguish of the systematic transfer of relatively well paying, once secure white-collar occupations presumably to technology hubs within Mother India.[36]

Nandan Nilekani, who along with seven other founding engineering genii fashioned Infosys Technologies Limited into a leader in global outsourcing, is one of the more prominent of the new business raja stratum put in place to help facilitate the final stage in the transition to the "borderless world" as given popular expression by international corporate management guru Kenichi "Mr. Strategy" Ohmae in 1990.[37] (Early on, Ohmae recognized the importance of CNN as an ideological tool.) The son of a textile mill manager that had resources enough to provide his son an elite English medium school education ((Bishop Cotton Boys' School; the "Eton of the East") that in turn led to undergraduate study at the ultra-competitive Indian Institute of Technology (IIT) in Bombay.

Nilekani has been seen on American corporate media peddling his vision of the unfolding globalist economy to worshipful interlocutors ranging from Charlie Rose and the obsequious Tavis Smiley on Public Broadcast Service (PBS) to Jon Stewart on *The Daily Show*.[38] Nilekani has been sanctified as Indian neo-colonial comprador by none other than neoliberal *nabob* Thomas L. Friedman of the *New York Times*, Pulitzer Prize winner, and author of bestselling books that retell the globalist master narrative.[39]

Recently, Nilekani has provided an astonishingly insightful historical and social analysis of contemporary India written from the perspective of one who has benefitted enormously from the transfer of intellectual labor to India from the US. In *Imagining India: The Idea of A Renewed Nation*, Nilekani begins with a discussion of the relationship of government sterilization programs ("family welfare") to economic take-off in this nation of over one billion persons; of whom forty percent remain in poverty. Much of the book (foreword by Thomas L. Friedman) is devoted to *ex post facto* explanations as to why the neoliberal economic model has succeeded while state socialism and the planned economy has failed.[40] He ends the 511-page apologia by affirming the need for Indian entrepreneurs such as himself to accept "their role in nation-building and public welfare" while shouldering the "burdens of equity and development."[41] Whether or not Nilekani is aware of it, his professed admiration for the "charity activities" of the Rockefeller Foundation, Ford Foundation, and Gates Foundation is perfectly consistent with their common commitment to the imposition of a globalist political economic order with eugenics science being their principal weapon of population control.[42]

The Empire Strikes Back

With India and its gifted immigrants to the US being crucial to the creation and implementation of novel methods to drive the American public deeper into financial bondage, CNN management conferred upon Canadian journalist Ali Velshi the title of "chief business correspondent" to provide co-ethnic cover for a number of South Asian sleaze-bags who have been recruited to hasten the demise of the dying economic order. His profile and role as hand-holder to those confused and frightened by successive financial scandals and related engineered crises functions on an international level as well. By 2012, Velshi was anchor of "World Business Today" on CCN International (CNNI) that reached over 200 countries beyond the US.[43]

One such gifted immigrant was legal loan-sharking wizard Shailesh J. Mehta. It was Mehta, an engineer by training, who led the way in mass marketing high interest Providian VISA credit cards to average folk struggling to maintain their standard of living despite flat wages and the decline in buying power due to inflation of the US fiat currency printed by the private Federal Reserve.[44]

Select South Asian Americans have been recruited by Wall Street to serve as "quants." Their charge was to devise and interpret elegantly abstract and hence utterly convincing mathematical models used to extract profit from non-productive and non-value-producing rapid-fire high-volume trading activity that is all but impossible to comprehend, never mind regulate and police. Occasionally, to satisfy the public thirst for vengeance, a quant has been ritually sacrificed before the camera in a ceremonial "perp-walk." Raj Rajaratnam, founder of the Galleon Group hedge fund, was subjected to one such public display of simulated justice after being arrested by the FBI in October 2009 for allegations of insider trading.[45] He subsequently was tried, convicted, and incarcerated.

Like his father, who holds a doctorate in the field, Neel Kashkari was trained as an engineer. After a time spent as an aerospace engineer, he earned an MBA at the Wharton School of Business and worked in the San Francisco office of Goldman Sachs before being called to government service in 2006 by Henry Paulson. Appointed Secretary of Treasury by President George W. Bush, Paulson had been CEO at Goldman Sachs (1994-98). As Interim Assistant Secretary for Financial Stability and point man for the Troubled Assets Relief Plan (TARP) Kashkari testified before US Congress concerning the multi-trillion dollar bailout of certain Wall Street banks including his own former employer Goldman Sachs.

At the close of his C-SPAN-televised dance around the issues, Kashkari tried to impress upon committee members how hard he was working to solve the problems relating to the financial meltdown. Congressman Dennis Kucinich (D-Ohio), serving as chair of the Oversight Subcommittee on Domestic Policy, in a riposte that resonated far and wide stated, "I don't think anyone questions that you're working hard. Our question is, who you're working *for*."[46] While licking his wounds with his wife at a remote cabin in the Sierra Nevada, Kashkari complained that his testimony before Congress felt "like three guys beat the crap out of me."[47]

In the field of international politics, Fareed Zakaria was re-cruited by CNN in 2008 as mouthpiece for the globalist Coun-cil on Foreign Relations that traces its institutional history to the Royal Institute of International Affairs. He sits on the board of directors for the avowedly non-partisan globalist organization that bears the omnipresent stamp of the Rockefeller family and has served as managing editor of its influential journal *Foreign Af-fairs*. Representing the new breed of contemporary Asian Amer-ican transnationals who have slipped effortlessly into positions of power and influence because of their utility to the Anglo-Amer-ican policy elite, Zakaria hails from Mumbai but is a naturalized US citizen. With breathless glee, in *The Post-American World* (2009) he expounds upon the much-heralded arrival of India as a dynamic site of economic growth second only to China over the past decade. Based upon his visits to the annual Davos conclave for the supranational over-class, Zakaria observes, "The world is courting India as never before,."[48]

His ease with political insiders, leaders of the highest order, and figures of world-historical stature stems from early exposure to movers and shakers within the privileged social milieu of his family. Zakaria is an attendee of private planning conferences such as Bilderberg and Davos where the globalist elite set the po-litical and economic agenda for years in advance. Rafiq Zakaria, his deceased father, was a politician allied with the Indian Nation-al Congress party and diplomat. His mother is a close associate of the industrialist Ratan Tata who owns the Taj Mahal Palace hotel in Mumbai, the site a terrorist attack in November 2008.

Drawing upon this family connection, Tata spoke in a "voice of suppressed rage" with Zakaria on CNN four days after the assault upon his prize symbol of post-colonial Indian affluence.[49] Like Infosys, Tata Consultancy Services (see *American Jobs* above) is one of the Indian companies responsible for gutting the American middle class in preparation for the globalist regional consolida-tion plan known as the North American Union under its "Securi-ty and Prosperity Partnership of North America" intended to deal the final blow to US national sovereignty.[50]

A student of Samuel P. Huntington at Harvard, where he earned a doctorate in political science, Zakaria the journalist is generally in line with the Trilateral Commission (Rockefeller again) world-view of his mentor whose name is stamped on one of its foundational statements *The Crisis of Democracy* (1975).[51] As a Muslim, however, Zakaria finds himself on the opposing side in the "clash of civilizations" as outlined by Huntington in an alarming treatise bearing the same title.[52] Nonetheless, Zakaria dutifully carries out his tacitly understood assignment to hose down fellow Muslims as evidenced by an interview with former Inter-Services Intelligence (ISI) chief Lt. Gen. Hamid Gul on his program *Fareed Zakaria GPS* (for Global Public Square). When asked who he believes was behind the attacks of 9/11, Gul without hesitation points the finger at the "Zionists" and "neocons." He elaborates by stating that the coordinated action was an "inside job" and that the plot was "planned in America."

Against the large number of articles, books, documentaries, and founding of professional organizations such as Architects & Engineers for 9/11 Truth that dispute the principal findings of the official government investigation, Zakaria spouts the government official line:[53] "Some of General Gul's views are simply false," he says at the close of the show. "There is a mountain of evidence about 9/11 that refutes his assertions."[54] Meanwhile, the number of books, DVDs, websites, and professional organizations that support the accusations of Gul continues to grow both in the US and internationally. Like many servitors of American empire that have been allowed to climb to positions of influence, only to have the ladder kicked out from under them, Zakaria found himself suspended indefinitely from *Time* magazine and CNN for having been caught plagiarizing from an article on "gun control" that appeared in the April 23, 2012 issue of *The New Yorker*.[55]

With Velshi occupying the business and economy chair and Zakaria hosting his own hour-long CFR globalist new world order vehicle, the last link in the CNN daisy chain is Sanjay Gupta, MD. The Atlanta-based neurosurgeon was the first of the South Asian American triumvirate (not counting Kiran Chetry) to be placed before the camera, having been brought into the fold in 2001. The timing was propitious since Gupta was then able to report on the suspicious weapons-grade anthrax attacks (as investigated in the excellent documentary *Anthrax-War* [2009]) launched as the USA PATRIOT Act was being held up in Congress and then quickly passed in the panic after 9/11 without having been read by those that voted for it.[56]

Gupta by all appearances is a dedicated medical professional and journalist who cares deeply about the welfare of humanity. His almost nonstop reportage from Port-au-Prince, Haiti, devastated by an earthquake in mid-January 2010, elevated him to heroic status when he was pressed into service to perform emergency surgery under trying circumstances.

Humanitarian derring-do notwithstanding, in his capacity as "chief medical correspondent" and host of the weekend program *Sanjay Gupta MD* (formerly *House Call with Dr. Sanjay Gupta*), he is a perfect fit for the globalist agenda as advanced by CNN.[57] He is an uncritical advocate of mass vaccination, as in the case of the laboratory-created H1N1 "swine flu" virus that originated in Mexico City during the spring of 2009. The flu scare, hyped in the US and abroad by Big Pharma and the World Health Organization, has been exposed as a "false pandemic" orchestrated to cash in on vaccine sales.[5] More generally, Gupta does the bidding of the United Nations and its sundry population reduction schemes as seen in the hour-long CNN special featuring Lucy Liu and other celebrities on behalf of UNICEF.[59]

Finally, as a brown man, Gupta wears the ideal racial camouflage that gives him instant credibility among the non-White worldwide audience for CNN. Within the US, the Asian American physician has been rendered respectable by doctor dramas featuring Ming Na (*ER*), Sandra Oh (*Grey's Anatomy*), or Kal Penn (*House*). His racial and ethnic identity offers a friendly and reassuring face to both the domestic market and the larger non-White world that – if news-manufacturing organizations such as CNN are to be believed – is teeming with diseased populations awaiting to be cured by advanced medical treatment and biotechnology courtesy of pharmaceutical cartels.

Cable Psy-Ops Network

The capitalist world system has experienced profound shifts since the day Lou Dobbs took his place with CNN in 1980 as its chief economics correspondent. In 1991, at the behest of the International Monetary Fund, economic liberalization of India under Prime Minister P. V. Narasimha Rao was implemented.

In the year 2000, China was admitted to the World Trade Organization. Unregulated immigration from Mexico and other Latin American countries was viewed as adding to the mounting woes of ordinary people suckered into improbably inventive speculative financial bubbles that were inflated and then propped up by Wall Street investment banks such as Goldman Sachs and Bank of America. Clearly, the neoliberal political economic order as designed by their minions in academia, publicized in journals of opinion, and propagated among the general public via mass communication outlets such as CNN has caused great hardship at minimum and, at the other extreme, deprivation for the vast majority of the world population. Neoliberalism as an overarching world-view and comprehensive system of repackaged capitalist depredation, like any other product, needed to be sold on the most sophisticated of advertising medium of all: Television.

Manfred B. Steger has emphasized the discursive strategies and ideological underpinnings of neoliberalism while others – both critics and advocates – have tended to look mostly at its material processes and the measurable effects of this historically-specific reinvention of political economic power and control wielded by hereditary oligarchs. Steger accurately simplifies the ideological project administered by corporate leaders and their public relations hirelings by isolating the "selling" of five truth-claims that argue for the goodness, rectitude, desirability, and inevitability of the neoliberal political economic order.[60]

Perhaps the most patently disingenuous and easily falsifiable claim is that the neoliberal world order will advance the spread and scope of democracy and thereby foster institutions that nurture human freedom, cultivate communal self-activity, and allow for productive work. On the contrary, David Harvey has characterized the neoliberal regime as "anti-democratic" in nature, held together as it is by the "authoritarianism of the neoconservatives" against those engaged in political opposition to this latest iteration of age-old tyranny.[61]

The particular warped genius of the psy-ops specialists at CNN who war-game approaches to the capture and colonization of the human mind is that they seem to have figured out an effective method of exploiting race and ethnicity as a means of making more palatable an odious, dehumanizing neoliberal control grid known in times past as totalitarianism. The military allusions here are not metaphorical; they are literal: The US Army has admitted to placing its psy-ops personnel at CNN Atlanta headquarters as part of its "Training With Industry" program.[62]

Apart from Anderson "360°" Cooper's admission that he spent his summer vacations from Yale interning with the CIA, CNN and its putative rivals Fox News and MSNBC each enjoy a close connection to both the military and the intelligence community.[63] Cooper, whose mother Gloria Vanderbilt entered the mass public consciousness by taking common blue jeans up-market through clever marketing as "designer" fashion, is a scion of not one but two illuminist bloodlines: Astor and Vanderbilt.

The equality revolution of the postwar period that reached its high point during the Civil Rights movement was subverted by PHOENIX Program targeted assassinations of the political and cultural opposition, infiltration by government-controlled assets as in COINTELPRO, and exploited by political opportunists of diverse ethnic and racial backgrounds, and eventually domesticated by institutions such as the university.

Perhaps the most insidiously effective institution to have successfully turned the "race" concept against itself and thereby stymie substantive transformation has been the corporate-media arm attached to the larger national security body. With its continuous MONARCH/MOCKINGBIRD/MK-ULTRA Program sensory bombardment meant to short-circuit the rational mind and substitute critical thought with fear, loathing, and submission to the neoliberal new world order so dear to its architects within the Anglo-American alliance, CNN is vital to the manufacture of political consensus.[64]

The departure of Lou Dobbs, however, came at a time when viewership of both network and cable television (not to mention corporate-print media) is dropping. Alternative online media podcasts, inexpensively produced independent documentaries, and music file-sharing programs have loosened the grip of the dominant media system. At the same time, the CNN of today demonstrates the way in which race and ethnicity has been subsumed by corporate-media mind managers and adapted to the needs of the neoliberal world system that requires constant ideological reinforcement to maintain its legitimacy among the ordinary subject population.

To thwart the cynical use of racial and ethnic identity by the military-corporate psy-ops experts, a more honest and nuanced approach to media criticism and analysis will be required. This includes getting past the mindless adulation and acceptance of every non-White person that wears the CNN logo. Ethno-nationalist groups – or what Dobbs archly dubbed "socio-ethnic centric special interest groups" – almost certainly will take offense to this call for a new level of honesty. But political maturity and realism requires an understanding that the heart of darkness dwells in all of humankind, even within those of duskier hue.

The welfare state entitlement groups, however, no longer have a Lou Dobbs to serve as a lightning rod for their ire. One year after being canned from CNN, as the left-globalist online news site *Media Matters* (funded by liberal-globalist financial oligarch George Soros) gloated, Dobbs resurfaced on the Fox Business Network; part of the News Corporation empire run by global media lord Rupert Murdoch under protection of his Asian American wife Denge Wenge (Wendi Deng).[65] In a calculated transformation designed to appease his detractors and give them the momentary sensation of victory, Dobbs has since backed away from the views he routinely spouted on CNN and now fully embraces the globalist political economic agenda.

Postscript

At the end of the first quarter of 2012, it was reported that CNN had sustained a fifty percent drop in viewership since the previous year. More importantly, the once-stellar news organization lost sixty percent of the twenty-five to fifty-four age group cherished by advertisers.[66] Cable TV in general is experiencing a general decline in audience. If the downward trend continues, it will be seen that "alternative" online news media operations such as *Infowars.com,* pioneered by anti-New World Order investigative journalist Alex Jones, *Breitbart,* or the *Drudge Report* collectively were the meteor that killed the dinosaur.

Endnotes

1) *Lou Dobbs Tonight* began as *Moneyline* in 1980 and launched with CNN itself. Upon his final appearance on November 13, 2009, Dobbs reportedly walked away from $9 million had he stayed on to complete a five-year contract that totaled $35 million. Michael

Shain and David K. Li, "Dobbs Gave Up on $9M," *New York Post* 13 Nov. 2009. Http://www.nypost.com/p/news/national/dobbs_gave_up_on_3EsCWZGeRuYrPsFuzm8YoJ.

2) Piers Robinson, *The CNN Effect: The Myth of News, Foreign Policy and Intervention* (London and New York: Routledge, 2002). This study is written from an orthodox "communication studies" framework that minimizes the influence of CNN in the facilitation of so-called humanitarian (military) intervention. It is useful, however, as a compendium of criticism lodged against CNN for the institutional legitimacy (whether valid or not) it carries through its state-managed reportage. See a similar, though slightly more critical assessment in Royce J. Ammon, *Global Television and the Shaping of World Politics: CNN, Telediplomacy, and Foreign Policy* (Jefferson, North Carolina and London: McFarland & Company, Inc., 2001).

3) See this classic encounter on *Democracy Now!* 04 Dec. 2007. Http://i2.democracy-now.org/2007/12/4/fact_checking_dobbs_cnn_anchor_lou.

4) His attempt to create what is known in the intelligence field as a "legend" can be found in Barack Obama, *Dreams of My Father: A Story of Race and Inheritance* (New York: Three Rivers Press, 2004). According to a team of *Newsweek* writers, the transformation in identity came during his stint at Occidental College in Los Angeles,. See Richard Wolffe, Jessica Ramirez, and Jeffrey Bartholet, "When Barry Became Barack." *Newsweek* 31 Mar. 2008. Http://www.newsweek.com/id/128633. In his autobiography, Obama writes of his awakening at college among "politically active black students," "Chicanos," and "Marxist professors and structural feminists...." *Dreams*, 100.

5) One of the more prominent "birthers," Pastor James David Manning of ATLAH World Ministry Church in Harlem, has characterized Obama – "The long-legged Mack Daddy" – as an "illegal immigrant" and usurper who should be tried for treason and if found guilty, executed. See *The Alex Jones Show* 26 Jan. 2010. His viral rants caused *YouTube* to exercise its censorship function by banning such posts. Similarly, the Secret Service has visited Manning at his offices in an attempt at intimidation and suppression of free speech. See his letter of complaint to Attorney General Janet Napolitano at *Atlah.org* 12 Jan. 2010. Http://atlah.org/atlahworldwide/?p=4628&cpage=1. See also Manning, "Long Legged Mack Daddy." *YouTube.* Http://www.youtube.com/watch?v=OLkok-NuIojw&feature=related.

6) See the Dobbs, Poe, Martin exchange on *Lou Dobbs Tonight* 23 Jul. 2009. Http://www.youtube.com/watch?v=bvYcFgXCJrE&feature=related. CNN/US president Klein declared the Obama "birther" issue dead and distanced his organization from such coverage by Dobbs. See Chris Ariens, 'Jon Klein on Birthers: "It Seems This Story is Dead"' on *Mediabistro.com* 24 Jul. 2009. Http://www.mediabistro.com/tvnewser/cnn/jon_klein_on_birthers_it_seems_this_story_is_dead_122546.asp.

7) Terry Moran and Melinda Arons, "Lou Dobbs Mulls Presidential Run, Switches Stance on Immigration." *Nightline* 13 Jan. 2010. Http://abcnews.go.com/Nightline/lou-dobbs-mulls-presidential-run-switches-stance-immigration/story?id=9545590. Interview was aired on 26 Jan. 2010 due to special coverage of the Haiti earthquake disaster.

8) See Jerome R. Corsi, *The Late Great U.S.A.: The Coming Merger With Mexico and Canada* (Nashville, Tennessee: WND Books, 2007).

9) John Bryne, "Dobbs' Rating Dive After Reporting on Obama Conspiracy Theory." *Raw Story* 31 Jul. 2009. Http://rawstory.com/blog/2009/07/dobbs-ratings-dive/.

10) Pew Research For the People & the Press, "Internet Overtakes Newspapers as News Outlets." Pew Research Center Publications 23 Dec. 2008. Http://pewresearch.org/pubs/1066/internet-overtakes-newspapers-as-news-source.

11) Rating woes were not unique to *Lou Dobbs Tonight.* As one of the Time Warner "brands," CNN on the whole does not fare well against the competition such as Fox News Channel. Jon Friedman, "Time Warner's Bewkes: Perform or Hit the Road." *MarketWatch* 05 Feb. 2010. Http://www.marketwatch.com/story/time-warners-mantra-

perform-or-hit-the-road-2010-02-05.

12) Angelo Falcón, "Lou Dobbs Is Gone from CNN: Now What? *New American Media* 13 Nov. 2009. Http://news.newamericamedia.org/news/view_article.html?article_id=41441077eb042ec359859b31c322ed7e.

13) Under pressure from high-level members of the military and government establishment such as Richard Helms, Henry Kissinger, and Colin Powell CNN had Arnett repudiate his involvement with the report "Valley of Death" (June 07, 1998) which concerned the illegal use of sarin nerve gas in Laos (1970) as part of the secret OPERATION TAILWIND. He subsequently was fired in April 1999. Producers April Oliver and Jack Smith, who conducted the principal research, also were fired. Jeff Cohen and Norman Soloman, "CNN's 'Tailwind' and Selective Media Retractions." *FAIR* August 1998. Http://www.fair.org/index.php?page=1429. See also Barry Grey, "Pentagon Pressure Behind CNN Firing of Peter Arnett." *World Socialist Web Site* 22 Apr. 1999. Http://www.wsws.org/articles/1999/apr1999/cnn-a22.shtml.

14) CNN/US version runs for a full hour while on CNN International the program is thirty minutes in length.

15) Elizabeth Jensen, "Connie Chung to Leave CNN." *Los Angeles Times* 26 Mar. 2003. Http://articles.latimes.com/2003/mar/26/business/fi-chung26.

16) Rather was put out to pasture by CBS, the self-described "Tiffany Network" in mid-2006 after forty-four years of service, twenty-four of which were as anchor. Rebecca Leung, "Dan Rather Signs Off." *CBSNEWS* 20 Jun. 2006. Http://www.cbsnews.com/stories/2006/06/19/national/main1727285.shtml.

17) "Full Transcript of Sanchez Remarks." *Democratic Underground.com.* Http://www.democraticunderground.com/discuss/duboard.php?az=view_all&address=389x9242751.

18) *United Nations Foundation.* Http://www.unfoundation.org/press-center/fact-sheets/.

19) Joseph Abrams, "Obama's Science Czar Considered Forced Abortions, Sterilization as Population Growth Solutions." *FoxNews.com* 21 Jul. 2009. Http://www.foxnews.com/politics/2009/07/21/obamas-science-czar-considered-forced-abortions-sterilization-population-growth/.

20) *Charlie Rose* 01 Apr. 2008. Http://www.charlierose.com/view/interview/9019.

21) Associated Press, "Ted Turner wants Yellowstone bison for his Montana ranch." *Missoulian* 19 Aug. 2009. Http://www.missoulian.com/news/state-and-regional/article_e79c2d0a-8cc3-11de-b22f-001cc4c03286.html.

22) See the documentary film *The Goebbels Experiment.* Lutz Hachmeister, dir. (First Run Features 2006). Kenneth Branagh reads from the 1924-1945 diaries kept by the Nazi minister of propaganda against archival footage, much of it heretofore unseen by the public.

23) Francis Fukuyama, *The End of History and the Last Man* (New York: Free Press, 1992).

24) *Project for the New American Century* Website. Http://www.newamericancentury.org/.

25) Peter Engardio, ed., *Chindia: How China and India are Revolutionizing Global Business* (New York: McGraw-Hill, 2006).

26) Ken Wills and Jim Wolf, "China: U.S. Arms Sales to Taiwan Hurt National Security." *Reuters* 31 Jan. 2010. Http://www.reuters.com/article/idUSTRE60T07W20100131.

27) CNN U.S., "Americans See China As Economic Threat." *CNN.com* Http://www.cnn.com/2009/US/11/17/obama.china/index.html.

28) Peter Lee, "China Feels US-Iran Fallout." *Asia Times Online* 13 Feb. 2010. Http://www.atimes.com/atimes/Middle_East/LB13Ak03.html.

29) Andrew Jacobs, "Tiger Farms in China Feed Thirst for Parts." *New York Times* 12 Feb. 2010. Http://www.nytimes.com/2010/02/13/world/asia/13tiger.html?hp.

30) Harry Wu, *Troublemaker: One Man's Crusade Against China's Cruelty* (New York: Times Books, 1996).

31) *China Digital Times*. Http://chinadigitaltimes.net/.

32) Bill Moyers, "Interview with Dr. Vandana Shiva." *Now* 05 Sep. 2003. Http://www.pbs.org/now/transcript/transcript_shiva.html.

33) Jagdish Bhagwati, *In Defense of Globalization* (New York: Oxford University Press, 2007).

34) Atul Vashistha and Avinash Vashistha, *The Offshore Nation: Strategies for Success in Global Outsourcing and Offshoring* (New York: McGraw-Hill, 2006).

35) *American Jobs*. Dir. Greg Spotts. The Disinformation Company 2005.

36) *Up In the Air*. Dir. Jason Reitman. DreamWorks 2009.

37) Kenichi Ohmae, *The Borderless World: Power and Strategy in the Interlinked World Economy* (New York: Harper Business, 1990).

38) *Charlie Rose* 02 Oct. 2007. Http://www.charlierose.com/view/interview/8721; *Tavis Smiley* 09 Apr. 2009. Http://www.pbs.org/kcet/tavissmiley/archive/200904/20090409_nilekani.html; *Daily Show* 18 Mar. 2009. Http://thedaily show.com/watch/wed-march-18-2009/nandan-nilekani.

39) Thomas Friedman, "Nandan Nilekani." *Time* 30 Apr. 2006. Http://www.time.com/time/magazine/article/0,9171,1187483,00.html.

40) Nandan Nilekani, *Imagining India: The Idea of a Renewed Nation* (New York: Penguin Press, 2009).

41) Ibid., 459.

42) John Harlow, "Billionaire Club in Bid to Curb Overpopulation." *TimesOnline* 24 May 2009. http://www.timesonline.co.uk/tol/news/world/us_and_americas/article6350303.ece.

43) Alex Weprin, "Ali Velshi Gets New Domestic Role at CNN, Adds CNNI Program." *Media Bistro* 03 Nov. 2011. Http://www.mediabistro.com/tvnewser/ali-velshi-gets-new-domestic-role-at-cnn-adds-cnni-program_b96174.

44) *Frontline*: "The Card Game" 24 Nov. 2009. Lowell Bergman & Oriana Zill de Granados, writer/producer. Http://www.pbs.org/wgbh/pages/frontline/creditcards/. Mehta discusses the over $180 million in quarterly profit he generated while CEO with Providian Financial.

45) Alex Berenson, "14 Charged With Insider Trading in Galleon Case." *New York Times* 05 Nov. 2009. Http://www.nytimes.com/2009/11/06/business/06insider.html?_r=1.

46) Allison Kilkenny, "Kucinich Hands Kashkari His Own Ass." *Allison Kilkenny: Daily News & Opinion* 15 Nov. 2008. Http://allisonkilkenny.wordpress.com/2008/11/15/kucinich-hands-kashkari-his-own-ass/. Article links to C-SPAN video of the encounter on YouTube.

47) Laura Blumenfeld, "The $700 Billion Man." *Washington Post* 06 Dec. 2009. Http://www.washingtonpost.com/wp-dyn/content/article/2009/12/04/AR2009120402016.html.

48) Fareed Zakaria, *The Post-American World* (New York: W. W. Norton & Company, 2009), 130.

49) Marie Brenner, "Anatomy of a Siege." *Vanity Fair* (November 2009), 135.

50) *SPP.com* Website. Http://www.spp.gov/.

51) Michel Crozier, Samuel Huntington, Joji Watanuki, *The Crisis of Democracy: Report on the Governability of Democracies to the Trilateral Commission* (New York: New York

University Press, 1975). For an early critique of this open declaration of centralized global control against popular democracy see Holly Sklar, ed. *Trilateralism: The Trilateral Commission and Elite Planning for World Management* (Boston: South End Press, 1980).

52) Samuel P. Huntington, *The Clash of Civilizations and the Remaking of World Order* (New York: Simon & Schuster, 1998).

53) *Architects & Engineers for 9/11 Truth* Website. Http://www.ae911truth.org/.

54) *CNN.com Transcripts* 07 Dec. 2008. Http://transcripts.cnn.com/TRANSCRIPTS/0812/07/fzgps.01.html.

55) Paul Harris, "Fareed Zakaria Suspended From Time and CNN For Plagiarising Content. *The Guardian* 10 Aug. 2011. Http://www.guardian.co.uk/media/2012/aug/10/fareed-zakaria-time-cnn-plagiarising.

56) *Anthrax-War*. Bob Coen and Eric Nadler, dirs. Transformer Films 2009.

57) *Sanjay Gupta MD* Website. Http://www.cnn.com/CNN/Programs/house.call/

58) *Swine Flu ABC* Website, "H1N1 'false pandemic' biggest pharma-fraud of century. avi" 23 Jan. 2010. Http://www.swine-flu-abc.com/html/45188.html.

59) *CNN.com/world* Website. "The Survival Project: One Child At A Time" 06 Jul. 2008. Http://www.cnn.com/SPECIALS/2008/survival.project/.

60) Manfred B. Steger, *Globalization: A Very Short Introduction* (New York: Oxford University Press, 2003), 95-112.

61) David Harvey, *A Brief History of Neoliberalism* (New York: Oxford University Press, 2007), 205.

62) Alexander Cockburn, "CNN and Psyops." *CounterPunch* 26 Mar. 2000. Http://www.counterpunch.org/cnnpsyops.html.

63) *Radar online.com* Website. "Anderson Cooper's CIA Secret" 27 Oct. 2008. Http://www.radaronline.com/exclusives/2006/09/anderson-coopers-cia-secret.php.

64) Two-hour special *We Were Warned: Cyber-Shockwave* featured an "all-star" panel of national security "experts" that war-gamed an all-out attack upon the Internet; yet another example of basic psychology used to heighten paranoia and panic among the population. For CNN promo see "Cyber Attack 'War Game.'" *American Morning* 16 Feb. 2010. Http://www.youtube.com/watch?v=d-T3ZxtBNtA&feature=related. *We Were Warned* aired 21 Feb. 2010.

65) Ben Dimiero & Eric Hananoki, "Inevitable: Fox Hires Lou Dobbs. *Media Matters* 10 Nov. 2010. Http://mediamatters.org/blog/201011100033.

66) Rick Kissell, "CNN Ratings Tumble Farther in May." *Variety* 30 May 2012. Http://www.variety.com/article/VR1118054829.

CHAPTER NINE

Ethnic Cover: Inquiry Into Norman Yoshio Mineta and Post-Racial Profiling

Ethnic Dimension

In *A Pretext For War*, the preeminent authority on the US intelligence apparatus James Bamford notes the carefully scripted, "Hollywood" manner by which the American public was steered into support for the pre-emptive military strike against Iraq that commenced Gulf War II.[1] He argues that the crafted scenario was based upon the 1962 Cuban missile crisis, only this time starring US Secretary of State Colin Powell in place of Adlai Stevenson who had gone before the United Nations Security Council to confront his Soviet counterpart about the presence of nuclear missile sites in Cuba. Bamford credits the secretive White House Iraq Group (WHIG) composed of "high-level administration officials" whose "job was to sell the war to the general public, largely through televised addresses and by selectively leaking the intelligence to the media."[2]

There was one major historical difference, however, between the Cuban missile crisis and the planning that led to the invasion of Iraq in 2003: The select team of White House conspirators that exploited sustained public outrage over the concerted 9/11 attacks reflected the "new" multicultural America that had its genesis in the Civil Rights Movement. That is, unlike the White male Eastern establishment individuals ("Wise Men") that predominated during the Cold War period, by the time George W. Bush was elected president, the political elite class had figured out how to integrate minorities into key positions to present a seemingly more inclusionary image of democratic governance.[3] This in turn enhanced the legitimacy of the ruling regime in the eyes of most Americans, the majority of whom have come to accept the changes in race relations that underwent significant transformation beginning in the 1950s.

In the autobiography by Colin Powell, it is clear that the immigrant roots of his parents and non-White racial identity loom large in his rise through the ranks of the military and subsequent achievements as a civilian.[4] Not only had he served as US Secretary of State (2001-05) under Bush, at one point Powell was discussed seriously as a presidential candidate. His immediate successor Condoleezza Rice was old enough to have attended racially segregated schools as a child in Birmingham, Alabama. The daughter of educators, Rice had lived through the early years of the civil rights movement.[5] Biographical profiles of the former US Secretary of State point to her exceptional talent in both music and academics that flourished within a highly accomplished family and larger African America community environment.[6] Yoshihiro Francis Fukuyama, notorious signatory of the Project For the New American Century (PNAC), met Rice in the early 1980s and presciently told an associate, "You know, we're all going to be working for Condi some day."[7]

To extend the dramatological analogy of the 9/11 plot as set forth by Bamford, it appears that this tragedy was cast with race-specific social actors to help manipulate a demographically diverse audience into backing the invasion of Afghanistan (Operation Enduring Freedom) the very next month to capture alleged terrorist mastermind Osama bin Laden.[8] Operation Iraqi Freedom followed in 2003, engendering an almost nine-year war and occupation by US troops until the end of 2011.

The present chapter is intended to introduce an important but overlooked descriptive and explanatory perspective on 9/11 Studies: The ethnic dimension. The primary reason for the avoidance of race and ethnicity in honest discussions of contemporary power politics is that three decades of political correctness in academia, publishing, and the press has draped perpetrators of certain protected groups in a veil of critical immunity, lest one be branded a bigot, or worse, a "racist."

The singular media moment that put a freeze on questioning the integrity or professional competence of racial minority figures in positions of authority took place on October 11, 1991 before the US Senate Judiciary Committee. It was then that Clarence Thomas as nominee to the US Supreme Court defended himself against accusations of sexual harassment in an emotionally gripping, seemingly extemporaneous denunciation of the treatment he had endured at the hands of the FBI, the press, and the Judiciary Committee itself:

> This is a circus. It's a national disgrace. And from my standpoint, as a black American, as far as I'm concerned, it is a high-tech lynching for uppity blacks who in any way deign to think for themselves, to do for themselves, to have different ideas. And it is a message that unless you kowtow to an old order, this is what will happen to you. You will be lynched, destroyed, caricatured by a committee of the US Senate rather than hung from a tree.[9]

This rhetorically masterful response recalled in an instant the ignoble history of race and racism in US history. Even when viewed today, the well-rehearsed soliloquy by Thomas is riveting for its sheer dramatic force. He not only played the "race card"; Thomas laid down a royal flush before the court of public opinion. His desperate strategy was enough to rescue Thomas from what until that moment had been almost certain defeat. He won confirmation by a narrow margin of votes and has sat as a justice with the US Supreme Court ever since.

It is argued here that Norman Yoshio Mineta, US Secretary of Transportation (2001-06) during the run-up to and aftermath of 9/11, was typecast to fill a highly visible role in a scripted public relations scenario intended to calm public fear over racial profiling, targeted round-ups of Muslims or Arab Americans, and the possible mass internment of civilians. Reassurances uttered by Mineta proved hollow. For while he enacted his assigned public relations part as DOT secretary, civil liberties were trampled upon by an array of government agencies. Most notably, without objection by Mineta, the Transportation Security Administration (TSA) in 2003 was moved from the DOT to the newly created Department of Homeland Security. The TSA has wreaked havoc with constitutionally protected freedoms ever since.

The concept of "ethnic cover" is introduced here to account for the calculatingly cynical casting of non-White actors (albeit with solid credentials and professional experience) in high-visibility roles to create an altogether new and uniquely American historical phenomenon: "Post-racial" multicultural fascism.

The Legend Begins

According to the storyline favored by both the ethnic press and corporate media, the career of Norman Yoshio Mineta began with his steady rise from local independent businessman involved in community service to iconic status as one of the more visible figures to have emerged from the rubble of the concerted attacks against US landmarks on September 11, 2001. The narrative is as familiar and predictable as the catalogue of immigrant sagas memorialized in American popular culture through the past century.

One such contemporary example that foregrounds the role of race in the biographical subject, *Dreams From My Father* (1995), helped launch the political career of an obscure transplanted Chicago lawyer who had adopted the professional name Barack Hussein Obama.[10] A second volume titled *The Audacity of Hope* (2006) helped sell Obama to a public desperate for relief from ruinous wars and precipitous economic decline presided over by President George W. Bush.[11]

Having been vetted, approved, and financed by the private banking establishment and globalist ruling class leadership, the biographically scripted racial identity of Barack Hussein Obama combined with his promise of messianic deliverance was sufficient to win him the US presidency. Like the three presidents that preceded him to office – George W. Bush, Bill Clinton, and George H.W. Bush – intrepid and daring investigative inquiry into the hidden past of Barack Hussein Obama implies strongly that he too enjoyed a special relationship with the world of covert operations, secret societies, and private tutelage. As an example, far-fetched as it might first seem, the well-researched documentary film *Dreams From My Real Father* (2012) presents compelling evidence that Soetoro/Obama is a third-generation intelligence asset.[12]

Contrary to the promise of salvation crafted through sophisticated behavioral science techniques and disseminated by the corporate media through trusted figures like Oprah Winfrey, the Wall Street-controlled Obama administration not only multiplied the theaters of war but also accelerated the process of economic decline and attendant social degeneration. One of the few sober critics of the Obama phenomenon, however, studied the trajectory of his career beginning in early life and concluded that he is a "controlled asset of the Rockefeller family and its allies."[13] Importantly, for many left-liberals of varied ethnic backgrounds including "Asian Americans For Obama '08," this "postmodern coup" meant the transcendence of the race bugaboo that has stuck to the history of the American republic like Tar Baby.[14]

It might be argued that Obama is more Asian Pacific American than African American. For he was socialized as a child in Indonesia and later in Hawaii. His adoptive father was an Indonesian called Lolo Soetoro. "Obama" the synthetic construct illustrates the way in which the "race" concept has been stripped of its liberal-progressive thrust and returned to its original pseudo-scientific use as a classificatory weapon of division and control; but in a far more subtle and canny fashion than that of the more obvious racial supremacists that followed Darwin and Huxley.

Similarly, the Mineta Story fits so neatly and universally into the morphology of the contemporary race/ethnicity narrative that it is as if a mighty public relations firm had scrupulously strung each biographical plot-point together into a flawless necklace of dissimulation. Indeed, it probably is no coincidence that immediately after retiring from public life Mineta was appointed in July 2006 vice-chairman at Hill & Knowlton, the storied public relations giant that maintains close institutional ties to the intelligence community.[15]

Hill & Knowlton perhaps is remembered best for its direct role in engineering public support for the invasion of Iraq (Operation Desert Storm) and Gulf War I. In 1990, the firm fabricated a gruesome story delivered by a Kuwaiti teenager named "Nayirah." Later revealed to be the daughter of Kuwaiti ambassador to the US, Saud bin Nasur Al-Sabah, the fake eyewitness "testified before Congress that she had seen Iraqi soldiers tear premature babies from their incubators, leaving them on the cold hospital floor to die."[16] In the seventy-minute documentary *The Great Conspiracy: The 9/11 News Special You Never Saw* (2004), eminent investigative journalist Barrie Zwicker places the "Nurse Nayirah" deception in line with a documented history of pretexts for war and false-flag attacks blamed on a designated "enemy."[17]

As a veritable fourth branch of government, Hill & Knowlton has an extensive history of dealings with high-level Asian Americans including Anna Chennault of "China Lobby" renown, Tongsun Park with "Korean CIA" connections, and the Rev. Sun Myung Moon of the Unification Church. According to historian Bruce Cummings, both "rice merchant, lobbyist, and bon vivant" Park and self-proclaimed messiah Moon (now deceased), founder of the *Washington Times*, are KCIA-controlled.[18] Robert Parry, award-winning investigative journalist and a reporter with the Associated Press when he broke the Iran-Contra story, has probed even more deeply into the doings of the Moon organization and its under-reported connection to the US-Japan political establishment.[19]

The mother of all research on the Moon organization and its deeper connection to the fascist international is *Gifts of Deceit: Sun Myung Moon, Tongsun Park, and the Korean Scandal* (1980), by Robert Boettcher.[20] The historical origins and institutional lineaments of the right-wing establishment in Asian American culture were laid bare in *Inside the League* (1986), an outstanding study by Scott Anderson and Jon Lee Anderson.[21] This body of literature, largely overlooked in the discussion of contemporary Asian American politics, connects Norman Yoshio Mineta to this ignoble heritage of such US-sponsored "political warfare" creations as the Asian People's Anti-Communist League formed in 1954 through its keystone client states Taiwan and South Korea.

As discussed below, Mineta early on had experience in the field of intelligence in a manner similar to the way Barry Soetoro/Barack Hussein Obama was brought along from the days of his youth in Indonesia and Hawaii along the path that led eventually to the White House.[22] Mineta, in sum, was a supporting cast member in an artfully crafted psychological operation in which race/ethnicity was deployed as a strategic force multiplier in the propaganda war on terrorism internationally and its parallel assault on civil liberties domestically.

Plot Twist

The Mineta Story, however, has a novel twist to it that keeps it from being utterly formulaic: Shortly after the US declaration of war against Japan, his family had been part of the over

100,000 men, women, and children taken from their homes and placed in military-guarded concentration camps situated in barren locations far from major population centers in the west. In the case of the Mineta family, they were transported by rail to Heart Mountain, Wyoming. Their forced removal from the verdant Santa Clara Valley where the immigrant Kunisaku Mineta and "picture bride" wife Kane had settled was the one of the few times he was seen weeping, according to his son.[23]

What today is considered to have been a grave historical "mistake," the mass internment of Japanese Americans is often invoked at times when Constitutional protections are threatened or transgressed upon. Countless documentaries, films, novels, biographies, curricular material, and scholarly work have been produced to the extent that the Internment Narrative has penetrated deep into the consciousness of the American public. As such, in the aftermath of 9/11, civil libertarians across the political spectrum were quick to warn against what today is called "racial profiling."

After their release, the family returned to San Jose and Kunisaku Mineta restarted the insurance business he had established in 1920. The elder Mineta had been serving as a translator for the civil courts when he was recruited into the insurance field despite, by his own admission, having no experience in the area. After completing his studies in business at the University of California while enrolled in the Reserve Officers' Training Corps (ROTC) and then serving as a commissioned officer with US military intelligence in South Korea and Japan (1953-56), Norman Mineta joined the family business, which by its very nature stood as a key institution in the racially segregated life of the Santa Clara Valley Japanese American community.[24] Such insurance operations are privy to detailed financial information, business contracts, family income, and private actuarial information that require the utmost discretion and secrecy be observed.

As a co-ethnic businessman, Mineta *père* would have had access to a detailed inside view of the local Japanese American community at a time when federal agencies used for surveillance were in their infancy (Internal Revenue Service founded 1913), were relatively undeveloped (US Census Bureau founded 1902), or did not exist in their modern form (Federal Bureau of Investigation, 1935). Possession of hard information on family assets real property holdings were necessary to execute the mass dispossession and outright theft visited upon Japanese American communities.

Intelligence Insurance

Apart from their more obvious function, insurance companies have strategic value in the ability to gather intelligence and sensitive information the world over for private security entities, governmental bodies, and multi-layered spy agencies. The international spy network established in the years following World War I by insurance pioneer Cornelius V. Starr gave rise to contemporary financial powerhouse American International Group (AIG). During World War II, Starr ran the ultra-secret Insurance Intelligence Unit code-named X-2 formed by William J. Donovan of the OSS.[25]

Succeeding Starr after his death in 1968 was Maurice R. ("Hank") Greenberg, who served as CEO until 2005 when he was forced to resign. Greenberg was described by a former longtime lieutenant at AIG as having enjoyed a "symbiotic relationship with the intelligence community" (CIA), which presumably continues to the present despite its 2008 "liquidity crisis" and subsequent financial bailout by the public to the tune of $182 billion.[26]

OSS veteran-turned-Wall Street lawyer-turned-CIA director William J. Casey desribed Greenberg – member of both the Council on Foreign Relations and the Trilateral Commission – as a trusted adviser. Like Greenberg, Casey was tainted by scandal as one of the major figures in the Iran-Contra affair, which unfolded during the mid-1980s before conveniently dying in 1987, without having had to testify before a Congressional bipartisan special investigative committee.

This is not to suggest that the family insurance business of odd origins operated by Kunisaku Mineta necessarily was involved in surveillance activity or colluded with the US military or government spy agencies. It is known and well-documented, however, that the identification, round-up, and mass incarceration of Japanese Americans would not have been possible without the complicity of co-ethnic government informants acting in accord with the marching orders issued by larger organizations such as the Japanese American Citizens League (JACL) that willingly supplied intelligence information to the FBI and Office of Naval Intelligence (ONI).[27]

In Los Angeles, for example, the individual who went by the Anglicized name of Tokie Slocum (born Tokutaro Nishimura), headed the so-called "Anti-Axis Committee" intended as a "public relations" move intended to "demonstrate the loyalty of Japanese Americans" or at least those *Nisei* who aided and abetted government attempts to exploit regional, nationality, language, and generational tensions within the larger community for purposes of political control and eventual physical containment.[28] So hated was Slocum, Fred Tayama, Togo Tanaka, and other Los Angeles-based leaders of the JACL that they were "placed on a death list for actively collaborating" with the administration at Manzanar War Relocation Center.[29]

Tellingly, there is a familial relationship between Norman Mineta and perhaps the most reviled figure in Japanese American history. Head of the national JACL Mike Masaoka married his older sister Etsu in 1943.[30] In recent years, perhaps beginning with the publication of the highly critical "Lim Report" in (1990), the reputation of the collaborationist element among *Nisei* has fallen considerably.[31] The JACL had commissioned the report, but then attempted to suppress the document once it was learned that complicity with government intelligence agencies on the part of certain figures within the leadership structure loomed large in the critical study. By contrast, the stand taken by the "resisters" or "renunciates" (often lumped together as "No-No Boys") is viewed far more favorably by many contemporary academicians, filmmakers, and journalists, as seen in the breakthrough documentary produced and directed by Frank Abe, *Conscience and the Constitution* (2001) aired on the Public Broadcasting Service (PBS).[32]

Nisei Spooks

Apart from the cohort of *Nisei* informants, spies, and provocateurs there was a sizable group that was recruited into the Military Intelligence Service (MIS) during World War II. Approximately 6,000 were trained as linguists to translate captured documents, interrogate prisoners of war, intercept Japanese language radio transmissions, and work undercover in enemy-held territory such as the Philippines.[33] Beginning with the occupation of Japan by the US (1945-1952), a few noteworthy *Nisei* intelligence operatives engaged in extra-legal activity ranging from petty racketeering to systematic state-level criminality of the highest order.

Largely ignored or de-emphasized in the scholarship on Japanese Americans, individuals like Keiichi "Kay" Sugahara were major dealmakers in the postwar *"Nichi-Bei kankei"* or "Japan-America relationship." While identified properly as one of the more prominent figures to have arisen from the Japanese American community within Los Angeles, his role as an OSS "operator" and major player in the unseemly history of postwar US-Japan relations is missed entirely. Sugahara, for example, is described only as a member of the "entrepreneurial elites" that were put in place by internment officials to discipline "leftist organizers" and others who defied the forced labor camp regime.[34] More fully, *New York Times* national security reporter Tim Weiner described Sugahara as having been "recruited by the OSS from an internment camp" during the war and involved in a multi-million dollar smuggling operation of tungsten involving legendary *kuromaku* (literally "black curtain" or political fixer) Kodama Yoshio, the CIA, and the Pentagon.[35]

Nisei contemporaries of Sugahara with similarly shadowy roles in the history of postwar America such as Shig Katayama, Taro Fukuda, and Victor Matsui are overlooked in the academic literature concerning Japanese Americans. According to William Blum, for example, Matsui during the late 1950s was involved in such CIA conspiracies as the plot to overthrow Norodom Sihanouk of Cambodia .[36] According to *NameBase*, an authoritative web-based database of cross-listed and hyperlinked books and articles dedicated to figures involved in espionage, corporate criminality, government misconduct, and conspiracies, a Victor Masao Matsui can be placed in numerous political hotspots during the course of his career with the US Foreign Service: Japan 1945-1952; Cambodia 1957-1959; Egypt 1959-1960; Pakistan 1962-1966; Madagascar 1965-1968; Ivory Coast 1970-1973; Zaire 1977-1979.[37]

The present discussion of *Nisei* "spooks" is far from being only of academic interest: As of 2005, Matsui was still active and speaking at "schools, clubs, government and national TV" according to a press release by the Japanese American Veterans Association (JAVA).[38] Such gatherings are ideal opportunities for contemporary propaganda efforts that target the enemy of the moment. Like Mineta, Matsui relies upon accounts of his personal tribulations as a young internee with his family at the Rohwer (Arkansas) War

Relocation Center to establish and maintain the theme of guilt, gratitude, and redemption through sacrifice that have been so effective in American imperial melodrama. Such was the tenor of an appearance Matsui made during "Asian-Pacific Remembrance Month" held at Fort Riley, Kansas; home of the "Big Red One."[39]

Historiography Deficit

The dark careers of Sugahara, Katayama, Fukuda, Matsui, and others expose a glaring weakness in the historiography of Japanese America: The overwhelming analytical weight placed on "The Internment" in historical interpretation has resulted in a one-sided view that privileges victim status over that of perpetrator. Through the routine exercise of community memory and formal scholarship, "The Internment" has ossified into a Foucauldian *épisteme* that has allowed for the imposition of a far more comprehensive system of civilian concentration camps in the present. While Executive Order 9066 signed by Roosevelt that spelled the destruction of the mainland Japanese American community is often cited, it was Executive Order 12148 issued by President Jimmy Carter in 1979 that set into motion the current system of mass roundup and indefinite detention.

Most of the material published or otherwise produced about the internment of Japanese Americans during World War II fails to connect it with the installation of massive centers that have been readied for large segments of the civilian population. By now, even a mainstream biography on the "Bush dynasty" notes, "In 2006, the Army Corps of Engineers awarded $385 million contract to Halliburton subsidiary Kellogg, Brown & Root for building 'temporary immigration detention centers.'"[40] It is not simply a matter of quibbling over historical interpretation that is here at stake. Rather, the Internment-centered view of Japanese American history has resulted in an analytical blind spot that has allowed criminality of the highest order to go unchecked in the present. The perversion and cynical exploitation of this one sordid episode of US national history has concealed state-level crimes that have eroded the very foundation of the American constitutional republic.

As seen in the wartime derring-do of Sugahara, Katayama, and most spectacularly, Taro Fukuda, Mineta was not the first

Japanese American to have worked in the intelligence trade. His years of meritorious service to holders of largely ill-gotten family wealth was rewarded by being presented the Presidential Medal of Freedom in 2006. The following year the government of Japan presented Mineta with the Order of the Rising Sun. While Fukuda died under highly suspicious circumstances, both Katayama and Sugahara prospered individually over the decades following World War II. Sugahara through his shipping business came to be known as the "Nisei Onassis" while Katayama amassed wealth enough to write checks from a Beverly Hills, California address in support of right-wing American political candidates.

The "Onassis" nickname for Sugahara might be more appropriate than imagined. The relationship between long-distance transportation firms such as that headed by Aristotle Onassis and highly profitable "black" operations is well documented. Onassis apparently enjoyed a working relationship with two veteran dope smugglers of the OSS, Paul E. Helliwell and Mitchell WerBell; names that frequently appear in the literature on "parapolitics."[41]

In pulling aside the curtain of public relations design that has draped the past of Norman Yoshio Mineta, it is revealed that he early on was steeped in the culture of discretion and secrecy as practiced by the insurance firm run by his father. Their agency would have maintained a veritable Domesday Book of personal assets and real estate holdings kept by the more prominent members of the local Japanese American community who in those days could trust no one but of their own to guard family treasures.

His experience as an officer in US Army intelligence in South Korea and Japan provided Mineta a closer look into the inner workings of total institutions like the military. At the height of the Cold War, East Asia was a hotbed of political intrigue among the American military, quasi-civilian operations like the Civil Air Transport (CAT), and the CIA during its first decade after its formation in 1947. After graduating from Reserve Officers' Training Corps (ROTC) at the University of California Mineta found himself in an administrative setting amidst Communist and nationalist insurgencies against which "secret wars" were waged alongside unsavory allies.[42]

In Japan, US occupation authorities slipped back into power prewar ultra-right figures such as Kodama Yoshio, Sasakawa

Ryoichi, and Kishi Nobusuke to buffer the rise of the Soviet Union and China. The Chinese Revolution gave even more cause for American foreign policy intellectuals such as George F. Kennan to argue for the return to power of the anti-communist fascist ruling class, however unsavory.[43] In South Korea, where Mineta also was posted, the US has backed a succession of military dictatorships in the name of political stability and the preservation of fledgling putative democracies against the military threat posed by Moscow and Beijing. In truth, a substantial body of scholarship exists, largely ignored by family foundation-controlled academia (e.g. Ford, Carnegie, Rockefeller) that credit the illustrious private banking families and their well-placed minions for both the beginnings and eventual triumph of Bolshevism and revolutionary movements in China, culminating in the one-party totalitarian state established as the prototype for the new world order being ushered in by these self-same bankers.[44]

Tapped Lackey

Such direct exposure to the shadow world of *realpolitik* on an international scale would serve Mineta well as he moved up through the hierarchy of secrecy and circumspection while in service to the state. In the aftermath of what many established researchers and citizens organizations refer to as the staged terror events of 9/11, his socialization into a business milieu that requires the keeping of confidences while circulating widely among current and prospective clients makes it understandable that he was identified by talent scouts and then "tapped" for progressively higher levels of political and corporate functions. His early childhood spent in captivity by the US government and encounters with residual anti-Japanese racism in the aftermath of the war in the Pacific made Mineta ever-eager to please his corporate and political patrons.

His political career began in 1967 by being appointed to a vacant city council seat in San Jose, California. He was elected mayor in 1971. Mineta served in the US House of Representatives from 1975 to 1995 during the rise to international prominence of the Silicon Valley region that was home to Pentagon-related information technology corporations and an array of robust start-up companies that caught the fancy of venture capitalists and

Wall Street institutional investors. Tellingly, he was chair of the Transportation and Public Works Committee from1992 to 1994. In 2001, San Jose International Airport was renamed "Norman Y. Mineta San Jose International Airport" in honor of the money and investment capital he helped steer into the area.

In 1995, he took a break from public service by abandoning his Congressional seat in midterm to hire on as vice-president with full-service weapons contractor Lockheed Martin (with deep Silicon Valley roots), a major recipient of Department of Defense largesse. Mineta was the first Asian American to hold a Cabinet post when he was rotated in as US Secretary of Commerce under President Bill Clinton in 2000. The following year, the succeeding Republican administration of George W. Bush brought back the former Congressman and private industry executive as Secretary of Transportation for the capstone of his career as a high level functionary for the postwar corporatist class.

As a political appointee, Mineta fit the professional profile. William Hartung notes that, "more than half a dozen important policy posts in the Bush administration were filled by Lockheed Martin executives, lobbyists, or lawyers."[45] Consistent with a personal history that began with US military intelligence decades earlier, the Transportation Security Administration (TSA) was rolled out during his watch following the airborne terror attacks of September 11, 2001.

After a decent interval following the dubious conclusions arrived at by the National Commission on Terrorist Attacks Upon the United States (9/11 Commission) and the controversy that its official report (2004) precipitated, Mineta retired from government service in July 2006 and was rewarded for decades of meritorious public service by immediately sliding into an executive position with Hill & Knowlton; a known institutional home to many "former" CIA officials. Despite the critical almost minute-by-minute eyewitness account he provided during his testimony on May 23, 2003 before the 9/11 Commission, these first-hand observations were not included in the final published report.[46]

Deep PEOC

The professional ascent of Mineta led him finally to that fateful date of September 11, 2001. On that morning he was taken out of a meeting at his office and then escorted to the Presidential Emergency Operations Center (PEOC) located in the East Wing of the White House. Before leaving his office, he claims to have seen on television the second plane (United Airlines Flight #175) hit 2 World Trade Center, the South Tower. Once safely relocated in the PEOC, Mineta witnessed a damning exchange between Vice-President Dick Cheney and a staff member who was reporting an aircraft closing in on the Pentagon. In testimony before the 9/11 Commission on May 23, 2003, Mineta recounted the following:

> During the time that the airplane was coming in to the Pentagon, therewas a young man who would come in and say to the Vice President, "The plane is 50 miles out." "The plane is 30 miles out." And when it got down to "the plane is 10 miles out," the young man also said to the Vice President, "Do the orders still stand?" And the Vice President turned andwhipped his neck around and said, "Of course the orders still stand. Haveyou heard anything to the contrary?[47]

His account cast Cheney – notorious for his extensive history of professional devilry that began during the Nixon administration – in a highly incriminating light according to a multitude of sources ranging from British social scientist Nafeez Mossadeq Ahmed to veteran "deep history" researcher Peter Dale Scott.[48] David Ray Griffin, a prominent critic within the community of scholars pursuing a more complete and truthful accounting of the terror attacks, has contributed ten books and many more damning articles on the events of 9/11.[49] In addition, a good number of professionals from diverse fields have joined together under the umbrella organization "9/11 Truth"; organizations such as "Architects and Engineers for 9/11 Truth" based in San Francisco, California.[50]

Mineta already had been positioned by administration planners to act as ethno-racial cover for government round-ups of Arab Americans. While attending a Cabinet meeting the day after 9/11, Congressman David Bonior of Michigan voiced (probably rehearsed) his concern to Commander-in-Chief George W. Bush that the large Arab American population in his state feared racial profiling. In a video interview (2006), Mineta paraphrased the (probably canned) response to Bonior by Bush: "The president said, 'David, you are absolutely correct, and we don't want happening to them what happened to Norm in 1942.'" [51] This staged exchange is right out of the playbook kept by public relations firms such as Hill & Knowlton. With the rigidity of his physical bearing and his doddering performance style, the well-worn tale as told by Mineta in the video is less than convincing.

Political Fixer

Over a decade prior to his post-9/11 public promise that no one group would be singled out through racial profiling, Mineta proved his worth as a Cabinet minority hireling in the furor that arose from the Wen Ho Lee spy case. Shortly after he was appointed Secretary of Commerce on July 20, 2000, Mineta gave a speech to the Organization of Chinese Americans to calm down the well-to-do attendees that were agitated by allegations of espionage that appeared to target co-ethnic scientists such as Lee.

It was at this annual convention of the OCA in Atlanta on July 29, 2000 that Mineta spoke with Alberta Lee, the daughter of the accused researcher who in 1980 had transferred to the top-secret X Division at the Los Alamos National Laboratories (LANL). He gave reassurances that "her father was not targeted because of his race and encouraged her to send that message to the Asian American community, which had threatened to withhold political donations to the Democratic National Committee."[52]

DNC chair Ron Brown already had proven successful at tapping into certain pockets of the Asian American community to raise money for the Clinton-Gore campaign and the political machine did not want to alienate this newly discovered source of revenue. Mineta was the perfect emissary to help calm the fears of fellow Asian Americans that had legitimate fears of political persecution. Mineta talked up the fact that a number of Asian Pacific Americans – seventy or so – had been brought into the administration and pointed out that the Small Business Administration had granted loans to APA-owned companies at higher levels over the previous year.

On the tenth anniversary of 9/11, the prestigious NHK (*Nippon Hōsō Kyōkai*) national public broadcasting organization of Japan aired a 100-minute documentary that featured internationally recognized movie star Ken Watanabe.[53] The actor traveled to different sites in the US to learn of the impact of the *"terror jiken"* (terrorist incident) on Americans. Its main purpose, however, was to introduce the concept of "racial profiling" (*jinshu purofaringu*) to a society that is relatively homogeneous. Moreover, there remains significant skepticism among the Japanese public concerning the government-approved 9/11 storyline. In 2009, Diet member Fujita Yukihisa publicly connected the orchestrated offensive of September 2001 with the "war on terror" that followed and wrote a book on the controversy.[54] The power of celebrity embodied by Watanabe was deployed by NHK to reassure his countrymen that 47,000 US troops that occupy Japan are necessary for its military defense.

In the documentary, Watanabe interviews Mineta about the attacks of 9/11and skillfully weaves in a discussion of his family origins Japan. At a choreographed press conference, following the emotionally charged events of 9/11, Secretary Mineta is shown as a calming influence on a fearful American public. Again, he invokes his personal history as a Japanese American concentration camp internee:

> The Arab American and Muslim American community are treated with the same dignity and the same respect afforded every citizen of the United States of America. And I know first hand about being judged by one's looks and by one's skin color. My own history as an American who by accident of birth is of Japanese ancestry is filled with the strength and determination of my parents and with the stories of the injustices that we as Japanese Americans faced.

Cutting back to the personal interview with Watanabe, Mineta reiterates, "Racial profiling was not a basis for security. And that came from ... as a result of my own personal experience."

Internment Redux

A decade after 9/11 Mineta has proven true to his word: There is no officially sanctioned racial profiling done by the TSA at the airport as such. Instead, *all* Americans and every traveler in the US are held under universal suspicion regardless of race, ethnicity, or gender: young or old, wheelchair bound or able bodied. Everyone is run through invasive and dangerously unhealthful full-body backscatter x-ray devices pushed by former Director of Homeland Security and co-author of USAPATRIOT ACT Michael Chertoff while he was still head of the newly created federal agency charged with tracking and tracing the American population under the pretext of safeguarding the public against imminent terrorist attack. After he left his government post, the consulting firm formed by Chertoff represented Rapiscan Systems; one of the principal suppliers of the very equipment that has been declared a threat to physical health, with high levels of radiation exposure linked to a "cancer cluster" among TSA employees, by medical investigators at the University of California, Johns Hopkins, and Columbia University.[55] Chertoff in specific had not registered as a lobbyist among the majority of others that formerly had worked as "lawmakers, congressional aides, and federal employees" only later to be hired by scanner-technology companies.[56]

Rapiscan Systems, based in Los Angeles, California enjoys lucrative government and corporate contracts thanks to the social panic created by the defense establishment and related civilian law enforcement firms that have benefitted from the budgetary largesse sanctioned by the US Congress since the 9/11 attacks on American soil. Rapiscan is a division of OSI Systems, Inc., whose chairman and CEO is named Deepak Chopra; not to be confused with the mystical medical media personality by the same name. Chopra of the harmful Rapiscan backscatter-radiation body scanners enjoys a special relationship with President Barack Hussein Obama, according to a letter of concern from research scientists at the University of California, San Francisco, addressed to Obama science czar John P. Holdren.[57] Along with other globalist corporations such as PepsiCo, GE, and United Technologies, Chopra accompanied the chief executive on the three-day trade mission to the land of his birth stating, "There is substantial opportunity to improve the trade relations with India for mutual economic gain."[58] Like the 9/11 attacks, the government of India installed the intrusive scanners in airports after what some have claimed to be the staged Mumbai attack in 2008.

Mineta was hired as senior vice-president Lockheed Martin in 1995, held shares in the defense giant and was granted stock options as part of a compensation plan that was in force even after his return to government service as Transportation secretary.[59] Once he was safely ensconced in his public relations job at Hill & Knowlton after providing symbolic reassurance to a population made apprehensive and suspicious of the centralized control grid being imposed by the military-industrial "cryptocracy," Lockheed Martin began raking in vast sums of money from the TSA, such as the $72 million contract to supply its "passenger screening and security equipments at airports across the east and central United States."[60]

Behind the public presentation of self as the personal protector of Arab and Muslim Americans and guarantor of civil liberties, Mineta more honestly stood as ethnic cover for a system of policing far more extensive and rationalized than that first tested on his own people during the 1940s. In the region of the country from which he hails, the Northern California branch of the American Civil Liberties Union and Asian Law Caucus based in San Francisco filed a Freedom of Information Act (FOIA) request with US Attorney General Eric Holder to obtain documents supporting its claim that the FBI was engaged in "domestic intelligence practices including the use of informants and infiltrators (such as those reportedly used in gyms, community centers and mosques), the FBI Junior Agent Program's recruitment of Muslim and Arab American children, and investigation of Muslin leaders and imams in northern California."[61] In the person of Norman Yoshio Mineta, the ignoble historical memory he embodies was turned on its head and used to bring the wider society into a far more dangerous level of militarized state control. A comprehensive report by the American Civil Liberties Union issued in late 2011 exposed a so-called "domain management" program by the FBI that "included mapping and gathering intelligence on racial and ethnic communities."[62]

With the December 2011 Congressional passage of the National Defense Authorization Act for 2012 that allows for the "indefinite detention" of American citizens, the career of Norman Yoshio Mineta – former concentration camp inmate and now-retired servant of the military corporatist system – has come full circle. If the mounting volumes of investigative articles, books, recorded conference proceedings, and video documentaries pertaining to the events of September 11, 2001 are accurate, in this signal moment in the history of Anglo-American empire, Mineta will be remembered for his complicity in a cabal that promises to radically redraw the geopolitical map for the benefit of the An-glo-American global banking establishment.

As part of this centrally controlled geopolitical entity called the "new world order," the US is the last remaining piece to fall into place, according to long-range globalist planners that have engineered recurrent economic crises, world wars, subversion, and staged events such as 9/11 to bring the masses to heel and make them beg for one-world governance, headed by supranational bodies, to provide financial stability (World Bank; International Monetary Fund), political order (United Nations), food (Monsanto; Cargill), spiritual sustenance (the Vatican), and propaganda (CNN). For those remaining Americans that dare resist the political economic takeover of the central banking cartel the leaked US Department of the Army document "Civilian Inmate Labor Program" (effective 14 February 2005) provides the specifics for dealing with dissidents, protestors, and foes of the new world order system.[63]

Endnotes

1) James Bamford, *A Pretext For War: 9/11, Iraq, and the Abuse of America's Intelligence Agencies* (New York: Anchor Books, 2005), 367.

2) Bamford, 318.

3) Walter Issacson and Evan Thomas, *Wise Men: Six Friends and the World They Made* (New York: Simon & Schuster, 1986).

4) Colin Powell with Joseph E. Persico, *My American Journey* rev. ed. (New York: Ballantine Books, 2003).

5) Condoleezza Rice, *Extraordinary, Ordinary People: A Memoir of Family* (New York: Crown Archetype, 2010).

6) Antonia Felix, *Condi: The Condoleezza Rice Story* (New York: Newmarket Press, 2002).

7) James Mann, *Rise of the Vulcans: The History of Bush's War Cabinet* (New York: Penguin Books, 2004), 149.

8) It has been claimed in numerous sources that Osama bin Laden was an American intelligence asset. His CIA identity is reported to have been "Tim Osman" or "Ossman." Videotape footage of bin Laden taking credit for the 9/11 debacle is thought by experts to have been faked. See David Ray Griffin, *Debunking 9/11 Debunking: An Answer to Popular Mechanics and other Defenders of the Official Conspiracy Theory* (Northampton, Massachusetts: Olive Branch Press, 2007), 128. Also, David Ray Griffin, *Osama Bin Laden: Dead or Live?* (Northampton, Massachusetts: Olive Branch Press, 2009).

9) An excellent piece that originally aired on *PBS NewsHour* reported by Roger Mudd presents testimony by both Clarence Thomas and his accuser Anita Hill. "Clarence Thomas: Supreme Court Nomination Hearings from *PBS NewsHour* and EMK Institute." YouTube. Https://www.youtube.com/watch?v=G3n-Sa0B2s8. Accessed 08.14.12.

10) Barack Obama, *Dreams From My Father: A Story of Race and Inheritance* (New York: Times Books, 1995).

11) Barack Obama, *The Audacity of Hope: Thoughts on Reclaiming the American Dream* (New York: Crown, 2006).

12) *Dreams of My Real Father: A Story of Reds and Deception.* Joel Gilbert, dir. Highway 61 Entertainment, 2012.

13) Webster Griffin Tarpley, *Barack H. Obama: The Unauthorized Biography* (Joshua Tree, California: Progressive Press, 2008), 238.

14) Webster Griffin Tarpley, *Obama: The Postmodern Coup* (Joshua Tree, California: Progressive Press, 2008).

15) Johan Carlise, "Public Relationships: Hill & Knowlton, Robert Gray, and the CIA." *Covert Action Quarterly* (Spring 1993). Http://mediafilter.org/MFF/Hill&Knowlton. html.

16) Karen S. Miller, *The Voice of Business: Hill & Knowlton and Postwar Public Relations* (Chapel Hill and London: University of North Carolina Press, 1999), 182.

17) *The Great Conspiracy: The 9/11 News Special You Never Saw.* Barrie Zwicker, dir. 2450 Video Distribution, 2004. See also, Barrie Zwicker, *Towers of Deception: The Media Cover-Up of 9/11* (Gabriola Island, British Columbia: New Society Publishers, 2006).

18) Bruce Cummings, *Korea's Place in the Sun: A Modern History* (New York: W. W. Norton & Company, 1997), 446-7.

19) Robert Parry, *Secrecy & Privilege: Rise of the Bush Dynasty From Watergate to Iraq* (Arlington, Virginia: The Media Consortium, Inc., 2004). Parry is a Democratic Party partisan and as such aims most of his criticism at Republicans. Nonetheless, via his *Consortiumnews.com* website he regularly provides is a wealth of valuable information and analysis on the inner workings of Washington political intrigue.

20) Robert Boettcher with Gordon L. Freedman, *Gifts of Deceit: Sun Myung Moon, Tongsun Park, and the Korean Scandal* (New York: Holt, Rinehart and Winston, 1980).

21) Scott Anderson and Jon Lee Anderson, *Inside the League: The Shocking Exposé of How Terrorists, Nazis, and Latin American Death Squads Have Infiltrated the World Anti-Communist League* (New York: Dodd, Mead & Company, 1986).

22) Jerome Corsi, *Where's the Birth Certificate?: the Case That Barack Obama Is Not Eligible to Be President* (Washington, DC: WND Books, 2011).

23) Academy of Achievement. "From Internment to the Halls of Congress." Interview 03 Jun. 2006. Http://www.achievement.org/autodoc/page/min0int-2.

24) "Guide to the Norman Mineta Papers." Norman Mineta Papers, MSS-1996-02-17, San José State University Library Special Collections & Archives, 3.

25) Mark Fritz, "Under Coverage." *Contingencies* May/June 2001, 18. For details of the relationship between Donovan and Starr see Sterling Seagrave & Peggy Seagrave, *Gold Warriors: America's Secret Recovery of Yamashita's Gold* (London & New York: Verso, 2003), 268.

26) Ron Shelp with Al Ehrbar, *Fallen Giant: The Amazing Story of Hank Greenberg and the History of AIG* (Hoboken, New Jersey: John Wiley & Sons, Inc., 2006), 10.

27) Deborah K. Lim, "The Activities and Relationships with Government Agencies Prior to December 7, 1941" in *Research Report Prepared for Presidential Select Committee on JACL Resolution #7* (aka "The Lim Report"), 1990. Http://www.resisters.com/study/ LimPartIA.htm#IA2.

28) Bill Hosokawa, *JACL in Quest of Justice: The History of the Japanese American Citizens League* (New York: William Morrow and Company, Inc., 1982), 140. It should be noted that Hosokawa himself was not a disinterested chronicler.

29) Lon Kurashige, *Japanese American Celebration and Conflict: A History of Ethnic Identity and Festival in Los Angeles, 1934-1990* (Berkeley and Los Angeles: University of California Press, 2002), 75.

30) J. K. Yamamoto, "Etsu Masaoka Remembered at JACL Convention." *Rafu Shimpo* 11 Jul. 15. Http://rafu.com/news/2011/07/etsu-masaoka-remembered-at-jacl-convention/.

31) Deborah K. Lim, "Research Report Prepared For Presidential Select Committee on JACL Resolution #7 (aka "The Lim Report"), 1990. Complete and uncensored document found at http://www.resisters.com/study/LimTOC.htm.

32) Frank Abe, dir., *Conscience and the Constitution*. Resisters.com, 2001. Http://www.pbs.org/itvs/conscience/.

33) Tad Ichinokuchi, ed., *John Aiso and the M.I.S: Japanese-American Soldiers in the Military Intelligence Service, World War II* (Los Angeles: Military Intelligence Service Club of Southern California, 1988). Privately printed.

34) Hayashi, Brian Masaru. *Democratizing the Enemy: The Japanese American Internment* (Princeton and Oxford: Princeton University Press, 2004), 102.

35) Tim Weiner, *Legacy of Ashes: The History of the CIA* (New York: Anchor, 2008), 664.

36) William Blum, *Killing Hope: US Military & CIA Interventions Since World War II*, 2nd ed. (London: Zed Books, 2003), 135. See also Kenton J. Clymer, *The United States and Cambodia, 1870-1969: From Curiosity to Confrontation* (New York: Routledge, 2004), 72.

37) *NameBase*, "Matsui Victor Masao." Http://www.namebase.org/xmas/Victor-Masao-Matsui.html.

38) Japanese American Veterans Association press release 27 Jul. 2005. Http://www.javadc.org/Press%20release%2007-27-05%20JAVA%20Speakers%20Bureau.htm.   It should be noted JAVA maintains an office on K Street in the heart of Washington, DC.

39) Katherine Rosario, "Japanese American Veteran Shares WWII Story." *News Viewer* Fort Riley, Kansas 02 Jun. 2011. Http://www.riley.army.mil/NewsViewer.aspx?id=5073.

40) Russ Baker, *Family of Secrets: The Bush Dynasty, The Powerful Forces That Put It In the White House, and What Their Influence Means For America* (New York: Bloomsbury Press, 2009), 483.

41) Peter Evans, *Nemesis: Aristotle Onassis, Jackie O, and the Love Triangle That Brought Down the Kennedys* (New York: HarperCollins, 2005), 252-55.

42) John Prados, *Presidents' Secret Wars: CIA and Pentagon Covert Operations From World War II Through the Persian Gulf*, rev. ed. (Chicago: Elephant Paperbacks, 1996).

43) Howard B. Schonberger, *Aftermath of War: Americans and the Remaking of Japan, 1945-1952* (Kent, Ohio: Kent State University Press, 1989).

44) While in residence at the Hoover Institution, British-born, US naturalized economist Antony C. Sutton wrote a pioneering series monographs on the funding by bankers of US enemies. Because of his embarrassing findings, Sutton was forced to leave due to political pressure. Antony C. Sutton, *National Suicide: Military Aid to the Soviet Union* (Stanford, California: Hoover Institution on War, Revolution and Peace, 1968-73). See also, *Wall Street and the Bolshevik Revolution* (New Rochelle, New York: Arlington House, 1974); *Wall Street and the Rise of Hitler* (Seal Beach, California: '76 Press, 1976).

45) William D. Hartung, *Prophets of War: Lockheed Martin and the Making of the Military-Industrial Complex* (New York: Nation Books, 2011), 192.

46) The transcript of the Mineta testimony can be found online from multiple sources and video material can be accessed on YouTube and other websites.

47) David Ray Griffin, "9/11 Contradictions: When Did Cheney Enter the Underground Bunker?" *The Canadian* 22 Jan. 2008. Http://www.agoracosmopolitan.com/home/Frontpage/2008/01/22/02147.html.

48) Nafeez Mosaddeq Ahmed, *The War On Freedom: How and Why America Was Attacked September 11, 2001* (Joshua Tree, California: Tree of Life Publications, 2002); Peter Dale Scott, *The Road to 9/11: Wealth, Empire, and the Future of America* (Berkeley and Los Angeles: University of California Press, 2007).

49) David Ray Griffin, *The New Pearl Harbor: Disturbing Questions About the Bush Administration and 9/11* (Northampton, Massachusetts: Olive Branch Press, 2004).

50) See *9/11 Truth.org* and its links to related websites maintained by diverse professional groups including *Architects and Engineers for 9/11 Truth.* Http://www.911truth. org/.

51) Norman Y. Mineta Interview, "From Internment Camp to the Halls of Congress." *Academy of Achievement* 03 Jun. 2006 (Los Angeles, California). Http://www.achievement.org/autodoc/page/min0int-8. Primary sponsor for the Academy is the Catherine B. Reynolds Foundation. Among "Platinum Patrons" is the Kingdom of Bahrain and The Carlyle Group. Other sponsors include global corporatists the likes of Mexican magnate Carlos Slim Helú (reportedly the richest man in the world), Philip F. Anschutz, and Mimi Haas.

52) Paul Sperry, "Cabinet Head Met With Wen Ho Kin." *WorldNetDaily* 25 Oct. 2000. Http://www.wnd.com/?pageId=7311.

53) *Watanabe Ken: America wo Yuku.* NHK World TV 11 Sep. 2011.

54) Heiner Buecker, "Major 9/11 Breakthrough in Japan, Spectacular Support for Yukihisa Fujita." *911 Truth.org* 25 Apr. 2009. Http://www.911truth.org/article.php?story=20090425150642797.

55) Paul Joseph Watson, "TSA To Test Body Scanner Operators For Radiation Exposure." *Prison Planet.com* 16 Jan. 2012. Http://www.prisonplanet.com/tsa-to-test-body-scanner-operators-for-radiation-exposure.html.

56) Dan Eggen, "Firms' Lobbying Push Comes Amid Rancor On TSA Use of Airport Full-Body Scanners." *Washington Post* 24 Dec. 2010. Http://www.washingtonpost.com/wp-dyn/content/article/2010/12/23/AR2010122304412.html.

57) Richard Knox, "Scientists Question Safety of New Airport Scanners." *NPR* 17 May 2010. Http://www.npr.org/templates/story/story.php?storyId=126833083.

58) Daniel Tencer, "Body Scanner CEO Accompanied Obama to India." *The Raw Story* 21 Nov. 2010. Http://www.rawstory.com/rs/2010/11/21/body-scanner-ceo-obama-india/.

59) Suzanne Herel, "Contract Awarded to Lockheed Where He Has Shares, Options." *San Francisco Chronicle* 23 Jul. 2002. Http://articles.sfgate.com/2002-07-23/news/17554968_1_lockheed-martin-coast-guard-united-airlines.

60) Paul Joseph Watson, "Lockheed Martin Wins $72 Million Contract to Install Body Scanners." *Prison Planet.com* 29 Jul. 2011. Http://www.infowars.com/lockheed-martin-wins-72-million-contract-to-install-body-scanners/.

61) "ACLU and Asian Law Caucus Seek Records on FBI Surveillance of Mosques and Use of Informants in Northern California." American Civil Liberties Union press release 09 Mar. 2010. Http://www.aclu.org/racial-justice-religion-belief/aclu-and-asian-law-caucus-seek-recordsfbi-surveillance-mosques-and-u.

62) Justin Elliot, 'Racial Profiling On An "Industrial Scale."' *Salon* 22 Oct. 2011. Http://www.salon.com/2011/10/22/racial_profiling_on_an_industrial_scale/.

63) Army Regulation 210-35. Issued 14 January 2005. By order of the Secretary of the Army Gen. Peter J. Schoomaker.

CHAPTER TEN

THE DREAM IS OVER: LENONO AND THE DEATH OF THE ASIAN AMERICAN MOVEMENT

Meet the Beatle

British subject John Winston Lennon and Japanese American artist Yoko Ono were among a cohort of high-visibility political activists that came under surveillance by COINTELPRO during the 1960s. Lennon commanded a formidable international youth following throughout his post-Beatles years as he evolved into a political activist. After he disengaged from the world of celebrity and retreated into domesticity in 1975, Lennon and his body of work – both in music and political theatre – still held in thrall large numbers of people committed to his grand vision of humanity struggling to be free. The music of the mid-to-late Beatles period through his post-Fab Four years succeeded in wedding his intensely personal confessionals and romantic longing to the politics of the possible that emerged for a brief moment in postwar world history from the late-1960s to the late-1970s.

The message delivered by Lennon was sincere and the passion genuine, making it doubly dangerous to an entrenched "power elite" that had declared boldly that the American Century would be theirs alone. Prior to his five-year break from "riding on the merry-go-round" ("Watching The Wheels"), much of his snarky but incisive invective was directed against the systematic violence of the Anglo-American alliance, whether expressed in public opposition to the Vietnam War or announcing at a press conference in 1969 the return of his Member of the British Empire medal out of disgust with the state-sponsored Biafra disaster resulting from the Nigerian Civil War.

As head of the FBI since its founding in 1935 to his death over thirty-five years later, J. Edgar Hoover with COINTELPRO oversaw what in practice was a comprehensive domestic spy operation.[1] The autocratic director of the agency was assisted by such experienced black-bag men as G. Gordon Liddy, later imprisoned for his 1972 involvement with the Watergate scandal that helped bring down the presidency of Richard M. Nixon. At the suggestion of Dixiecrat segregationist Sen. Strom Thurmond of South Carolina, in 1972 the former pop idol and the Japan-born avant-garde artist were served notice by the Immigration and Naturalization Service that the couple was no longer welcome in the US. Ono and Lennon were active supporters of the Black Panthers, contributing both money and lending their talents as performing artists to advance the cause of African American liberation. Less known, however, is their direct involvement with the Asian American movement.

The historiographic conventions of much scholarship and journalism dictate that African Americans (with a secondary nod to Chicano/na Movement) be given priority if not exclusivity in writing about the civil rights movement, while discussions of the counterculture is apportioned to White youth and its taste leaders like The Beatles. Given a slight shift in framing and closer scrutiny, however, it is seen that Asian Americans (Japanese Americans more specifically) played a key role in the transformative postwar decades of the 1960s and 1970s.

One of the more incisively adventurous pieces of scholarship to correct this interpretive myopia is that by Laura Pulido in *Black, Brown, Yellow, and Left* (2006).[2] In this richly detailed volume she places Mexican American and Asian American radical political activity on a par with that of African Americans, rather than simply as offshoots or adjuncts to the history of struggle against race-based expressions of inequality.

Moreover, Pulido offers a perceptive analysis of Asian American women who asserted their claim to organizational leadership and decision-making along with their male counterparts. Their collective defiance is shown in a photograph by Mike Murase that appeared in a special issue of the *Gidra* (Los Angeles-based Asian American radical newspaper) devoted to women in the movement: Nine unsmiling women sit arrayed around a sofa addressing the camera directly with barely contained anger save for one of them who is giving the one-fingered peace sign to the implied viewer.[3]

Besides Yoko Ono, another Japanese American targeted by COINTELPRO was Richard Aoki, an early ranking member of the Black Panther Party. He was also active in Asian American radical politics while a student at the University of California, Berkeley, where he assumed a leading role in the Third World Liberation Front.[4] In a critical biography of Newton, Aoki is described with a trace of condescension as a "Japanese American who saw himself as a revolutionary."[5] This affiliation was not, however, so far fetched as it might appear to outside observers. During this period in California social history the system of residential racial segregation lumped together "Orientals" with other non-White people such as "Negroes," and "Mexicans." As such, Aoki grew up as just another kid from the Oakland community that produced such figures as Bobby Seale, Huey Newton, and Bobby Hutton.

Consistent with its program of armed self-defense as guaranteed by the Second Amendment to the US Constitution, Aoki – a military veteran – helped supply the nascent Black Panther Party for Self Defense with firearms. The BPP had been influenced by the community work of Robert F. Williams in rural North Carolina. As president of the local chapter of the NAACP he had both men and women organize themselves and train with firearms to ward off violent attacks against their community by the Ku Klux Klan and other groups. Williams wrote of this struggle in the seminal text *Negroes With Guns* (1962).[6]

While Aoki within recent years has gained the adulation of a certain segment of younger Asian Americans desperate for political anti-heroes, less known are figures such as Mike Tagawa.[7] He apparently became radicalized during the mid-1960s while stationed at Travis Air Force Base in Northern California. As a regular visitor to Berkeley, the active duty Air Force medic became involved with the anti-war movement. After returning home to Seattle in 1968, Tagawa joined the local chapter of the BPP but left two years later to organize more specifically on behalf of Asian Americans.[8] Guy S. Kurose was the third of at least three Japanese American direct participants in Black Panther politics. Prior to his death, he had made a career of providing community-based services to youngsters tempted by gang life.[9]

Sansei involvement in Black and Chicano politics and culture grew organically since as non-Whites they had been restricted to the same urban neighborhoods and shared institutions such as public schools.[10] Similarly, the characterization of Asian American political activists as only imitative ("performing Blackness") of Black nationalist figures in both matters of style and ideology is both simplistic and clichéd.[11] Bounded neighborhoods of non-White inhabitants (including that of the professional class) in cities such as Los Angeles or Oakland and a shared postwar mass-mediated popular culture heavily inflected by commercial Negro music (e.g. Motown "The Sound of Young America") and strong Mexican American influences (e.g. Ritchie Valens [Valenzuela]; Thee Midniters), the movement that emerged from this milieu moved far more fluidly and unselfconsciously across ethnic-specific lines when compared to the state-mandated (hence controlled) "multiculturalism" of the present.[12]

Moreover, the generation of African American intellectuals that preceded Black power advocates, some of whom held a deluded fascination with Maoism, looked to the revolutionary tradition of East Asia for ideas and inspiration; as in the founding in 1912 of the Republic of China. Prior to the US declaration of war against Japan, not a few African American writers and political leaders took hope in the fact that a non-White nation could defeat Russia militarily (1905) and then dare to contest the European colonial powers of Britain, France, and the Netherlands for control of Asia.[13]

The decolonization tactics of Gandhi when combined with the rich tradition of African American Protestantism provided the moral force for the modern civil rights movement as seen in the short-lived but powerful career of the Rev. Martin Luther King, Jr. Without question, a great deal of moral inspiration and political precedents for the Black revolution came first from the Asian world.

Ono Sideboard

Interviewed for the documentary *The U.S. vs. John Lennon* (2007), "dirty tricks" specialist Liddy decades later still conveys a sick delight in the woes visited upon the former leader of The Beatles.[14] Government inter-agency spying by the FBI and CIA, institutional harassment, physical intimidation, and costly battles fought within the legal system were among methods used to bring Lennon and Ono to heel. Unlike the arrogantly unapologetic Liddy, a seemingly repentant former FBI agent says, "We were being used by the government to stop dissent, just plain and simple." At the opposite end of the political spectrum, Noam Chomsky serves to remind that the situation was "serious" to the point of political assassinations being carried out by government hirelings. He speaks specifically of the "Gestapo-style" killing of Illinois Black Panther Party chairman Fred Hampton and Mark Clark by the Chicago Police Department and the FBI in December of 1969.

Accusations that the attack was a targeted assassination were born out in independent investigations by criminalist Herbert MacDonell and noted forensic pathologist Cyril Wecht, MD. A well-known commentator and author of several true crime books written for the non-expert, Wecht points to police misconduct in the assassination of Hampton. The government cover-up that followed demonstrated "how easily the coroners and medical examiners in many cities can be improperly influenced by politics."[15]

The expert opinion of Wecht, who has investigated a good number of politically sensitive deaths, only confirms claims of government conspiracy made decades ago in the revelatory documentary film *The Murder of Fred Hampton* (1971).[16] Thus, there were both sensational and lesser-known precedents leading to the murder of John Lennon in December 1980, all politically motivated. These murders might even be understood as the US domestic version of the PHOENIX Program run by the CIA in Southeast Asia to eliminate key civilian leaders.

Although in *The U.S. vs. John Lennon* Yoko Ono is recognized for her part in the personal and artistic evolution of John Lennon, it does not assign her proper credit for being the *intellectual* force behind their shared Dada-radical politics. Well before she first crossed paths with Lennon on November 9, 1966 at a preview of her exhibition at the Indica Gallery in London, Ono was an established presence within the Fluxus circle whence she arose. Her name, for example, is invoked more than once by prominent interviewees in a well-executed documentary film on poet-provocateur Allen Ginsberg.[17]

It was Paul McCartney rather than Lennon who was responsible for the coming together of high-art circles and the vibrant pop scene in swinging London of the mid-60s. It was McCartney who had an interest in the work of Karlheinz Stockhausen and other contemporary experimentalists in music. In more recent years, according to one critic who meticulously dissected the landmark double album *The Beatles* (1968)," McCartney challenged the "public's image of him as the cozy, domestic Beatle and of Lennon as the great radical experimenter."[18] In short, the perceived intellectualism of Lennon by those outside his circle, while not inaccurate, nonetheless was overstated.

Respected journalist Al Aronowitz, who was close personally to key figures in the world of 1960s countercultural expression, introduced The Fab Four to Bob Dylan. He in turn initiated the group to the wondrous mind-expanding properties of marijuana, famously, on August 24, 1968 at the Delmonico Hotel in New York.[19] Tellingly, Aronowitz suggested that the government persecution of Lennon through the Immigration and Naturalization Service (INS) had more to do with attempting to silence Yoko Ono. It was the "offensive" Ono that the Feds were after. By deporting Lennon, Aronowitz claims, "they would also be rid of her."[20]

Supporting this view is long-time New York radio personality Alex Bennett, who got his professional start during the 1970s and knew both Ono and Lennon quite well. "Lennon was almost like an idiot savant," Bennett observes, alluding to his singular talent as a musician. "The bright one was Yoko." Bennett stated that he could get into "deep philosophical" discussions with Yoko in a way that he could not with Lennon. The Leftist radio veteran, who more recently hosted a program on SIRIUS Satellite Radio, observes without a trace of rancor that Lennon was "simply mouthing what other people had to say." Sadly, he concludes, "You would be very disappointed if you met John Lennon. Very disappointed."[21]

Australian journalist Murray Sayle, who lived in Japan for three decades, was among the first mainstream critics to give Ono her due as an artist, intellectual, and political force. He pronounced her a "prophetess" who along with Lennon caused a worldwide youth audience to "reconsider its own values" through collaborative efforts that were at once aesthetic gestures and political expressions.[22] Although the beneficiary of privileges enjoyed by her elite banking family, Ono as a child saw her homeland reduced to ruin during World War II. Such firsthand experience with widespread suffering perhaps accounts for her commitment to the ideological pacifism shared widely by her countrymen in the postwar period.

By the time Lennon came out of retirement to create what became *Double Fantasy* (1980), interviews with the rejuvenated self-described "house husband" indicated that he had moved past sixties-style radicalism. He was still viewed, however, as a formidable threat to those that jealously guard their monopoly on political-economic power. According to Phil Strongman, a British journalist whose work among all others arguably does the best in discussing the historical significance of The Beatles as a social phenomenon, presents a compelling argument that the reemergence of John Lennon at the beginning of the Reagan-Thatcher era might have served as a catalyst to convert millions of "fans" into thinking political actors, who might draw upon their collective idealism and romanticism to militate for substantive change against the prevailing global order.[23]

Whether intellectually limited or not in comparison to Ono, most sources concur that for better or worse Lennon quite clearly was held under her sway. A well-produced documentary (there are many of dubious worth) titled *Inside John Lennon* (2003) featured interviews with his sister Julia Baird and those who knew him as a youth in Liverpool.[24] Len Garry, a band mate with the storied Quarrymen, says that Lennon after meeting Ono "went a bit strange after that, in my opinion." Independently, Bill Harry founder of *Mersey Beat* magazine and author of the *John Lennon Encyclopedia* observes, "That was the end of the real John Lennon ... because Yoko used him as a vessel for her own ideas." Baird laments that once he melded with Ono, Lennon disappeared from her life as if he was body-snatched.

The two merged as a business entity as well: Lenono Music was an arm of an investment enterprise that Ono ran successfully from their apartments in The Dakota. Given her distinguished maternal lineage of Yasuda *zaibatsu*, privileged international experience, and upbringing in a family of accomplished individuals both male and female, the dominance she maintained over her far less sophisticated spouse born and raised in Liverpool should not surprise.[25]

Frederic Seaman, formerly a personal assistant to John Lennon, paints an even less flattering portrait of Ono. When he absconded with private journals that Lennon had kept, Seaman found himself in a morass of legal problems and a criminal conviction that he blames on "Yoko's ability to influence overzealous prosecutors."[26] Shortly after the murder of his employer, Seaman tendered his resignation out of disgust for what he characterizes as Ono's attempt to capitalize on the death of her husband. "I could see that far from being the grief-stricken widow she played for the media and for the detectives investigating John's murder," he writes, "Yoko was determined to take advantage of this once-in-a-lifetime opportunity to forge a more positive public image and make money."[27] The observations by Seaman, however, are prejudiced by suspicions that in addition to his self-admitted thievery he might have been functioning as a mole with "Project Walrus" that had Lennon under surveillance, subject to psychological operations, and possibly targeted for assassination.[28]

In light of more recent killings such as that of Tupac Amaru Shakur on September 7, 1996, a wider politically-motivated plan to assassinate Lennon seems all the more plausible. Shakur, whose lineage connected him with Black radicalism of the 1960s, was both impossibly talented and a charismatically attractive figure whose popularity cut across color lines among American youth. His work was discussed seriously by a broad spectrum of artists, writers, and university-housed intellectuals.[29] Like Lennon, Jim Morrison, Jimi Hendrix, and Bob Marley, Shakur was a dangerous presence in the eyes of the Illuminist forces he called out in his final, posthumously released studio album, *Don Killuminati* (1996).[30]

Tele Revolution

In February 1972, Lennon and Ono did a memorable star turn as weeklong co-hosts of *The Mike Douglas Show*. Douglas began the shows by imparting his Easy Listening spin on songs made famous by The Beatles including "Michelle" and "With A Little Help From My Friends." In improbable contrast, the couple had invited a number of counterculture types as guests, including New Left gadfly Jerry Rubin, corporate reformer Ralph Nader, and Bobby Seale. At the time a political firebrand who had struck fear in the imagination of Middle America, Seale spoke passionately of a community-based political philosophy he called "inter-communalism."[31] All involved were well behaved and exhibited a level of intelligence to a degree that long ago was abandoned on American television and would be incomprehensible to viewers of *The Jerry Springer Show*, *The Oprah Winfrey Show*, *Dr. Phil* or the multiple incarnations of Geraldo Rivera.

A generation older than the other guests and apparently oblivious to the larger cultural and political significance of this gathering on the same stage, rock 'n' roll great Chuck Berry was introduced by a worshipful Lennon. He then backed up Berry on rhythm guitar as they ran through "Johnny B. Goode" and "Memphis." Ono and Jerry Rubin sat in the background onstage each beating, incongruously, a hand drum. Douglas, a "square" singer from the Big Band era, was both respectful of his guests and solicitous of the divergent political views presented to his audience. Confounding attempts by government control masters to engineer social division along generational, racial, gender, political affiliation, and regional lines, Mike Douglas brought these different streams together and offered a glimpse into the new America that was beginning to take form before the Reagan reactionary rollback kicked in with a vengeance during the 1980s.[32]

In *Come Together: John Lennon In His Time* (1991) author Jon Wiener devotes several pages describing the week of shows with Lennon and Ono.[33] (The five programs were released as a VHS box set and then in DVD format.) Movement provocateur and jester Jerry Rubin is given extensive treatment by Wiener. He neglects to mention, however, the most arresting of all the musical performances given that entire week, by the duo of Joanne Nobuko Miyamoto and Chris Iijima (February 15, 1972). Rubin later remade himself into a hip capitalist scoring well enough as a multi-level marketing promoter to live in a nice penthouse on the West Side of Los Angeles until he was run over in heavy traffic while trying to cross the street during rush hour. Conversely, Miyamoto and Iijima never veered from their commitment to social justice.

As the duo "Yellow Pearl," Miyamoto and Iijima sang "We Are the Children," one of the more lyrical songs that appeared on their landmark album *A Grain of Sand: Music For the Struggle of Asians in America* (1973).[34] Accompanied solely by his nylon string guitar, the arrangement blended the high tenor of Iijima with the soaring soprano of the soulfully beautiful Miyamoto. She was already an experienced professional performer whose formal training in the arts had won her roles on Broadway (*The King and I*; *Flower Drum Song*) and in the film *West Side Story* prior to her political awakening. *A Grain of Sand* gave voice to the nascent Asian American Movement, placing it alongside – not secondary to – the history of political contestation by Puerto Ricans and Blacks whom they worked with while in New York. In both song and political involvement, Miyamoto and Iijima were consistent in emphasizing the points of commonality between the Asian American movement and other groups that at the time identified with the struggles of the "Third World."

A thirty-five minute independent documentary titled *A Song For Ourselves* (2009) traces the career of Yellow Pearl and places their art within the larger political context in which massive cultural tremors shook the terrain. The strength of the documentary lies in its foregrounding of the Asian American historical experience and the political movement that arose during the 1960s to challenge complementary systems of subordination while creating culturally specific alternatives to the systemic distortions and exclusionary institutional behavior of corporate media combines.[35]

In more recent years, both Miyamoto and Iijima prior to his death remained as committed to communities of color as when they appeared before the television audience on *The Mike Douglas Show* decades before. Through her Great Leap organization Miyamoto continued to teach the performing arts in Los Angeles. Iijima capped his career at the University of Hawai'i, Manoa on the faculty of law and led a program that served Native Hawaiians and other groups underrepresented in the profession.

About one year prior to appearing before a more middle-of-the-road audience on *The Mike Douglas Show*, Lennon and Ono were given in-depth exposure to the presumably more urbane audience on *The Dick Cavett Show* (1969-75). Beginning September 11, 1971 the couple appeared on three separate broadcasts.[36] These programs constituted Lennon's post-Beatles debut on American television. As it later was revealed in declassified government documents, the pair had a less appreciative audience in FBI sources that monitored their activities and wrote reports colored with unintended humor owing to its unfamiliarity with the counterculture. The ABC late-night television program hosted by Cavett was unique for the arch humor and understated but often biting wit of its Yale-educated host who had a fondness for palindromes (TUMS spells "SMUT" backwards).

Guests of Cavett included an inventive admixture of established celebrities in the popular arts and the theatre, literary figures such as Truman Capote, and a sprinkling of cutting-edge creative sorts like Jimi Hendrix (very stoned) that personified the spirit of the counterculture.[37] "We plan for our sound to go inside the *soul* of the person ... and see if it can awaken some kind of thing in their minds," said Hendrix during a fifteen-minute appearance, "because there are so many sleeping people."[38]

While Lennon was murdered at the relatively advanced age of forty, Hendrix was among other youth culture figures such as Jim Morrison, Phil Ochs and Bob Marley who met with an early death under murky circumstances.[39] Each evening the show brought with it the possibility that it might reel beyond the usually light and inoffensive chattiness characteristic of the talk-show format. As an example of the intelligent unpredictability of the program, the December 2, 1971 live airing of a triangulated verbal set-to between an obnoxious and combative Norman Mailer, his haughty literary rival Gore Vidal, and ringmaster Cavett has become a key moment in television lore.[40]

Working Class Martyr

Ironically, through this calculated use of the most effective postwar technology of mass mind control – television – Lennon and Ono succeeded in reaching a much larger segment of the population far beyond the youth counterculture that was their principal audience. Once more, it had been Ono who convinced Lennon that they could use his pop star celebrity as a vehicle for cultural and political change. The idea was that ruling class legitimacy would be undermined by their mélange of provocative pronouncements, staged put-ons, and inspired mass media happenings combined with a liberating rock 'n' roll attitude that itself derived from the inchoate rebellion of the rural and urban American underclass.

Their growing mainstream exposure and public challenges to the Nixon administration, however, caused his henchmen to deal with the couple as credible threats to the American Republic and got Lennon placed on the president's "Enemies List."

More immediately, the rumored involvement of Lennon and Ono with a series of concerts staged to subvert the 1972 re-election campaign of Nixon made it even more imperative that they be silenced. According to Lennon, Jerry Rubin and Abbie Hoffman pressured the couple to appear at the Republican National Convention in San Diego, but they were reluctant to do so.[41] Allen Ginsberg, also at the meeting, argued that another brutal and violent police riot such as that which had taken place in Chicago during the 1968 Democratic National Convention might result.

"That was enough to get Immigration on us," Lennon concluded. "They started attacking us through the Immigration Department, trying to throw us out of the country."[42] So commenced years of US government efforts to have Lennon deported while secretly subjecting the two to general harassment, wire taps, gang stalking, and assorted dirty tricks. It was such political pressure that dissuaded him from joining a national tour that "would combine rock music with anti-war organizing and voter registration."[43]

The year 1972 was to be the first presidential election cycle in which newly enfranchised eighteen-year-olds would be eligible to vote, in accordance with the Twenty-Sixth Amendment to the US Constitution passed and ratified in 1971. Already, in local elections, the impact of the youth vote had been felt. As such, the potential of eleven million young voters mobilized by the proven cohesive force of expression through music performance posed a tangible threat to the Nixon regime.

The Nixon presidency was beleaguered by popular opposition to the Vietnam War, widespread domestic racial rebellion, and a vital counter culture whose politicization posed a challenge to the legitimacy of American empire itself. Even influential elements within his own political class at the *Washington Post* or the *New York Times* held the veteran politician in low regard. Nixon biographers, filmmakers, and past professional acquaintances such as David Frost have dissected the near-pathological zeal that Nixon exhibited in going after enemies both real and imagined.[44] Lennon was one such enemy.

Wiener mentions the importance of the Asian American Movement to both Lennon and Ono near the conclusion of *Come Together*, before it segues into an anti-climactic epilogue that sketches a profile of confessed assassin Mark David Chapman. In a show of support for Japanese American unionists militating for wage equity on a par with that of White employees and fairness in managerial practices, Lennon, Ono, and their young son Sean were due to visit San Francisco for a labor rally in December 1980.

Lennon and Ono already had issued a statement of solidarity with their Asian American brethren who had organized in Los Angeles, California. This proved to be the last public political gesture by John Ono Lennon prior to his killing. At the request of labor leader and community activist Shin'ya Ono, Yoko's cousin, the couple sent the following message to workers in the Little Tokyo district of Los Angeles that were pressuring Japan Food Company (JFC) to deal fairly with non-White employees. Note that they described themselves as an "Oriental family":

> We are with you in spirit. Both of us are subjected to prejudice as an Oriental family in the Western world.
>
> In this beautiful country where democracy is the very foundation of its constitution, it is sad that we have to fight for equal rights and equal pay for the citizens.
>
> Boycott it must be, if it is the only way to bring justice and restore the dignity of the constitution for the sake of all citizens of the U.S. and their children.
>
> Peace and love,
>
> John Lennon and Yoko Ono.
> New York City,
> December, 1980.[45]

The protest against JFC was part of a larger ongoing struggle against Japanese multinational corporations that had run roughshod over Japanese American workers, community members, and local institutions during the rise of Japan to economic prominence during the 1970s and 1980s

Shin'ya Ono had been active in the student movement at Columbia University and had aligned himself with the Weathermen faction of the Students for Democratic Society (SDS). He had relocated to the West Coast and then worked on behalf of organized labor and on issues specifically affecting the Japanese American community. Ono famously was captured in a press photograph as he was about to be clubbed by one of 2,000 policemen brought in to suppress street actions and public protest during the "Days of Rage" (October 8-11, 1969) in Chicago.[46]

For Shin'ya Ono, a teacher by profession, his politics were thoroughly grounded in radical theory and practice. By contrast, his cousin Yoko was less dogmatic and more of a revolutionary romantic. Her public pronouncements and art projects, while specifically confronting issues of war, economic exploitation, subordination of women and racism, still managed to convey can almost childlike innocence in both conception and execution.

Of possibly even greater political consequence was the exposure and halo of legitimacy Lennon gave to groups and individuals he endorsed. Shin'ya Ono – in his steady involvement with an array of community groups, labor organizations, and anti-war activity – was but one of a good many Asian Americans that realized a new level of political awareness during the 1960s.[47] When combined with the celebrity power and personal commitment of Lennon and Ono, the nascent Asian American political movement demonstrated its ability to disrupt and potentially overthrow the color-caste system and resultant social subordination that had greeted the first immigrants to the US over a century earlier. It was this admixture of pop celebrity and radical politics – a new and potentially incendiary development in the history of revolutionary movements – that so threatened the ruling elite. On December 8, 1980, upon his return to The Dakota after a recording session, John Ono Lennon was laid low by four shots from a handgun wielded by Mark David Chapman.

Imagine Overpopulation

The assassination of John Winston Lennon stands as a historical turning point, from the politics of hope, change, and possibility ("Imagine") to one of an oppressive and boldly assertive new world order, wherein the human soul and the music that is its expression has been commandeered and controlled by the corporatist media oligopoly. Both Yoko Ono and Lennon were profoundly in sympathy with the universal life force in contrast to that of his former countrymen such as H. G. Wells (1866-1946),

Bertrand Russell (1872-1970) and most notably Aldous Huxley (1894-1963). These world famous individuals and others of their patrician ilk who shared the globalist political agenda held nothing but disdain for the lower orders of humankind. Through various means – science fiction, popular history, academic philosophy, cinema, essays, and public lectures – this contempt for humanity and sacred life was guided by the pseudoscientific principles of eugenics that had its epistemological-political origins not coincidentally in the Victorian age of British high imperialism.[48]

In one of the storied appearances of Ono and Lennon on *The Dick Cavett Show* discussed above, its host invites members of the studio audience to address questions to his guests. A presentable non-"hippie" White woman with a Canadian accent in her early twenties directs an obviously rehearsed question specifically to Yoko Ono by asking, "how you as a woman feel about overpopulation in the world and its relation to polluting the environment." Lennon tries to answer for her but Cavett cuts him off and redirects the question to its intended target. Her answer is adamantly out of sync with the ideals of the nascent environmental movement through which eugenics depopulations schemes were to be imbedded in deceptively benign form. By her unhesitant and well-reasoned response it is obvious that Ono already had given the issue serious thought:

> Well, I think the problem is *not* overpopulation as people believe it to be. But it's more of the *balance* of things. But, you know, like food: Some parts of the world it's wasted food and some parts, you know, nobody has food. And that kind of balance, if that is solved, I don't think we need to be worried so much about overpopulation.

Lennon chimes in by stating unequivocally, "I think it's a bit of a joke the way, ah, people have made this overpopulation thing into kind of myth. I don't really believe it, you know.... I think we've got enough food and money to feed everybody." Cavett attempts to interject his own view on "overpopulation," but this time it is Lennon who cuts him off by expanding on his original statement:

> Yeah, I don't believe 'overpopulation,' you know. I think that's just a kind of myth that government has thrown out to keep your mind off Vietnam and Ireland and all the important subjects.

251

When Cavett objects to this assertion – "Oh, I think you're wrong about that" – Lennon mocks him with an affected rejoinder, "Oh, I don't care." This elicits mild laughter from the audience.[49]

The first "Earth Day" had been rolled out on April 22, 1970, not long before Lennon and Ono did their three-day stand on *The Dick Cavett Show* in 1971. This was at the dawn of the "environmental movement" and the period in which basic principles of "ecology" began to be beamed into the minds of the general population. In 1968, entomologist Paul R. Ehrlich of Stanford University sounded a dire warning in advocating radical conservationism with the publication of *The Population Bomb*. Although even his critics miss the historical connection, the ideas advanced by Ehrlich complemented the earlier intelligence-testing franchise (Stanford-Binet) operated by psychologist Lewis M. Terman. Both he and Paul B. Popenoe (1888-1979) were "quite influential in eugenic-sterilization work" and involved with the Human Betterment Foundation.[50]

As a mass-market paperback geared to the educated general public, *The Population Bomb* could be found on bookracks at drug stores and newsstands for 95 cents. The book with its lurid cover and sensationalist advertising text ("POPULATION CONTROL OR RACE TO OBLIVION?") set off a controlled chain-reaction in the popular press and made an indelible impression upon generations of college and university students who ate up its highly palatable half-truths.

As revealed by the retort to Cavett by Lennon, both he and Ono were in possession of a prescience and ability for deep understanding that challenged the very foundation of the new world order system: population control.[51] That the couple had a ready audience for their views and damning analysis made them all the more dangerous to those whose wealth, power, and influence financed such neo-Malthusian propaganda as *The Population Bomb*.

In the case of this particular title, the Sierra Club – whose institutional roots reach back to 19th century American nativism and the "conservation" movement – was co-publisher of the paperback with Ballantine Books. Jonathan Peter Spiro in *Defending the Master Race* offers a detailed exposition on the scientific and political substrate underlying the conservation movement, eugenics theory, population control policy, anti-immigration agitation, and rule by the "Nordic race" threatened with extinction by "hordes" of inferior peoples.[52]

In the aftermath of its stand on current immigration, criticism of the mostly White professional, upper-middle class leadership and membership rolls of the Sierra Club forced it to install Allison Chin, an Asian American woman from the biopharmaceutical-industrial sector, as its president to cover its politically correct "diversity" flanks.[53] Other characters like Stanford Law School graduate Sanjay M. Ranchod have been made board members of the Sierra Club as part of its "efforts to attract more minorities."[54]

True to its institutional roots, the Sierra Club and related "green" front organizations remain firmly anchored to private family foundations and the corporatist powers that have used "environmentalism" to tighten their control of both public and private resources while providing justification for ever-expanding pretexts for taxation in the name of protecting "nature." EarthWatch Institute, for example, "was created using tax-free money from the Rockefeller Foundation."[55] Similarly, The Ford Foundation is the corporatist power behind the National Resources Defense Council.

Target Assassination

In light of the innumerable books, articles, and video material that chart the modern American history of political assassination since the breakthrough publication of *Rush To Judgment* (1966), the murder of Lennon – on the day before he and Ono were to leave for the West Coast to support fellow Asian Americans – is consistent with the *modus operandi* of the national security establishment.[56] The late Col. L. Fletcher Prouty referred to a "secret team" of players that neutralize enemies of the regime at the behest of high-level controllers within the shadow government.[57] As a U.S. Air Force officer, he served as Chief of Special Operations for the Joint Chiefs of Staff. Under President John F. Kennedy he was USAF liaison to the CIA. Outside independent contractors also have been used against targeted victims. Contract killers, mob hit-men, former military marksmen, moonlighting police officers, and security guards have been known to perform "wet work" for government agencies.

James E. Files claims to have been one such individual, having gotten the attention of CIA spook David Atlee Phillips while serving in the 82nd Airborne Division operating secretly in Laos during the Vietnam War.[58] Under direction from his controller Phillips, Files described in extensive interviews the logistics of the John F. Kennedy shooting in Dealey Plaza.[59] He had positioned himself on the "grassy knoll" armed with a prototype Remington X-200 "Fireball" that fired special .222 caliber wax-tipped mercury-filled rounds. Other documentary sources point to Corsican hit-men that were brought into the US via American mafia connections to eliminate Kennedy. This was thought to provide a layer of deniability for domestic criminal networks that otherwise might be held suspect.[60] Recent highly credible first-person revelations by the former lover of Lee Harvey Oswald, Judyth Vary Baker, point to the participation of CIA operatives and mafia associates in a parallel kill-Castro/kill-Kennedy conspiracy.[61]

With few exceptions, respected researchers in JFK assassination history such as Jim Marrs, Robert J. Groden, and Dick Russell find the account by Baker to be independently verifiable and therefore credible.[62] As he lay dying, the legendary CIA operative E. Howard Hunt confessed to being in Dealey Plaza on that fateful day in the fall. Government documents and photographs implicate CIA official George H.W. Bush as attending the ritual slaying.[63] Incredibly, Bush, unlike everyone else in America, has claimed a lapse in memory as to his whereabouts on November 22, 1963. Lower level but proven gunmen such as William Harvey, Antonio Veciana, Frank Sturgis, Lucien Sarti, and David Morales were key participants. Morales was later linked to the assassination of Robert F. Kennedy in June 1968 as his campaign for the presidency gained momentum.

Among the first to raise doubts over the findings of the Warren Commission (September 1964) was Mae Brussell, an independent researcher who produced an innovative program devoted to political conspiracy aired by independent radio station KLRB-FM in Carmel, California.[64] In an interview conducted in December 1980, almost immediately after the Lennon assassination, she described him as a "spiritual force" on a par with Gandhi; one who could rally anti-war protestors against plans by the Reagan administration to rebuild the "Pentagon war machine" that would be set upon smaller countries such as El Salvador and Guatemala as a run-up to potential conflict with the USSR.[65] More astounding in the interview was a highly prescient and far-reaching analysis of CIA and FBI involvement in running operations executed to silence opposition to government policies. In the years since Brussell began her pioneering efforts in conspiracy research, a mountain of books, articles, and films have been produced to confirm the information she uncovered through an impressively comprehensive and deep research agenda that she began airing publicly in 1971 on the program *Dialogue: Assassination,* hosted by Gloria Baron.

Along with a number of independent researchers and writers influenced by Brussell, Paul Krassner of *The Realist* and, with Abbie Hoffman and Jerry Rubin, founder of the Youth International Party (Yippies), owed much to her highly sophisticated and nuanced understanding of *sub rosa* politics and the deformed history it spawns. Krassner had known both Lennon and Ono well enough to share confidences with them. He has recounted one memorable private conversation that took place in 1972 when the couple spent the weekend at his home in Watsonville, California, south of San Francisco. The work of Mae Brussell came up in their chat. Krassner said she had asserted that the deaths of figures in popular music such as Jimi Hendrix, Janis Joplin, and Jim Morrison were in fact *political* assassinations carried out against leaders of the youth rebellion.

At the time, Lennon denied that there was such a link among these revered figures; rather, that they self-destructed. Lennon, not long after, changed his mind about the Brussell scenario. Krassner writes that only a few months after their conversation, Lennon told him, "Listen, if anything happens to Yoko and me, it was not an accident."[66]

Even Jon Wiener, a cautious and circumspect academic historian of high repute, felt compelled to touch upon Operation CHAOS, a CIA domestic surveillance program initiated in 1967 that targeted political dissidents, in his account of the landmark lawsuit *Weiner v. Federal Bureau of Investigation* (1983). This, however, is years after Brussell made more explicit claims concerning Operation CHAOS in a way that is far more comprehensive than conveyed by Wiener in *Gimme Some Truth* (1999). In reviewing government material received in accordance to the Freedom of Information Act (FOIA), his legal team sent the professor to the library at UCLA to find more information on MSCHAOS. There, he read of a well-coordinated conspiracy at the highest level of government to subdue specific individuals viewed as disruptive or threatening to the political order. "The CIA sent Operation CHAOS domestic intelligence reports on political dissent first to President Johnson and later to Nixon," Wiener writes, "as well as to Henry Kissinger and John Dean, counsel to the president."[67] For Brussell, however, Operation CHAOS was nothing less than a systematic and comprehensive effort by government forces to track, catalogue, harass, defame, drug, blackmail, and in certain cases eliminate leaders of the 1960s counterculture.[68]

Due to the contributions of independent researchers, investigative journalists, documentary filmmakers, "alternative" historians, and a subset of academic specialists, scenarios that might have been seen as outrageously implausible back then are now accepted by a fairly large segment of the lay public and even among the more naïve and sheltered types found at the university.

Less than one week after the assassination of Lennon, Mae Brussell, mother of five and daughter of Rabbi Edgar Magnin of Los Angeles, presented a remarkably comprehensive analysis on her radio program (renamed *World Watchers International*) on Sunday December 14, 1980. She followed it up with a second broadcast (December 20, 1980). Both programs were dedicated exclusively to the subject of the Lennon killing. The combination of passion and intellectual clarity that shines through in these one-hour programs, despite the shock, grief, and outrage Brussell expresses, is all the more remarkable for its timeliness and relevance to more recent killings of a suspicious nature that probably were politically motivated.[69]

She begins by telling of her friendship with John Lennon and Yoko Ono, who had reached out to Brussell after the publication of her first essay "Why Was Martha Mitchell Kidnapped" (August 1972) for *The Realist*. At the invitation of the couple, who had helped fund the counterculture publication, Brussell and her family spent the day with Lennon and Ono in San Francisco. They had been fans of The Beatles from the early days when they first stormed into the American popular imagination in early

1964. The Brussell family was also among the fortunate crowd at Candlestick Park on August 29, 1966 for what was to be the final large-scale public concert appearance of The Beatles.

Before launching into an impassioned but reasoned analytical breakdown of the murder, Brussell explained the degree to which The Beatles and the "music scene" at large had been "very much a part of our family life through all of these turbulent years." Together, they attended such phenomenal politico-cultural events as the Monterey Pop Festival in the fabled summer of 1967. Not only was the music enjoyable for its own sake, Brussell stressed that it was liberating and instructive as well. Indeed, she named the Beatles as among the three most important influences in her life, the other two being Virginia Woolf and Henry Miller.

Eleven minutes into the broadcast, in an emotion-filled outburst, Brussell dedicates her observations on the Lennon murder to the memory of her daughter Bonnie who, at age fourteen, was killed in an automobile crash that Brussell suspected was not an accident. She connects the "murder" of her daughter with similar losses suffered by other "researchers and writers and politicians." Brussell then addresses a grieving Yoko Ono directly, "We paid our dues many times over, so 'Yoko, we know what sorrow is.'"

Brussell understood as few individuals do even today the dark and violent elements that populate ordinary reality. "Rock music and musicians were becoming the largest social, cultural, and political force for world peace," she stated. "This energy, talent, and enthusiasm was spreading around the world." Because of the political potential demonstrated by the popular acceptance of the new music "Operation CHAOS and other federal government programs were formed to disrupt, reject, and eliminate the combined skills of too many." Brussell blamed the families of the murder victims and their "apathy" for not investigating the deaths; she blamed the fans for being blinded by adoration. Moreover, she understood that it was the function of the corporate "mass media" to conceal the nature of these criminal actions carried out on behalf of the power elite.

Influenced heavily by the meticulous research and analytical genius of Brussell, a barrister based in London (with decades of professional experience in the courts and a wide-ranging career as a journalist and television pundit) published the first systematic investigative account of the Lennon assassination. He presented a case that implied strongly that John Ono Lennon had been silenced by dark elements within the political establishment. He is careful, however, not to make direct accusations; perhaps to avoid running afoul of laws concerning libel in Britain. Fenton S. Bresler (called to the bar in 1951) already had carved out a multifaceted career as an author and public intellectual before undertaking the investigative inquiry that culminated in the magisterial *Who Killed John Lennon?* (1990). He therefore had little to gain professionally by launching his own investigation.

After Brussell, Bresler found it suspicious that the flighty and mysteriously peripatetic Chapman would somehow secure an assignment as counselor in a refugee camp at Fort Chaffee, Arkansas, tending to newly-arrived Vietnamese families that had been evacuated after the final collapse in 1975 of the US-supported regime in South Vietnam. Prior to this assignment, with little experience, Chapman was sent by the YMCA, in June 1975, to Beirut, Lebanon. As Lebanon was the site of a brutal civil war, Chapman was exposed directly to grave danger and violence; a prelude to the bloodletting he himself would perpetrate only five years later. Bresler cites Brussell once more in floating the possibility that both the Beirut and the Fort Chaffee assignments for the YMCA had a "CIA undertone."[70] While taking care not to place blame on the seemingly benign organization, Bresler notes that elements within the YMCA and CIA have maintained a complementary relationship through the years.

Brussell has made the point that, integral to the Vietnam War, were mind control programs and assassination squads run by the military and CIA operatives that targeted civilians. Today the literature on the PHOENIX Program is much more extensive than it was when Brussell was active. Independent researchers, investigative journalists, and even a number of academics have published work that supports her courageously original claims.

The comprehensive and shockingly detailed volume *The Phoenix Program* by Douglas Valentine (1990) is one of the better examples of scholarship that has substantiated the general assertions that Brussell made years earlier.[71] Lest the account by Valentine be dismissed out of hand by those with an inability to conceive of a dark, evil, and cynical world that is the very antithesis of that put forth by Lennon in his music and politics, perhaps the first-person account by Vincent Hichiro Okamoto might offer a glimpse into the mind-set of an apparently rational and highly-decorated commissioned US Army officer who was a member of an assassination team while serving in Vietnam:

> The problem was, how do you find the people on the blacklist? It's not like you had their address and telephone number. The normal procedure would be to go into a village and just grab someone and say, 'Where's Nguyen so-and-so?' Half the time the people were so afraid they would say anything. Then a Phoenix team would take the informant, put a sandbag over his head, poke out two holes so he could see, put commo wire around his neck like a long leash, and walk him through the village and say, 'When we go by Nguyen's house scratch your head.' Then that night Phoenix would come back, knock on the door and say, 'April Fool, motherfucker.' Whoever answered the door would get wasted. As far as they were concerned whoever answered was a Communist, including family members. Sometimes they'd come back to camp with ears to prove they killed people.[72]

After completing Ranger training, Okamoto was sent to Vietnam as an intelligence-liaison officer. Once returned to civilian life, he earned a law degree at the University of Southern California and worked as an attorney before being appointed judge to the Superior Court of Los Angeles County by Governor Gray Davis in April 2002.[73]

The youngest of ten children, Okamoto was born during World War II in the Poston, Arizona concentration camp. In his personal history, it is seen that individual and group suffering ensures neither compassion nor guarantees against inflicting even greater evil upon other human beings. According to Douglas Valentine, the current "war on terror" and its Office of Homeland Security is connected historically to both the PHOENIX Program and CHAOS. The Vietnamese secret police "established a nation-wide informant network to identify VCI and their sympathizers." All it took was an "anonymous informant" to have a suspect "arrested and detained indefinitely under the An Tri (administrative detention) Laws."[74]

As a former internee with his family in a model American behavioral science concentration camp, Okamoto (ROTC; like Norman Yoshio Mineta) is the ideal civic leader put in place to cover for snitch and assassination programs intended for the American people.[75] The "targeted killings" of civilians was justified by the Obama administration thanks to senior legal advisor (2009-2012) and legal theorist Harold Hongju Koh while on rotation through government from Yale Law School. The domestic version of the PHOENIX Program beta-tested by Okamoto and his band of brothers in Southeast Asia was declared legitimate by the scholar Koh who once had been a vocal critic of his former student John Choon Yoo.[76]

In light of current attacks against any and all by agencies of the private banking cartels that engineer social problems, facilitate the international drug trade, manipulate the economic system, and stage-manage wars, the hit on John Lennon might be understood as an early example of targeted assassination.

Dream Is Over

In his first solo album, *John Lennon/Plastic Ono Band* (1970) the penultimate song, titled simply "God," intones repeatedly that the "dream is over."[77] By this it was meant that he had moved beyond the epiphenomenal illusion of scripture ("I don't believe in Bible." "I don't believe in Gita."), boyhood heroes ("I don't believe in Elvis."), divinities ("I don't believe in Jesus." "I don't believe in Buddha.") youth cult leaders ("I don't believe in Zimmerman." "I don't believe in Kennedy."), and pop idols ("I don't believe in Beatles."). He knew himself as a free and sovereign being ("I don't believe in kings." "I don't believe in Hitler."). In this emotionally raw, soul-baring, album of collected confessions, Lennon strips away the impedimenta of his intensely lived celebrity existence. Specifically in "God," he reduces his reality to two indissoluble elements:

> I just believe in me,
> Yoko and me.
> And that's reality.

By "dream," Lennon did not mean the abandonment of the commitment to peace, social justice, and beloved community that he shared with Yoko Ono. As demonstrated by his appearances on *The Dick Cavett Show* and *The Mike Douglas Show* that followed the release of *Plastic Ono Band*, Lennon remained steadfast in the fundamental beliefs that he held constant throughout his life until it was brought to an end on December 8, 1980.

If, as argued in these pages that John Lennon and Yoko Ono are integral to the history of the Asian American movement, with his murder went the spirit and substance of resistance and revolution that characterized it in its classic form prior to 1980. Since the Asian American movement was an integral element of the New Social Movements of the 1960s, with John Ono Lennon no longer around to rally the conscience of his passionately devoted followers worldwide, this made it infinitely easier for the Reagan Revolution of the 1980s to usher in the new era of hard-right political economic policy that led to the current state of seemingly insoluble crises caused by the wanton destruction of domestic industry, concerted attacks on organized labor, scaling back or elimination of social programs, defunding of public education, and all-out war against the formerly productive, prosperous, and vital middle class.

Today, brutal police state practices proliferate and intensify in anticipation of large-scale rebellion against endemic joblessness combined with rollbacks in social services, mounting onerous taxation, and insurmountable consumer debt-slavery. As stated with precision by James Petras, "The growth of 'Homeland Security' and the 'War on Terror' parallels the decline of Social Security, public health programs, and the great drop in living standards for hundreds of millions."[78]

Writing in 2010, Joseph E. Stiglitz and Linda J. Blimes calculated that the Iraq war has cost American taxpayers $3 billion; far more than the $50 to $60 billion estimated in 2003 during the Bush administration.[79] Former Assistant Secretary of the US Treasury, Paul Craig Roberts, updated costs associated with the Afghan debacle and Iraq invasion during the Bush and Obama regimes and asserts that $6 trillion in public debt has been incurred in prosecuting these ill-fated wars. At the same time, the US has begun to "encircle" militarily and strategically substantially more formidable future enemies: Russia and China.[80]

Multiple shooting wars and the destabilization of sovereign nations through stealth, state-level criminality such as drug profiteering (Afghanistan), gun running (US-Mexico), and human trafficking (UN/US private contractors). This tripartite set of interlocking criminal activity is straight from the playbook of nineteenth century British and American empire-building. It has been updated for the twenty-first century through the co-optation of the equality revolution centered upon gender, race, and all-out class warfare waged by financial oligarchs on behalf of the illuminist banking families whose lineage reaches back to the emergence of long-distance trade and pre-capitalist economic formations.[81]

For her part, Yoko Ono has been rendered politically ineffective subsequent to the murder of John Winston Lennon. The formidable intellect, demonstrated creative ability, and bold attacks on state violence, exploitative institutional behavior, and militarism have been put in abeyance since the killing of her husband. Instead, apart from an occasional appearance on cable TV to keep the Lennon legacy alive, most of her public presence has been confined to Twitter. There, Ono regularly tweets the sort of brief but incisive words superficially similar to those that once were her trademark as a cutting-edge conceptual artist. Today, her pronouncements ring hollow for their almost unreal disengagement from the world and an utter lack of political grounding.

A new generation, however, has discovered Yoko Ono. She is now considered "cool" and fewer observers today think of her as the Oriental woman who broke up The Beatles. The formerly boutique CD label Rykodisc assembled select music pieces for its six-disc *Onobox* collection.[82] There are books of hers that have been published for consumption by the art museum and gallery set. She records or performs on occasion with Sean Ono Lennon and select Japanese musicians such as Yuka Honda (former Cibo Matto) and Cornelius (Oyamada Keigo) formed as the "new" Plastic Ono Band. Most of it is rock-based self-referential pastiche for would-be hipsters. Others purchase her recordings more out of duty than from devotion to her decidedly modest musical vision.

Yoko Ono in part represents all that might have been possible for a free, vibrant, and open Asian American movement that brought together art, politics, sexual expression, and intellectual inquiry informed existentially by a shared understanding of war, displacement, race-discrimination, the oppression of sisters, wives, mothers, and the living connection to the vibrant nations of the Pacific Rim. Instead, the murder of John Ono Lennon forced her into silence. Finally, the relative absence of oppositional voices has left the path clear for corporatist-identified, national security establishment-serving Asian Americans to take center stage in the cultural, political, economic, and intellectual life of the US.

The dream is over.

Endnotes

1) Anthony Summers, *Official and Confidential: The Secret Life of J. Edgar Hoover* (New York: Pocket Star Books, 1994).

2) Laura Pulido, *Black, Brown, Yellow, and Left: Radical Activism in Los Angeles* (Berkeley and Los Angeles: University of California Press, 2006).

3) Michael Dooley, "Gidra Takes on the American War Machine." *Salon.com* 22 Feb. 2012. Http://www.salon.com/2012/02/23/gidra_takes_on_the_american_war_machine/.

4) An interview with Aoki is found in Fred Ho, ed. *Legacy To Liberation: Politics and Culture of Revolutionary Asian Pacific America* (San Francisco, California, AK Press, 2000).

5) Hugh Pearson, *The Shadow of the Panther: Huey Newton and the Price of Black Power in America* (Reading, Massachusetts: Addison-Wesley Publishing Company, 1994), 112.

6) Robert F. Williams, *Negroes With Guns* (New York: Marzani and Munsell, 1962). See also the film documentary *Negroes With Guns: Rob Williams and Black Power*, dir. Sandra H. Dickson and Churchill Roberts (California Newsreel, 2005).

7) Such adulation proved misplaced when it was revealed that Aoki had been a longtime FBI informant. See Seth Rosenfeld, *Subversives: The FBI's War on Student Radicals, and Reagan's Rise to Power* (New York: Farrar, Straus and Giroux, 2012).

8) Mike Tagawa: Seattle Black Panther Party History and Memory Project." Seattle Civil Rights and Labor History Project. Http://depts.washington.edu/civilr/tagawa.htm. Accessed 05 Jun. 2008.

9) Dennis Fitzgerald, "Guy Kurose Devoted Life to Helping Youth." *It's About Time.* Http://www.itsabouttimebpp.com/Memorials/Guy_Kurose_Devoted_Life.html. Accessed 05 Jun. 2008.

10) Scott Kurashige, *The Shifting Grounds of Race: Black and Japanese Americans in the Making of Multiethnic Los Angeles* (Princeton, New Jersey: Princeton University Press, 2010).

11) Daryl J. Maeda, "Black Panthers, Red Guards, and Chinamen: Constructing Asian American Identity Through Performing Blackness, 1969-1972. *American Quarterly* (v. 57 n. 4 (December 2005)."

12) Walter Takaki played saxophone in a band called The Silhouettes with Valenzuela while attending Pacoima Junior High School (Los Angeles County, California) and affected the "waterfall" hairstyle and attire associated with the "*pachuco.*" Beverly A. Mendheim, *Richie Valens: The First Latino Rocker* (Tempe, Arizona: Bilingual Review Press, 1987).

13) Gerald Horne, *Race War!: White Supremacy and the Japanese Attack on the British Empire* (New York New York University Press, 2004).

14) David Leaf and John Scheinfeld, *The U.S. vs. John Lennon.* Lions Gate, 2007.

15) Cyril Wecht, M.D., J.D. with Mark Curriden and Benjamin Wecht, *Grave Secrets* (New York: Onyx Books, 1998), 201. Legal action taken by survivors prevailed in court and the city of Chicago paid $1.8 million in penalties.

16) Mike Gray and Howard Alk, dirs. *The Murder of Fred Hampton.* FACETS, 2007.

17) Jerry Aronson, dir. *The Life and Times of Allen Ginsberg.* New Yorker Films, 2007 [1994]. Ono herself discusses her relationship with Ginsberg on the newer two-disc edition.

18) David Quantick, *Revolution: The Making of the Beatles' White Album* (London: Unanimous Ltd., 2002), 153.

19) David Segal, "The Rock Journalist At a High Point In Music History." *Washington Post* 03 Aug. 2005. Http://www.washingtonpost.com/wp-dyn/content/article/2005/08/02/AR2005080201920.html.

20) Geoffrey Giuliano, *Lennon In America: Based In Part On the Lost Lennon Diaries 1971-1980* (New York: Cooper Square Press, 2000), 50. Aronowitz is interviewed extensively in the documentary the documentary DVD (uncredited) *Bob Dylan: 1966-1978: After the Crash.* Chrome Dreams, 2006. See also Joel Gilbert, dir. *Bob Dylan: World Tours 1966-1974.* (MVD Visual, 2004).

21) Bruce David and Carolyn Sinclair, *"Alex Bennett: Permission to Speak Freely."* Hustler *(April 2006),* 45-46.

22) Murray Sayle, "The Importance of Yoko Ono." *Japan Policy Research Institute* No. 18 (November 2000). Www.jpri.org/publications/occasionalpapers/op18.html.

23) Phil Strongman, *John Lennon: Life, Times & Assassination* (Liverpool, United Kingdom: The Bluecoat Press, 2010).

24) *Inside John Lennon.* Written by Henry Stephens. Passport International Pictures, 2003.

25) Philip Norman, *John Lennon: The Life* (New York: Ecco, 2008), 469-71.

26) Fredric Seaman, *The Last Days of John Lennon: A Personal Memoir* (New York: Birch Lane Press, 1991), 246.

27) *Ibid.,* 239.

28) Alex Constantine, "Case Closed: The CIA Murder of John Lennon." *Antifascist Encylopedia* 05 Dec. 2010. Http://www.antifascistencyclopedia.com/?p=47775.

29) John Potash, *The FBI War on Tupac Shakur and Black Leaders: U.S. Intelligence's Murderous Targeting of Tupac, MLK, Malcolm, Panthers, Hendrix, Marley, Rappers & Linked Ethnic Leftists* (Baltimore, Maryland: Progressive Left Press, 2007).

30) Tupac Shakur (as Makaveli), *The Don Killuminati: The 7 Day Theory* (Death Row/Interscope, 1996).

31) *Mike Douglas Show with John Lennon and Yoko Ono.* Rhino/WEA, 1998.

32) Thomas Bodenheimer and Robert Gould, *Rollback!: Right-Wing Power in U.S. Foreign Policy* (Boston: South End Press, 1989).

33) Jon Wiener, *Come Together: John Lennon In His Time* (Urbana and Chicago: University of Illinois Press, 1991).

34) Yellow Pearl, *A Grain of Sand: Music For the Struggle of Asians in America* (1973). Paredon Records (PAR1020). The record album included integral member Charlie Chin, although he did not perform on the *Mike Douglas Show.*

35) Tadashi Nakamura, dir. *A Song For Ourselves.* Third World Newsreel, 2009.

36) *The Dick Cavett Show: John & Yoko Collection.* Daphne Productions, 2005.

37) *Jimi Hendrix: The Dick Cavett Show* (DVD). Daphne Productions, 2002.

38) Steven Roby, *Black Gold: The Lost Archives of Jimi Hendrix* (New York: Billboard Books), 129.

39) Alex Constantine, *The Covert War Against Rock* (Los Angeles: Feral House, 2000).

40) Troy Patterson, "The Guest From Hell." *Salon.com* 02 Aug. 2007. Http://www.slate.com/articles/arts/television/2007/08/the_guest_from_hell.html.

41) Sherman H. Skolnick in 1972 suggests that the "Chicago 7" (Rennie Davis, Tom Hayden, David Dellinger, Jerry Rubin, Lee Weiner, John Froines, and Abbie Hoffman) were "The King's Men" only playing the role of revolutionaries. See Sherman H. Skolnick "'Chicago 7'" Are They For Real?" *Skolnick Report* 17 Mar. 2004. Http://www.skolnicksreport.com/awm1.html.

42) David Sheff, *All We Are Saying: The Last Major Interview With John Lennon and Yoko Ono* (New York: St. Martin's, 2000), 115-116.

43) Jon Wiener, "The US vs. John Lennon." *The Nation* 12 Sep. 2006. Http://www.thenation.com/blogs/notion/120879.

44) Sir David Frost with Bob Zelnick, *Frost/Nixon: Behind the Scenes of the Nixon Interviews* (New York: Harper Perennial, 2007). See *Frost/Nixon: Complete Interviews*. Jorn Winther, dir. Liberation Entertainment 2009.

45) Wiener, *Come Together*, 304.

46) The photograph of Shin'ya Ono and his seminal essay appear in Harold Jacobs, ed., *Weathermen* (Berkeley: Ramparts Press, 1971). Ono spent five months in Cook County Jail after his arrest along with about 300 other protestors. See also Jeremy Varon, *Bringing the War Home: The Weather Underground, The Red Army Faction, and Revolutionary Violence in the Sixties and Seventies* (Berkeley and Los Angeles: University of California Press, 2004). Relevant documentaries include *Underground*. Emile de Antonio, Mary Lampson, Haskell Wexler, Weather Underground Organization, dirs. MPI Home Video, 1998; *Rebels With A Cause*. Helen Garvy. dir. Zeitgeist Films, 2003.

47) Ono died of Parkinson's Disease on June 13, 2007 in Japan, where he had moved with his family. Terri Oshiro, "Tribute to Shinya Ono." *Azine: Asian American Movement Ezine*, 27 Aug. 2007. Http://www.virtualot.net/news/2007/shinya_ono1.html.

48) Andrew Gavin Marshall, "The New Eugenics and the Rise of the Global Scientific Dictatorship." *Global Research* 05 Jul. 2010. Http://www.globalresearch.ca/index.php?-context=va&aid=20028.

49) "John Lennon – Overpopulation is a Myth." *The Dick Cavett* Show 11 Sep. 1971. YouTube Https://www.youtube.com/watch?v=Emi1wf1q6os.

50) Wendy Kline, *Building A Better Race: Gender, Sexuality, and Eugenics From the Turn of the Century to the Baby Boom* (Berkeley and Los Angeles: University of California Press, 2005), 141.

51) Adele, E. Clarke, *Disciplining Reproduction: Modernity, American Life Sciences, and "the Problems of Sex."* (Berkeley and Los Angeles: University of California Press, 1998).

52) Jonathan Peter Spiro, *Defending the Master Race: Conservation, Eugenics, and the Legacy of Madison Grant* (Lebanon, New Hampshire: University of Vermont Press, 2009), 272.

53) Felicity Barringer, "Bitter Division For Sierra Club On Immigration." *New York Times* 16 Mar. 2004. Http://www.nytimes.com/2004/03/16/us/bitter-division-for-sierra-club-on-immigration.html.

54) Mireya Navarro, "In Environmental Push, Looking to Add Diversity." *New York Times* 09 Mar. 2009. Http://www.nytimes.com/2009/03/10/science/earth/10move.html.

55) Michael S. Coffman, *Saviors of the Earth?: The Politics and Religion of the Environmental Movement* (Chicago: Northfield Publishing, 1994), 101.

56) Mark Lane, *Rush To Judgment: A Critique of the Warren Commission Inquiry Into the Murders of President John F. Kennedy, Officer J. D. Tippit, and Lee Harvey Oswald* (New York: Holt, Rinehart, and Winston, 1966.)

57) L. Fletcher Prouty, *The Secret Team: The CIA and Its Allies in Control of the United States and the World* (New York: Skyhorse Publishing, 2008).

58) Wim Dankbaar, ed. *Files on JFK: Interviews With Confessed Assassin James E. Files, and More New Evidence of the Conspiracy That Killed JFK* (BookSurge Publishing, 2005).

59) James E. Files, *The Murder of JFK: Confession of An Assassin* (MPI Home Video, 1996).

60) Nigel Turner, prod. *The Men Who Killed Kennedy* A&E Home Video, 2011 [orig. 1988].

61) Judyth Vary Baker, *Me & Lee: How I Came to Know, Love and Lose Lee Harvey Oswald* (Walterville, Oregon: Trine Day, 2011).

62) Jim Marrs, *Crossfire: The Plot That Killed Kennedy* (New York: Basic Books, 1993); Harrison Edward Livingstone and Robert J. Groden, *High Treason: The Assassination of JFK & the Case for Conspiracy* (New York: Carroll & Graf Publishers, Inc., 1998); Dick Russell, *The Man Who Knew Too Much*, rev. ed. (New York: Carroll & Graf Publishers, 2003).

63) Russ Baker, *Family of Secrets: The Bush Dynasty, the Powerful Forces That Put It in the White House, and What Their Influence Means for America* (New York: Bloomsbury Press, 2008).

64) *The Mae Brussell Website*. Http://www.maebrussell.com/index.html.

65) Mae Brussell, "Interview With Mae Brussell On The Assassination of John Ono Lennon." *Maebrussell.com* December 1980. Interviewed by Tom Davis. Http://www.maebrussell.com/Mae%20Brussell%20Articles/John%20Lennon%20Assassination.html.

66) Paul Krassner, *Confessions of a Raving, Unconfined Nut: Misadventures in the Counter-Culture* (New York: Simon & Schuster, 1993), 214.

67) Jon Wiener, *Gimme Some Truth: The John Lennon FBI Files* (Berkley and Los Angeles: University of California Press, 1999).

68) Mae Brussell, "Operation Chaos: The CIA's War Against the Sixties Counter-Culture." *Mae Brussell Website* November 1976. Http://www.maebrussell.com/Mae%20Brussell%20Articles/Operation%20Chaos.html.

69) These include the murders of bioweapons expert David Kelley (2003); "DC Madam" Deborah Jean Palfrey (2008); and media figure Andrew Breitbart (2012) who just had announced at the Conservative Political Action Committee (CPAC) conference that he was going to release a damning videotape of Barack Hussein Obama while in college.

70) Fenton Bresler, *Who Killed John Lennon* (New York: St. Martin's Paperbacks, 1990), 123.

71) Douglas Valentine, *The Phoenix Program* (New York: Morrow, 1990).

72) Christian G. Appy, *Patriots: The Vietnam War Remembered From All Sides* (New York: Viking Press, 2003), 361.

73) Kenneth Ofgang, "County's Newest Judge Sworn In, Promises to Protect Rights." *Metropolitan News-Enterprise* 30 Apr. 2002. Http://www.metnews.com/articles/okam043002.htm.

74) Douglas Valentine, "Homeland Insecurity: Phoenix, CHAOS, The Enterprise, and The Politics of Terror in America," in Tom Burghardt, ed., *Police State America: U.S. Military "Civil Disturbance" Planning* (Toronto: Arm The Spirit/Solidarity, 2002), 148.

75) William Saletan, "Drones Over America." *Slate* 07 May 2013. Http://www.slate.com/articles/technology/future_tense/2013/05/domestic_drones_and_polls_has_targeted_killing_made_us_afraid_of_civilian.html.

76) Jonathan Masters, "Targeted Killings." *Council on Foreign Relations* 30 Apr. 2012. Http://www.cfr.org/counterterrorism/targeted-killings/p9627.

77) John Lennon, *John Lennon/Plastic Ono Band*. Apple/EMI, 1970.

78) James Petras, "The Western Welfare State: Its Rise and Demise and the Soviet Bloc." *Global Research* 04 Jul. 2012. Http://www.globalresearch.ca/index.php?context=va&aid=31753.

79) Joseph E. Stiglitz and Linda J. Bilmes, "The True Cost of the Iraq War: $3 trillion and Beyond." *Washington Post* 05 Sep. 2010. Http://www.washingtonpost.com/wp-dyn/content/article/2010/09/03/AR2010090302200.html.

80) Paul Craig Roberts, "The Collapsing US Economy and the End of the World." *Institute for Political Economy* 08 Jul. 2012. Http://www.paulcraigroberts.org/.

81) Carl A. Trocki, *Opium, Empire, and the Global Political Economy: A Study of the Asian Opium Trade* (London: Routledge, 1999); Timothy Brook and Bob Tadashi Wakabayashi, eds. *Opium Regimes: China, Britain, and Japan, 1839-1952* (Berkeley: University of California Press, 2000); Arthur Herman, *How the Scots Invented the Modern World: The True Story of How Western Europe's Poorest Nation Created Our World & Everything In It* (New York: Three Rivers Press, 2001); Konstandinos Kalimtgis, David Goldman, and Jeffrey Steinberg, *Dope, Inc.: Britain's Opium War Against the U.S.* (New York: New Benjamin Franklin House, 1978); John Coleman, *The Conspirator's Hierarchy: The Committee of 300*, 4th ed. (Carson City, Nevada: World In Review, 2006); Pratap Chaterjee, *Iraq, Inc., A Profitable Occupation* (New York: Seven Stories Press, 2004); Peter Dale Scott, *The War Conspiracy: JFK, 9/11, and the Deep Politics of War* (Ipswich, Massachusetts: Mary Ferrell Foundation Press, 2008).

82) Yoko Ono, *Onobox*. Rykodisc, 1992.

Andrea Wong

RACE, ETHNICITY, TECHNO-FASCISM AND THE RESTORATION OF THE AMERICAN REPUBLIC

Silicon Valley Girls

The foregoing essays radically question the prevailing view of Asian Americans as a uniformly oppressed ethno-racial group. One of the key arguments of this volume is that since 1965, Asian immigrants from US Cold War client states specifically have been recruited to meet the demand for intellectual labor required by the massive military-corporate science and technology complex. Earlier in the twentieth century, such social thinkers as H. G. Wells, Aldous Huxley, and Bertrand Russell posited the necessity of a science and technocratic dictatorship to manage a future world society free of the conflicts, divisions, and terror that have plagued human civilization consistently throughout all stages of its development. Its political manifestation is the European Union of today, whose origins can be traced to attempts at creating a unified world government in the aftermath of World War I.[1] The US is now in the process of forced merger with this super-union that has been the dream of the hereditary ruling elite for generations. Advances in technology has made the prospects for a new world order coming into being ever more possible.

Included among this identifiable demographic group of scientists and engineers are cadres of government-subsidized social and behavioral scientists, mental health specialists, legal theorists in schools of law, and the dominant majority in the arts and humanities that have been flogging variants of race, class, and gender theory for the past forty years. Together, they have trained and socialized two or more generations of undergraduates in related forms of identity politics within a comprehensive and total welfare state system stuffed with state and government agencies, departments, and bureaus established ostensibly in place to "protect" vulnerable minorities from discrimination. These individuals are now the political establishment in academia, government, business, and even the military.

Within corporate oligopoly media, carefully selected and meticulously groomed Asian Americans have broken into the executive ranks in recent years. One such example is Andrea Wong, currently president of international production for Sony Pictures Television. A more recent example of young, ambitious, attractive, and super-intelligent Chinese American women being tapped for high-visibility roles as media globalists in the China Century is Clara Shih.

Named the top-ranked undergraduate student in Computer Science at Stanford University, she then earned an MS degree with an emphasis on "User Experience and Design." *Fortune, Business Week, New York Times*, and other approved news organs of the corporatocracy have tagged her as an up-and-comer. That both Wong and Shih have close ties with Stanford University is no coincidence. With the rise of Silicon Valley and the enormous investment of private corporations and public funds disbursed by government, Stanford has become the preeminent academic training ground for Asians and Asian Americans competing to enter the ranks of the technocratic elite.

Wong grew up the daughter of teacher and a nurse in Sunnyvale, California in the heart of Silicon Valley. She earned a degree in electrical engineering at MIT, an institution considered an unofficial arm of the CIA. After graduation, Wong worked briefly at the Pacific Stock Exchange in San Francisco before returning to school to earn an MBA at Stanford University in 1993.

Lured by the whirl of network television, Wong was scouted, tapped, and fast-tracked at ABC and then NBC. Due to such network TV ratings successes as *The Bachelor* (2002 to present), *The Biggest Loser* (2004 to present), and *Dancing With the Stars* (2005), Wong was hired to rescue the ailing Lifetime Networks to make it "more appealing to younger women" and "urban sophisticates" while not losing its core audience of younger mothers in middle America.[2] Viewed more critically, Lifetime programs served up "liberal feminism" to the masses via a "telefeminist formula" that was used in "defusing, appropriating, and absorbing selected elements" of the oppositional women's movement.[3] As an entertainment media executive, Wong proved exceptionally prescient in tapping into and exploiting the dreams and aspirations of the post-feminist female audience hungry for fictional storylines and social simulacra upon which to model their unsatisfying lives.

More immediately and with greater lasting damage, Lifetime delivered a captive female demographic targeted by pharmaceutical giants that pushed anti-depressants on women using "direct-to-consumer (DTC) advertising." In 1997, the Federal Drug Administration "issued new guidelines that relaxed rules for broadcast ads. Now, Big Pharma could go straight to the public."[4] Lifetime, the cable network ostensibly devoted to elevating and strengthening the "liberated" American woman, instead helped crush her spirit with a combination of psychotropic drugs, fantasy surrogate relationships, self-pitying victim-heroine narratives, and trance-states induced by the very act of watching TV.[5]

The utility of Andrea Wong goes far beyond that of generating profits for the stockholders of Sony: She has been recruited by corporatist institutional fronts to supply insights into the engineering of the universal mass audience mind. As an example, *The Biggest Loser* – a meta-game-show that makes a contest out of massive weight loss – has franchises in countries that include China, Brazil, United Kingdom, Ukraine, Australia, Mexico, the Philippines, Spain, Slovakia, and other parts of the world where the corporate global food oligarchs such as Nestlé, PepsiCo, and General Mills have inflicted obesity on the populace.

Her inclusion by the Aspen Institute as an "emerging leader" indicates the value Wong brings to this "liberal" think tank arm of the Rockefeller Brothers Fund [6] Among high-level globalist viceroys that have attended Aspen conferences or retreats in more recent years since its first public session held in 1950 are Kofi Annan, Condoleezza Rice, Margaret Thatcher, Jimmy Carter, and Bill Clinton. Wong belongs to an exclusive club that includes media and entertainment heavyweights Michael Eisner (ex-Disney) and Gerald M. Levin (ex-Time-Warner).

Consistent with her position among upper echelon mind management strategists, Wong also enjoys membership in the Visiting

Committee of the MIT Media Lab. Founded by Nicholas Negroponte, younger brother of the notorious covert operative and the first Director of National Intelligence John Negroponte, the "lab" has extensive connections to the military-university-corporate national security complex. The Pentagon through its Defense Advanced Research Projects Agency (DARPA) has been one of the key funding sources for MIT going back to its Cybernetics Group during the 1940s-1950s.[7]

Green crypto-fascist and self-described "eco-freak" Stewart Brand of *Whole Earth Catalog* (1968-72) renown, writes glowingly of Negroponte and his visionary operation that functions as both an academic department and one of many MIT laboratories. He leads the concluding chapter of *The Media Lab: Inventing the Future at MIT* with a quote from his hero: "What needs to be articulated, regardless of the format of the man-machine relationship, is the goal of humanism through machines."[8]

Negroponte in his own book *Being Digital* sneeringly elaborates upon his vision of the cyberfascist state made possible through the merger of artificial intelligence with the man-machine. For one, he views the nation-state as a "mothball" that will "evaporate," going from solid to gas as "some global cyberstate commands the political ether." Second, gone will be the irritation of "nationalism," which according to Negroponte will have disappeared along with "smallpox."[9]

Andrea Wong, daughter of Silicon Valley, has come full circle in her appointment to the advisory position at MIT. It remains to be seen, however, whether her insertion into this select position within the transnational entertainment complex will advance the globalist agenda against the strong anarchic and libertarian strains within the diverse IT community. The Electronic Frontier Foundation in San Francisco, California is a noteworthy example of organizations formed to protect civil liberties and American political sovereignty against attacks by corporatist technocrats.

Perhaps the selection of venture capitalist Joichi Ito as director of the MIT Media Lab is meant to mute criticism of its anti-democratic tendencies in service to its corporate-military controllers. Neither an academic nor researcher (Ito is a college dropout), he grew up in both Tokyo and the Silicon Valley steeped in the nascent Internet culture. To his credit, Ito was involved in the open-source movement and active in the non-profit organization Creative Commons, which has addressed issues of copyright and intellectual property in the digital age.[10] Even so, that Ito has expressed the ambition to become what he calls a "global citizen" is cause for concern. His status as "guild master" in the widely acclaimed *World of Warcraft* (*WoW*) massively multiplayer online role-playing game (MMORPG) also might be an indication of what Ito envisions for the future of the humanity in "real life" or "RL" as it is abbreviated in yet another all-consuming immersive online experience, *Second Life.*

Neo-Prometheus

The contributions of European expatriate intellectuals in the sciences at the Institute For Advanced Study in Princeton, New Jersey are well known. The rise of fascism in through western and central Europe induced many great minds to leave for the US. The University of Chicago also has been important to the ascendancy of the science-driven, military-enforced US technocratic social system. Less known is the role of successful Wall Street investor and gentleman scientist Alfred L. Loomis.

In the 1930s, Loomis began to put his substantial fortune at the service of advanced research by establishing a facility in Tuxedo Park, New York that attracted some of the best international talent in the field of physics. Among his many and diverse interests, Loomis experimented with electrodes attached to the scalps of subjects whose brain waves were then measured.[11] This research was undertaken well before the government-sponsored MK-ULTRA mind control programs began during the 1950s.

Several decades later, the curiosity of Loomis and the German psychiatrists that inspired his interest in the workings of the brain has culminated in a "man-on-the-moon kind of project" recently funded by the Defense Advanced Research Program Agency (DARPA) for the sum of $26 million. The goal of the University of California, San Francisco (UCSF) research team led by neurosurgeon Dr. Edward Chang is to engineer an "implantable brain device" intended ostensibly to treat depression and post-traumatic stress disorder.[12]

The substantial commitment by the Obama administration to neuroscience harkens back to the 1950s when successful experiments were conducted with electronic stimulation of the brain (ESB). Numerous studies were funded by the Office of Naval Intelligence (ONI), National Security Agency (NSA), Central Intelligence Agency, National Institute of Mental Health (NIMH) and related government entities involved with developing and implementing mind control systems.[13]

Among ten campuses within the system, UCSF is the only institution dedicated to graduate education in health and biomedical sciences. It ranks near the top nationally for its research-focused MD and PhD programs. Its School of Pharmacy is the number one recipient of funding from the National Institute of Health, as is the School of Dentistry. Its most recent Nobel laureate (2012) is Shinya Yamanaka, a Japanese national who has been showered with accolades for his innovative stem cell research.

In 2013, Yamanaka received the Breakthrough Prize in Life Sciences that carries with it a $3 million award. Thanks to the efforts of Yamanaka and his rivals, embryonic stem cells have been created without the use of eggs or destroying embryos in the process. It is argued that this bio-innovation sidesteps the considerable political opposition to stem cell research based on moral, ethical, or religious grounds.[14]

The Wall Street investment community expects to profit handsomely thanks to the contributions of Asian American transnationals like Yamanaka that are laying the groundwork for what is being promoted as the life sciences economy. The more insidious implication of such research, however, is its application in the "reprogramming" of human cells and cloning.[15] This is the realization of the "brave new world" (1932) envisioned in the modern period by Huxley and his fellow advocates of eugenics.

In *Brave New World Revisited* (1958) this inheritor of Darwinian pseudo-science warned of the looming "Age of Over-population" that would lead to permanent social crisis, conflict, and totalitarianism.[16] In 1962, to a raptly attentive audience at the University of California, Berkeley Huxley summarized his "ultimate revolution" based on the manipulation of behavior and mind control through mass media and pharmacological intervention over a pacified population that had been led to "love their servitude."[17]

Setting an early precedent for later Asian immigrant scientists that settled in the US was astrophysicist Subrahmanyam

Chandrasekhar. After suffering professional ridicule from senior colleagues, he left the clubby social climate of British academic life at Cambridge and took residence at the University of Chicago in 1937. Chandrasekhar remained there for the remainder of his illustrious career, mastering a number of related subspecialties within physics and astrophysics. He missed the opportunity to work on the Manhattan Project by invitation of J. Robert Oppenheimer, but instead contributed to the war effort at Aberdeen Proving Ground. Chandrasekhar was named co-recipient of the Nobel Prize for Physics in 1983, although he felt that that the award did not acknowledge the innovative work produced during the latter part of his career.[18]

While Chandrasekhar devoted his career to speculating on the nature of the infinite expanding universe, a self-identified bioethicist with the Department of Philosophy at New York University called S. Matthew Liao argues that humankind itself has become an obstacle to environmental (as the cliché has it) "sustainability."[19] An academic journal article titled "Human Engineering and Climate Change" authored by Liao and two others proposes that *homo sapiens* be reduced physically in size as a rational solution to dwindling resources and environmental crises hyped by certain scientists, policy makers, and investment bankers.[20] Bizarre as it might seem, Liao and others within the academic establishment – both in the humanities and the sciences – are representative of the UN-led Agenda 21 and its aggressive push for "sustainable development" that some argue will lead to massive depopulation and greater concentration of wealth.[21]

Fanciful or not, the mere suggestion by Liao of this proposed godlike reengineering of humanity lowers the threshold of moral and ethical objections to future intervention by technicians. In this, Liao is heir to the occult alchemical romanticism of Percy Bysshe Shelly; its perverse expression being akin to that of Dr. Victor Frankenstein ("The Modern Prometheus") and his monstrously synthetic creation.[22] In an academic discipline struggling to attract both students and research dollars while remaining intellectually relevant, work such as this represents the handover of philosophy and the tradition of humanistic inquiry to the corporatist state that already has absorbed most other sectors of the contemporary research university.

Dishonor Before Death

Beyond their over-representation in allied science and technology fields, certain select Americans of Asian heritage have succeeded in entering the inner circle of government, business, and the military. Even the perceived elite among contemporary Asian Americans, however, cannot yet claim stable and enduring social advantage. Gen. Eric K. Shinseki, for example, once stood at the apex of military rank in his capacity as US Army Chief of Staff leading to the Iraq War in 2003.

A public dispute with US Secretary of Defense Donald Rumsfeld, however, exposed the pretense that Shinseki truly wielded decision-making power against the corporate elite that controls the global economic system and commands the US military as its enforcement arm. Iraqis numbering in the hundreds of thousands were killed in the aftermath of what had been only a technical argument between Shinseki and Rumsfeld over troop numbers rather than fundamental disagreement over whether war was even justified.

After having retired from the military, Shinseki was appointed Secretary for Veterans Affairs in 2008 by the first self-acknowledged non-White president of the US. Both shared a common heritage in the State of Hawaii, although in the case of Obama it remains unclear that he had been born there.[23] The second career public humiliation for the West Point graduate came in 2014 when VA hospital scandals began to surface. At first, President Obama voiced his obligatory support of the highest-ranking Asian American ever to serve in the US military. Shinseki needed to be held in place long enough to create a sensational distraction from the fiasco of the Patient Protection and Affordable Care Act (2010); so-called Obamacare.[24] (Critics have argued that the Veterans Administration and its medical care system is the prototype for state-monopoly health care in America.[25])

At no time during the VA furor did government functionaries or elected representatives take the opportunity to question whether the US should be sending US soldiers "off to fight, become maimed, and die in the endless conflicts overseas that have no connection to US national security."[26] In late May 2014, President Obama accepted the resignation of Shinseki, who had characterized the VA as having "systemic" upper-level management problems.[27] In the annals of US military history, Shinseki will be the first ever to fall on his sword twice for his president and commander-in-chief: Once as a general; the second time as a civilian.

A profile in *The New Yorker* characterized Shinseki as the "nineteen-fifties ideal of the straight-arrow, all-American boy." He was a Boy Scout awarded the "God and Country" merit badge, was president of the student body at Kauai High School, and married his homecoming queen sweetheart. His uncles had served in the US Army during World War II with Daniel K. Inouye, who later sat for decades as US Senator and recommended Shinseki for admission to West Point.[28] Combat experience during the Viet Nam War left him with a severe foot injury after stepping on a land mine that almost ended his military career.

Similar to the career-ending set-ups Shinseki experienced, Major General Antonio M. Taguba found himself being forced out of a distinguished career spanning three decades for conducting an inquiry into prisoner abuse at Abu Ghraib that greatly displeased Donald Rumsfeld and senior military officers. In "The General's Report" published in the *New Yorker*, the intrepid Seymour M. Hersh reviewed many of the horrors inflicted upon detainees by Military Police with the full knowledge and cooperation of commanding officers and O.G.A.s ("Other Government Agencies"), meaning the CIA.[29]

It is clear that Taguba was placed in a no-win situation so that high-level perpetrators including Lieutenant General Ricardo Sanchez, Commander of Coalition of Ground Forces in Iraq, would escape blame and punishment. The article by Hersh clearly indicts Rumsfeld as well, a latter-day Mephistophelian presence who has the distinction of being both the youngest (under Gerald R. Ford 1975-1977) and oldest (George W. Bush 2001-2006) Secretary of Defense in US history.

In the realm of government, Asian Americans in elective office exercise little substantive political power on behalf of the electorate regardless of color. Office holders ranging from smaller municipalities to the US presidency are beholden to the corporate interests that put them in place. It matters less, for example, that Gov. Piyush "Bobby" Jindal of Louisiana is born of South Asian immigrant parents than that he is politically subordinate to the supra-national corporate behemoth BP; formerly British Petroleum. Its corporate rebranding and adoption of the slogan "Beyond Petroleum" does not alter the reality that BP is synonymous with the House of Windsor and its vast wealth.

Jindal, who adopted he name "Bobby" at age four after a character in the 1970s sitcom *The Brady Bunch*, could do little but play out the role of governor in the aftermath of the 2010 Deepwater Horizon oil rig catastrophe that devastated much of the fauna and flora of the Gulf Coast, gravely harmed the health of residents, and further crippled the already hurting local economy. Former Schlumberger executive and oil industry expert Ian R. Crane quickly went public with his accusation of foul play surrounding the well-timed mega-accident.[30] By contrast, Gov. Jindal raised few incisive questions concerning BP misdeeds and instead pointed his finger at the Obama administration for its lack of response to the disaster.[31]

Before being appointed by President Obama as Ambassador to the People's Republic of China, Gary F. Locke served as governor for the State of Washington (1997-2005). He was the first governor of Asian descent to be elected in the continental US. Prior to becoming ambassador, Locke was Secretary of Commerce (2009-2011) by which time the US as a debtor nation was firmly in the grip of China as planned by globalist bankers.

The move into the ambassadorial post in Beijing (2011-2014) seemed to follow naturally in an age of politically expedient ethnic typecasting. His tenure, however, did not go over well with the Chinese leadership as seen in an insulting farewell published by the China News Service. In particular, his moralizing about human rights and urging a lessening of geopolitical tension between Japan and China was not appreciated. The *New York Times* reported that Locke, a third-generation Chinese American, was dismissed as "being a banana – 'yellow skin and white heart'" used only for the "advantage for Obama's foreign policy."[32]

Race to the Bottom

These essays should not be construed as dismissing the reality of race-based social discrimination altogether. (Prior to their current visibility on Wall Street, for example, Indian Americans of elite social origins with Harvard MBAs such as Rajat Gupta were denied "ask backs" by leading corporate recruiters that visited campus.[33]) Nor should the possibility of targeted group persecution be ignored during these times of extreme hardship among the larger population caused by an imploding economy and rampant high-level criminality within government, business, and the military. For the second decade of the twenty-first century finds the US economy severely underperforming. Record numbers of Americans receive some form of government assistance for food. The unemployment rate, even those reported by official sources as 6.7 percent, remains high. As of June 2014, the "real" unemployment rate stands at close to 25 percent of the eligible population including "discouraged workers."[34] The blue-collar "labor aristocracy" that once enjoyed a level of income that made it the envy of the undeveloped world has all but vanished.[35] Indicators of social decay and cultural degradation abound.

The once-confident American middle class has been rocked by flat if not regressive rates of income growth even as its ranks shrink due to reductions in force, relocation, and direct competition from highly-trained overseas labor and domestic specialized replacement workers in fields once thought immune to economic crisis including engineering, information technology, and biotech laboratory research.[36] In this larger context, "race" and "ethnicity" are second-order explanatory concepts within a more comprehensive new world order theoretical perspective that posits a calculated but not preordained attempt to decimate the American middle class through the radical restructuring of the US economy by central planners under the employ of the hereditary elite and the central banks they control through Wall Street and the City of London.[37]

The heavily guarded conference held over three-days in late May 2014 by the Bilderberg Group in Copenhagen, Denmark offered a glimpse of the supra-national power structure that almost has completed its mission of destroying national sovereignty and enfolding the wreckage into the globalist system. Independent journalists and ordinary citizens reported on the commingling of ultra-elite globalist managers, corporatist media, private think tankers and consultants, elected and appointed government representatives, and royalty such as H.R.H. Princess Beatrix of the Netherlands to assess its previous plans while setting the political-economic agenda for the coming year.[38]

Among the contingent from the USA were China expert Cheng Li of the Brookings Institution and Clara Shih mentioned above. In 2009, Shi co-founded Hearsay Social with headquarters in San Francisco, California. Her value as an Anglo-American media and computer science asset is seen in the M.Sc. degree she earned at Oxford University as a Marshall Scholar.[39] Other than Yiping Huang, professor of economics at Peking University, there were few academics in attendance; a further indicator of the exclusive nature and seriousness of purpose shared among these unacknowledged legislators of the new world order.

Bilderberg 2014 reaffirms the central importance of the People's Republic of China as the political-economic wedge being used to weaken the US economy and complete its conversion to a full-blown social-democratic welfare state as seen throughout Europe. The resultant mass unemployment and economic chaos combined with large-scale immigration from countries pillaged by foreign banks are preparing Americans for the radical restructuring of the US and its incorporation into the "global cyberstate." The new techno-totalitarian society will combine advanced robotics, neuroscience, bioengineering, social media, nanotechnology, psychopharmacology, virtual reality entertainment, and artificial intelligence in steady-state rule over what remains of humanity in the aftermath of population reduction campaigns and "enviro-eugenicist" initiated by globalist think tanks such as the Club of Rome.[40]

The more immediate threat to the Asian American population are those among the large number of self-employed small business owners concentrated in urban areas. With a population of 47 million dependent upon government-issued EBT cards, these communities rich with Asian American immigrant families and their businesses are especially vulnerable should food riots break out as warned in a report issued by the World Bank in May 2014.[41]

The wide-scale sustained assault on Koreatown during the Los Angeles Riot of April 1992 was but a preview of what might occur across the nation given the confluence of rising food prices, rampant unemployment, open political corruption, and a catalytic event such as a particularly brutal assault by the police-military force trained to treat the American people as the enemy. During what Korean Americans call *Sai-I-Gu*, neither police agencies nor the National Guard provided protection to residents and their businesses. Nor did government agencies offer much relief in the aftermath. Moreover, there is a strong suggestion that police intelligence units and agent provocateurs might have been involved in this most massively destructive and costly riot in US history.[42]

American Restoration

It is hoped that the present volume will allow for a far more nuanced and honest reassessment of contemporary American society at a critical moment in the history of the republic. Its political-economic foundations purposely have been undermined by social engineers and "economic hit men" in obedience to the dictates of globalist bankers that wish to see the US reduced to little more than a techno-totalitarian outpost of the new world order system.[43] The restoration of the American republic to a sovereign nation based upon individual liberty, private ownership, and freedom from government control will require a fundamental rethinking by Asian Americans concerning their general support of "big government" and uncritical fellow-feeling toward undeserving non-White minorities such as Barack H. Obama.[44] As its youth generation cycles through the public education system and the university, it remains to be seen whether such foundational values can withstand the indoctrination to state-approved race and gender politics, economic collectivism, and obedience to centralized world government and its premier institutions such as the United Nations, World Bank, and International Monetary Fund.

In the contemporary supranational popular culture disseminated via videogames, cinema, graphic novels, and the Internet, the world-view is that of Hobbes, Shelly, Darwin, Huxley, Mao, and Philip K. Dick, rolled into one. Perhaps in anticipation of its annihilation by nuclear radiation, Japan has led the way internationally in visualizing the posthuman world.[45] All told, the future will bring a neo-feudal social system populated by loveably stunted Hobbit-like creatures managed by inducted "guild masters" (*WoW*) that oversee the mecha and cyborgs programmed to terminate troublesome internees held captive within the universal panopticon while routine discipline and punishment is administered on the spot by "street judges" that police the Mega-City.

It is to be expected that countless others will follow the path taken by such unsavory characters (immortalized on cover) as Steven Chu, Neel Kashkari, Vikram Pandit, David Ho, Norman Mineta, Margaret Chan, John Choon Yoo, Viet Dinh, Wendy Lee Graham, and Barry Soetoro/Barack H. Obama. Such individuals are an unfortunate constant in social life and are found in all human groups regardless of race and ethnicity. Nor will behavior that ranges from questionable to outright evil deter the next succession of high-level mercenaries from stepping forward to engage in similarly abhorrent activity. Criminal psychopaths thrive on transgression and predation to satisfy their will to power and lust for dominance. Many rise to leadership in competitive fields where unbridled aggression, lack of empathy, and risk-taking is well rewarded.

More modestly, it is hoped that the concepts of "race" and "ethnicity" will be understood as having been co-opted by the political establishment; turned into simply a rhetorically-loaded means of whipsawing the public into acceptance of behavior that otherwise would be rebuked and punished. Race, ethnicity, class, gender, and more recently "sexualities" will be seen for their cynical and opportunistic use within mainstream contemporary political discourse; as slippery and outworn analytical terms that exploit historical victim-status as a cover and justification for all manner of unacceptable individual actions. Such behavior specifically includes willing participation in massive financial fraud, involvement in government criminal conspiracy, engaging in unethical medical practices, sexual exploitation, and placing intellect at the service of evil to justify torture, mass murder, and genocide.

There are signs, however, that the restoration of the once sovereign and free (hence prosperous) American constitutional republic is underway.[46] Moreover, counter-hegemonic anti-globalist political agitation is multiplying the world over from the grassroots to elected officialdom as seen in the growing popularity of the United Kingdom Independence Party (UKIP) founded in 1993.[47] In June 2014, the Tea Party movement in the US scored a major victory when academic economist and political novice Dave Brat defeated the mighty House Majority leader Eric Cantor

(R-Virginia) in a primary election that was not even close. "It was an operatic fall from power, swift deep and utterly surprising," observed the *Washington Post*.[48] Top new world order theoretician and *consigliere* Zbigniew Brzezinski warned of this sea change in a 2008 opinion piece published in the *New York Times*:

> For the first time in history almost all of humanity is politically activated, politically conscious and politically interactive. Global activism is generating a surge in the quest for cultural respect and economic opportunity in a world scarred by memories of colonial or imperial domination.[49]

This article might also be read, however, as a call to fellow travelers among the elite globalist stratum to accelerate the political-economic and military end game that they hope will bring comprehensive, worldwide, centrally controlled tyranny into being at last. Hence the intensification of police brutality against American citizens, relentless government persecution of "whistle blowers," political assassination of writers and journalists such as Andrew Brietbart and Michael Hastings, staged sensational violence such as school shootings meant to frighten the population into surrendering its right of self-defense, violent repression of political speech as seen at the University of California, Davis on November 18, 2011, and US military provocations waged against nations resisting being pulled into the widening gyre of the European Union, North American Union, and more recently, the Trans-Pacific Partnership.

Lawlessness within government, fundamental questions of legitimacy concerning its leadership, an oppressive and violently dangerous federal and state bureaucracy, and an unchecked two-tiered system of justice does not inspire confidence among those Americans educated and socialized to protect themselves against the abrogation of civil liberties by elected officials or appointed autocrats. As representatives among the criminal elite – servitors of empire – begin being brought to justice, the base level morality, decency, and honesty that is vital to the health of the republic will begin to dilute the heavy concentration of accumulated cynicism, deceit, and evil that slowly is poisoning civil society. The American people then will be on its way toward the restoration of the free and sovereign constitutional republic that once provided the preconditions for the emergence of a historically unique and economically thriving middle class.

To be sure, US national history has not been without bloody conflict nor has it been absent expressions of social inequality that range from mild to horrific. Global governance – however seductive it is made to appear on contemporary government-sponsored movies, TV, and popular fiction – offers a false solution to problems engineered by globalists themselves.[50] Consider that the new world order global governance system has its origins in the British imperial Round Table (1909) as conceived by Alfred Milner and the Rt. Hon. Cecil John Rhodes who funded this select group with his considerable fortune.[51] The Round Table gave direct rise to the Royal Institute of International Affairs (RIIA), Council on Foreign Relations (CFR), and Institute of Pacific Relations (IPR). Its postwar lineal descendants are the globalist think tanks Tavistock Institute of Human Relations, Bilderberg Group, and the Club of Rome. These are among the major anti-democratic private think tanks that have been pushing the US toward a non-productive debtor economy held together by a techno-fascist control system that will inspire an atavistic barbarism harsh enough to make the general population beg for more police repression in exchange for an illusory security.

Alfred Milner of Roundtable fame declared himself a "British Race patriot" at the height of imperial power during the reign of Queen Victoria as it was coming to a close in the early twentieth century.[52] Yet over a century later "race" and "ethnicity" as heuristic concepts are going stronger than ever in Anglo-American academia, arts and letters, and even has made an alarming resurgence in contemporary medical science.[53] The Anglo-American oligarchs through its private family foundations and other tax-avoidance mechanisms appear only too glad to fund research initiatives, colloquia, endowed chairs, and entire academic departments devoted specifically to issues deriving from race-identity and problems of ethnicity.

Race and ethnicity theory, however, no longer possess the cutting-edge force it might have had when these dual concepts began to enter mainstream academic discourse at the university beginning in the late 1960s. Almost in an inverse relationship, civil rights activism on campus began to wane as it was institutionalized with the "help" of families such as Rockefeller.[54] More recently, the preoccupation with race and ethnicity theatrics has been useful to the ruling class as a diversion from the quickening encroachment of its new world order system.

Race-guilt is endemic to the general public. Routinization has set in. Over the past forty years, generations of school children and university students have been educated in the real and undeniable historical struggles of Asian Americans and other "minority" groups. Meanwhile, the trans-generational foreign banking elite is reshaping the world economy to suit its needs exclusively while putting its wealth to work in attacking the health and very existence of all humanity through its monopoly on science and technology. To stay the hand of the global oligarchs, the recuperation and restoration of the American republic – sovereign and free – is the starting point of a long and admittedly arduous struggle. There is no better guide for this process than the revolutionary but practical wisdom found in the US Constitution and Bill of Rights.

It is hoped that the present volume represents one resolute step toward the restoration of the American republic by looking directly and honestly at the omissions and contradictions of race-theory, current and past immigration policy, left-liberal-progressive politics, and social class as applied specifically to contemporary Asian Americans. To shirk the responsibility of unflinching self-appraisal is professional negligence at minimum. Worse, turning away from the premonitory truths of the present will have devastating consequences for the future. Too much is at stake to not force a reappraisal of contemporary Asian America now that so many among its servitor stratum are helping to destroy the constitutional republic whose greatness has been built upon the strength, talent, ambition, and vision of its immigrant peoples.

Endnotes

1) Christopher Booker and Richard North, *The Great Deception: Can the European Union Survive?* 2nd ed. (New York: Continuum, 2005).

2) Jake Halpern, "Project Lifetime." *Stanford Magazine* July/August 2009.Http://alumni.stanford.edu/get/page/magazine/article/?article_id=29608.

3) Eileen R. Meehan and Jackie Byars, "Telefeminism: How Lifetime Got Its Groove, 1984-1997" in Robert C. Allen and Annette Hill, eds. *The Television Studies Reader* (London: Routledge, 2004), 92-104.

4) Fran Hawthorne, *The Merck Druggernaut: The Inside Story of a Pharmaceutical Giant* (Hoboken, New Jersey: John Wiley & Sons, Inc., 2003), 149.

5) Greg Guma, "Messing With Our Minds: Psychiatric Drugs, Cyberspace and 'Digital Indoctrination.'" *Global Research* 11 Nov. 2013. Http://www.globalresearch.ca/messing-with-our-minds-psychiatric-drugs-cyberspace-and-digital-indoctrination/5357710.

6) The Aspen Institute, "Aspen Institute Names Emerging Leader as 2010 Henry Crown Fellows." The Aspen Institute 25 Mar. 2010. Http://www.aspeninstitute.org/news/2010/03/25/aspen-institute-names-emerging-leaders-2010-henry-crown-fellows.

7) Jeffrey Steinberg, "From Cybernetics to Littleton: Techniques of Mind Control." *Executive Intelligence Review* 05 May 2000. Http://www.larouchepub.com/other/2000/2718_cybernetics_to_littleton.html#fnB1.

8) Stewart Brand, *The Media Lab: Inventing the Future at MIT* (New York: Viking, 1987).

9) Nicholas Negroponte, *Being Digital* (New York: Vintage Books, 1996), 238.

10) John Markoff, "M.I.T. Media Lab Names a New Director." *New York Times* 25 Apr. 2011. Http://www.nytimes.com/2011/04/26/science/26lab.html?_r=1&src=ISMR_HP_LO_MST_FB#.

11) Jennet Conant, *Tuxedo Park: A Wall Street Tycoon and the Secret Palace of Science That Changed the Course of World War II* (New York: Simon & Schuster, 2002), 108-116.

12) Erin Allday, "UCSF Team Wins $26 Million Grant to Build Brain Implant." *San Francisco Chronicle* 27 May 2014. Http://www.sfgate.com/health/article/UCSF-team-wins-26-million-grant-to-build-brain-5505946.php.

13) Armen Victorian, *Mind Controllers* (Miami, Florida: Lewis International, Inc., 2000), 147-154.

14) Gautam Naik, "Stem-Cell Advance May Skirt Ethical Debate." *Wall Street Journal* 07 Jun. 2007. Http://online.wsj.com/news/articles/SB118113311623826356.

15) Mark Johnson, "Holy Grail of Stem Cell Research Within Reach." *Journal Sentinel* 16 Dec. 2008. Http://www.jsonline.com/features/health/36202594.html.

16) Aldous Huxley, *Brave New World* and *Brave New World Revisited* (New York: Harper Perennial, 2005), 243.

17) Aldous Huxley, "The Ultimate Revolution." *Information Clearinghouse* 02 Feb. 2009. Http://www.informationclearinghouse.info/article24712.htm.

18) Arthur I. Miller, *Empire of the Stars: Obsessions, Friendship, and Betray in the Quest for Black Holes* (Boston: Houghton Mifflin, 2005).

19) James Dellingpole, *Watermelons: The Green Movement's True Colors* (New York: Publius Books, 2011).

20) Ross Andersen, "How Engineering the Human Body Could Combat Climate Change." *The Atlantic* 12 Mar. 2012. Http://www.theatlantic.com/technology/archive/2012/03/how-engineering-the-human-body-could-combat-climate-change/253981/.

21) Rosa Koire, *Behind the Green Mask: U.N. Agenda 21* (Santa Rosa, California: Post Sustainability Institute Press, 2011).

22) Scott Douglas de Hart, *Shelly Unbound: Discovering Frankenstein's True Creator* (Port Townsend, Washington: Feral House, 2013).

23) Joel Gilbert, *Dreams From My Real Father: A Story of Reds and Deception* (DVD). Highway 61 Entertainment 2012.

24) Garth Kant, "'Gang of 80' Vows to Put the Kibosh on Obamacare." *WorldNetDaily* 22 Aug. 2013. Http://www.wnd.com/2013/08/gang-of-78-vows-to-put-the-kibosh-on-obamacare/.

25) Avik Roy, "No, The VA Isn't A Preview of Obamacare – It's Much Worse." *Forbes* 23 May 2014. Http://www.forbes.com/sites/theapothecary/2014/05/23/no-the-va-isnt-a-preview-of-obamacare-its-much-worse/.

26) Ron Paul, "The VA Scandal is Just the Tip of the Military Abuse Iceberg." *Infowars* 26 May 2014. Http://www.infowars.com/the-va-scandal-is-just-the-tip-of-the-military-abuse-iceberg/.

27) William Branigin, "Shinseki Resigns Amid VA Scandal Over Veterans' Health Care." *Washington Post* 05 May 2014. Http://www.washingtonpost.com/politics/shinseki-apologizes-for-va-health-care-scandal/2014/05/30/e605885a-e7f0-11e3-8f90-73e071f3d637_story.html.

28) Peter J. Boyer, "A Different War." *The New Yorker* 01 Jul. 2002. Http://www.newyorker.com/archive/2002/07/01/020701fa_fact_boyer.

29) Seymour M. Hersh, "The General's Report: How Antonio Taguba, Who Investigated the Abu Ghraib Scandal, Became One Of Its Casualties." *The New Yorker* 25 Jun. 2007. Http://www.newyorker.com/reporting/2007/06/25/070625fa_fact_hersh.

30) Ian R. Crane, *BP: Population Reduction and the End of An Age* (DVD). IanRcrane.co.uk, 2010.

31) Josh Harkinson, "Bobby Jindal: Oil Spill Hero or BP's BFF?" *Mother Jones* 02 Jun. 2010. Http://www.motherjones.com/mojo/2010/06/bobby-jindal-bps-best-friend.

32) Michael Forsythe, "A Parting Shot At U.S. Ambassador, Inspired By Mao." *New York Times* 28 Feb. 2014. Http://sinosphere.blogs.nytimes.com/2014/02/28/a-parting-shot-at-u-s-ambassador-inspired-by-mao/?_php=true&_type=blogs&_php=true&_type=blogs&_php=true&_type=blogs&_r=2.

33) Anita Raghavan, *The Billionaire's Apprentice: The Rise of the Indian-American Elite and the Fall of the Galleon Hedge Fund* (New York: Business Plus, 2013), 77-84.

34) John Williams, "Alternate Unemployment Charts." *Shadow Government Statistics* June 2014. Http://www.shadowstats.com/alternate_data/unemployment-charts.

35) Mike Whitney, "The True State of the U.S. Economy." *CounterPunch* 4-6 Oct. 2013. Http://www.counterpunch.org/2013/10/04/the-state-of-the-economy/.

36) Evelyn Iritani, "Sending Biotech Research to China." *Los Angeles Times* 02 Jun. 2007. Http://articles.latimes.com/2007/jun/02/business/fi-chibio2.

37) John Coleman, *The Vanishing Middle Class* (Las Vegas, Nevada: World International Review, 2010).

38) Kit Daniels, "Leaked Secret Agenda From Bilderberg 2014 Revealed." *Infowars* 30 May 2014. Http://www.infowars.com/leaked-secret-agenda-from-bilderberg-2014-revealed/.

39) "Bilderberg 2014: Full List of Official Attendees." *Vigilant Citizen* 31 May 2014. Http://vigilantcitizen.com/latestnews/bilderberg-2014-full-list-official-attendees/.

40) Jurriaan Maessen, "Club of Rome Found Proposed 'Global Matrix' of Manufactured Consent." *ExplosiveReports.Com* 19 Jun. 2013. Http://explosivereports.com/2013/06/19/club-of-rome-founder-proposed-global-matrix-of-manufactured-consent/.

41) José Cuesta, "Food Price Watch." The World Bank Group May 2014. Http://www.worldbank.org/en/topic/poverty/publication/food-price-watch-may-2014.

42) Alex Constantine, *Blood, Carnage and the Agent Provocateur: Truth About the Los Angeles Riots and the Secret War Against L.A.'s Minorities* (Los Angeles, California: Constantine Report, 1993).

43) John Perkins, *Confessions of an Economic Hit Man* (New York: Plume, 2005).

44) Andrew Kohut, et al., "The Rise of Asian Americans." Pew Research Center 04 Apr. 2013, p. 17. Http://www.pewsocialtrends.org/2012/06/19/the-rise-of-asian-americans/.

45) Steven T. Brown, *Tokyo Cyber-Punk: Posthumanism in Japanese Visual Culture* (New York: Palgrave Macmillan, 2010).

46) Maira Sutton, "TPP Is Right Where We Want It: Going Nowhere." *Electronic Frontier Foundation* 25 Apr. 2014. Https://www.eff.org/deeplinks/2014/04/tpp-right-where-we-want-it-going-nowhere.

47) Nigel Farage, *Flying Free* (London: Biteback Publishing, Ltd., 2011).

48) Robert Costa, Laura Vozzella, and David A. Fahrenthold, "Republic House Majority Leader Eric Cantor Succumbs to Tea Party Challenger Dave Brat." *Washington Post* 11 Jun. 2014. Http://www.washingtonpost.com/local/virginia-politics/eric-cantor-faces-tea-party-challenge-tuesday/2014/06/10/17da5d20-f092-11e3-bf76-447a5df6411f_story.html.

49) Zbigniew Brzezinski, "The Global Political Awakening." *New York Times* 16 Dec. 2008. Http://www.nytimes.com/2008/12/16/opinion/16iht-YEbrzezinski.1.18730411.html .

50) Oliver Boyd-Barrett, David Herrera, and Jim Baumann, *Hollywood and the CIA: Cinema, Defense, and Subversion* (New York: Routledge, 2011).

51) Carroll Quigley, *The Anglo-American Establishment: From Rhodes to Cliveden* (San Pedro, California, GSG & Associates, 1981).

52) Martin Meredith, *Diamonds, Gold, and War: The British, the Boers, and the Making of South Africa* (New York: PublicAffairs, 2007), p. 365.

53) Troy Duster, *Backdoor To Eugenics* (New York: Routledge, 1990).

54) Clarence B. Jones and Joel Engel, *What Would Martin Say?* (New York: Harper Perennial, 2008), 174

INDEX

X

Y

Z